I Can Begin Again

Dr. Claire,

May God bless you as you join me while we paint the canvas of my life together.

Nola Katherine

www.NolaKatherineIrwin.com
icanbignagain@verizon.net

I Can Begin Again

Inside the Mind of an Adult
Who Was Abused as a Child

Nola Katherine
Trewin

Library of Congress Control Number:		2010907738
ISBN:	Hardcover	978-1-4535-1162-6
	Softcover	978-1-4535-1161-9

To order additional copies of this book, contact:
Xlibris Corporation
1-888-795-4274
www.Xlibris.com
Orders@Xlibris.com
59152

Book Notes

I Can Begin Again will take you into the complex and perplexing mind of an adult who bears the scars of child abuse. It was the voices of abused children past, present and yet to come who beckoned the author to tell her own story of childhood sexual abuse. For thirty years God would not let her rest until she finally listened and obeyed His call on her life to reach out and help others who are stuck in the grips of this devastating affliction. This very personal story will help adults who were abused as children understand who they are and why they behave the way they do. It will prove they do not have to remain stuck in their pain, and it will show each of them how to reclaim the power that was stolen from them as a precious, innocent child. This revealing account will encourage those who have endured *any type* of abuse to believe they can do more than just survive . . . they *can* begin life again!

The author also brings insights to those of you who live with one who has been shattered by child abuse. It is her hope that understanding will bring healing to relationships that are often torn apart because of the confusing behavior of the wounded child living within the adult. She will also open the eyes of abusers who have no clue what they are actually doing to their precious, innocent victims. It is her prayer that her story will save other innocent children from becoming victims.

There are many subjects covered in this book, and everyone who reads it will take from it something of value. Please won't you join the author as God, the Master Artist, guides her brush while she paints the canvas of her life for you? Cry with her, laugh with her and be touched . . . perhaps even changed . . . by the power of her incredible story. And then share it with others—everyone knows someone who has been abused.

About the Author

Throughout her adult life, Nola Katherine has led Bible studies, prayer groups and retreats on forgiveness. She has spoken to small groups and been asked to share parts of her personal story within her own church and other congregations. Three times she has been the guest of Dr. Gene Getz on his weekly program, *Renewal Radio*. However, she feels her most purposeful moments have been one-on-one and sometimes unexpected encounters with those who are suffering. She is especially drawn to those who suffer the devastating effects of child abuse. For this reason, she has chosen to overcome her fears and allow herself to become a vulnerable, open book. It is her desire for others to experience the freedom she now has from the horrific power her abusers had over her for forty-plus years. She believes that no one should ever have to carry their abuser's anger, guilt and shame . . . especially for so long.

Nola Katherine lives in the Dallas area with Jake, her soul-mate of forty-one years. Her three children, their spouses, and her five grandchildren bring her immeasurable joy and keep her young! She is thankful to God for His presence in her life and that of her family.

Praises for *I Can Begin Again*

"Your book was one of the more socially relevant and inspiring manuscripts that I've read and edited. I felt you; I was close to tears reading and rereading your life story, not to mention your family's story. It's one material people can learn from. Your readers will surely feel the same when they read it. It was a story of hauling oneself out from the quagmire brought about by the harsh circumstances life has to offer. 'Denial was my game. Confusion was its name.' were two powerful lines that will eventually lead one person to living life again—to the fullest."

—Belle Miles, Copy Editor

"I don't even know what to say. I am only on chapter 6. Your story is not only so parallel in personality traits of my own (even the handwriting *thing* because I do it too all the time and cannot figure out why my handwriting varies), but for once in my whole life I am actually sitting here and bawling and grieving and comforting my inner child. After years of dysfunction I have a long way to go. Even my therapist has tried for years to get me to do this; I never really could tap into what she was trying to get me to do. But I'm getting it now. I will continue to read . . . thank you for allowing me to read your manuscript . . . a divine appointment has been kept. Thank you."

—Stefanie M.

"I am halfway through your book, and so far, I am loving it. It is helping me. It is drawing me to have more healing, and God's love is all over your words. I am praising Him for your story, which is much needed in the world and in the Church, the Body of Christ. People will get a feel for what goes on in 'our' (survivors of child abuse) heads and hearts."

—Trudy S.

"I just finished reading your book in a two-evening marathon. It was hard to stop at one thirty in the morning. It was fantastic, very profound, and well written. I particularly liked your technique of the painting and how you interjected the thoughts and emotions of the abused adult child and the survivor. It was an excellent rending of your experiences and truth about healing the body, mind and soul; very honoring to God's work and the love of Jesus. It was very insightful; clearly the hand of the Holy Spirit throughout. It gave me some reinforced insights into the pain and abuse of pornography and awakened some of my own abuse as a child victim myself. I have a lot to process and think about."

—Jerry C.

"Throughout the ages God had used women to save His people; Deborah, Ruth, Esther, Mary. Each one of them were 'raised up for such a time as this.' In each case, God called each woman to step out of her personal circumstances for the good of many. So it is with you. We know that while abuse is a horrible thing, we also know that God will use your life to His glory. He has a master plan for everything. I am honored to have been a part of that plan. I am amazed at the lengths that the Lord went in order to get you and me together. What are the odds that we would be friends with the same people and end up at the same table at the same retreat, 200 miles from my home? Who could have known that you and I would become closer than sisters? Well, the Lord Almighty, of course! He knew all along that He had a story of forgiveness and healing, and you had a talent for telling that story. To complete the process, He gave me a talent for editing. A divine appointment, indeed! You have been raised up. *How beautiful are the feet of those who bring good news, who proclaim peace, who bring good tidings, who proclaim salvation, who say 'Your God reigns!' Isaiah 52:7.*"

—Linda F.

In Memory of Sharon Wilkinson

You finally had your own breakthrough and now you are truly free.
Thank you for showing me the way. Someday we will laugh
together again. I love you.

"To Nola Katherine, who has given so much to so many and deserves so
much more herself. I envy you for all the progress you've made. I hope
to make that breakthrough someday. Thanks to you and your family for
the loving support. Thanks to God for putting you in my life." Sharon
Wilkinson, 1990

Dedication

To all the abused children who have survived to become adults.
To the unimaginable number of children who have been cruelly abused.
To the inconceivable number of children who are being
or will be horrifically abused.
And to the One whose footprints are painted on the canvas of my
life—Jesus, the One who carried me when I could not walk.

Acknowledgments

Above all, I give praise to God for using my life story to His glory, for my good and the good of others. I will be eternally grateful that He never let go of me. Without His loving guidance, there would be no story to tell, no book to write.

I give many, many kudos to my husband for his unconditional love, his soulful encouragement and his patience with my limited computer skills. His honest editing toward the end of this overwhelming task allowed me to let go at last. I love you, Jake, for letting true love walk in. I know that it has not always been easy.

I embrace the sincere, heartrending feedback I received from my grown children and daughter-in-law. I will never forget the Sunday afternoon when together with Jake, we waded through my very rough manuscript. It was so much fun. We laughed and we cried and shared our souls with each other. Katherine, Jay, Kim and Zoe, you are truly great kids. Your suggestions, accolades and encouragement are so precious to me. I love and appreciate you so very much. *That* word will never be the same for me!

I am especially thankful to my retired pastor and friend Dr. Gene Getz for inviting me to tell my story on his weekly program *Renewal Radio*. By giving me the opportunity to speak openly about the childhood abuse, he gave me the courage to move forward and finalize the writing of my story. His advice and encouragement were priceless gifts to me. Thank you, Gene, for being God's inspirational voice to me and so many others.

Lorrie S., Jerry C., Trudy S., Stefanie M. and Dan L., thank you for touching me in a place where I allow few to go. Each of you has confirmed, in very different ways, that I must get my story out there for others to read. Your sincere, honest feedback and your own vulnerability have been invaluable to me. Through you, God revealed once again that His Holy Spirit is leading me. This book is about Him and His purposes and not about me.

Janie O. was the first person outside of my immediate family to read my story. I was terrified to allow her into my private world, but I felt God had arranged for us to have lunch together for the purpose of opening that door. We have been friends for over forty years, and like everyone else in my life, she had no clue about the extent of the painful and shameful secrets I carried within me. Thank you, Janie, for your enthusiastic encouragement and suggestions. It was so much fun to giggle with you about my native Texas tongue—I tend to write like I talk! You gave me the courage to be vulnerable.

Madeliene D. was truly God's instrument in helping me realize that my story had to be written very clearly. The short time we spent together looking at my manuscript was eye-opening for me and caused me to rewrite and reorganize some of my thoughts. Thank you, Madeliene, for always being there for me just when I need you.

Lois H. was my daily cheerleader. The Holy Spirit always sent her to me just when I needed her the most, and that was indeed almost daily. Thank you, Lois, for hanging in there with me throughout this long journey. Your prayers sustained me. I thank God for our special spiritual bond that is so sweet and precious.

I thank my dear friends Gaye C., Pam E., Helen C., Clarice H., Frances F., Donna J., Jeanne W., Juanita M. and my niece Stephanie D. for simply reading completely through my story and not only grieving for the pain my precious child suffered, but also for rejoicing in her healing. In addition, Jennifer S. and Lois S. graciously spent time editing and helping me get my manuscript on the road to recovery. The love, support and encouragement from each of you cheered me on.

Thank you, Jo Ann F., my forever, fun-loving friend. You touched my heart with your honest and loving comments. The Jesus in me loves the Jesus in you. I cherish our special connection. You know my heart.

Linda F., you have been such a blessing to me. Your devotion to God and prayer brought great peace to me. How can I ever thank you enough for embracing me (a total stranger) and my story as if it were your own? You courageously challenged my text where needed, and I sincerely appreciate all of your hard work. Thank you for being God's willing vessel.

Carol L. came to me in the midnight hour of the completion of my manuscript. As a retired school teacher, a dear friend and one of the smartest people I know, she helped me put on the finishing touches. In the process, God had a much bigger plan that we could not see. Carol, I love and appreciate you so very much.

My niece, Matthea S., also came to me in my midnight hour. Her trained eye as an English teacher caught things that all of the rest of us missed. Thank you so much for your quick response. You are precious to me.

Anita B., Cindy M. and Beth C. also reviewed my manuscript at the last moment. Thank you so much for your valuable feedback.

Iva M. did an amazing job of taking old photos and making them usable and turning colored photos into black and white. There are no words to convey how grateful I am to you. And many thanks to my son, Jay, for designing the perfect layout for them. You are the best!

Last but certainly not least are the many who have diligently prayed for me these past two years. There are too many prayer warriors to list individually, but I must mention my church family, the Nelson Life Group, my immediate family and relatives, my friends who live nearby and those who live across this great United States of America. I felt your prayers daily, and I know that I would not be where I am today without you. Please don't stop praying. This book needs to reach many.

In closing, I want you to know that I send many prayers to God for each of you, and I thank Him for putting you in my life. Individually you brought something of value to my manuscript and I coveted your feedback, which I took very seriously. Most importantly, you loved me enough not to judge me, and for an adult who was abused as a child, that is monumental. You all have a very special place in my heart and a special part in the completion of this book. Please know that I love and appreciate *all ya'll* passionately. May God's choicest blessings always be with you. nk

Contents

Foreword

I have chosen to use two letters and a personal experience as a foreword to my book. They each touch the very heart of my story. The first letter was sent to me by an abuser of children, and the second is from a woman who was abused as a child. The short story is a moment shared with my young son.

I am filled with many mixed emotions as I invite you to enter through the doors of my life as an adult within whom there is a precious abused child. Because I know there are millions of stories like the ones behind the following letters, I welcome you with open arms.

June 26, 1996
Dear Nola Katherine,

I want you to know how grateful I am for your openness in sharing your pain and forgiveness with me in the terrible childhood abuse you suffered. I have needed to meet someone like you for many years. I believe nothing happens by chance. God plans and arranges the healing we need in our lives in His own time.

I need to tell you about some of my greatest pain that I've carried for thirty years. And though I know in my heart that God, through Jesus, forgives me, I am still often haunted by the shame, guilt and self-hatred. This pain was the most difficult thing for me to share in my first recovery group because at the time my youngest daughter was eight years old, the same age as one of the little girls I victimized when I was fifteen years old.

I told the men that if anyone ever did to my daughter what I had done to those two innocent little girls, I would kill them. I am still often tortured by what I did in coercing them into my sickness as a young man. Even though I've been forgiven and the Lord has led me to a wonderful new life and pathway of healing, I carry this shame and anguish because I can never go back to them or find them. They were neighbors in a place 1,200 miles away, and of course I have no idea where they are or how their lives are today.

I pray God has shown His grace and mercy on them and healed them. I guess that's one reason I needed to meet you and hear your story. I needed to meet a little girl victim and to see God's grace and healing love in your life. Maybe you needed to meet the fifteen-year-old perpetrator inside me.

I want you to know how sorry and angry I am for what you went through, and for what happened to you in your childhood. You were robbed of your childish joy and innocence. Your soul was murdered. I'm so terribly sorry for the pain and death you suffered.

I am thankful for seeing how the Lord Jesus has reached into your life to resurrect your soul and give you new life, hope, joy and forgiveness. I pray you will continue to heal and grow spiritually, mentally and emotionally day by day. I have carried such self-loathing, pain and self-hatred for so much of my life. I have been unable to forgive myself as Jesus has forgiven me. But when my brother died, the years of lonely secrets, hidden pain and dark shame finally surfaced. It was then that God led me into new paths of recovery. I am thanking Him now, and thanking you that our paths crossed. I needed this next step on my journey. I didn't even know what I had needed, but He knew. I never sexually victimized any little girls ever again. But for many years I have victimized so many, many girls and women with my lust by turning them into objects of my desires deep in my heart and soul. I have hated myself in my deepest pain, not realizing that I too was a childhood victim in so many ways. Pornography was one more tool that fed my addiction. Now I am on a pathway to freedom by God's grace and you have helped me along that pathway.

Thank you so very much.

In Christ,
Jerry C.

June 2008
Dearest Nola Katherine,

It has been sixteen awesome years since I met you and gave my life to Jesus. He sent you into my life at a time when He knew that I needed Him, and He sent just the right person. Jesus used the power of your testimony and ministry, and my life was radically impacted and transformed.

You were giving a retreat on forgiveness at a friend's home over a Mother's Day weekend, and I attended because I thought that I would support the friend who was giving the retreat. What I did not realize was that the Holy Spirit had already started to work on me. I had had anger and rejection issues for years. There were times that I had contemplated suicide and had been in trouble at schools where I had taught. At least three different principals had reprimanded me for my behavior in the way I treated students with verbal abuse. I even had a letter to that fact put in my permanent record file after numerous complaints by parents. Students were removed from my classroom at parents' requests.

The first evening of the retreat you discussed why God wants us to forgive. The group took turns reading different Scripture passages on forgiveness. This really annoyed me, and I still have the paper that you gave us with my definition of forgiveness blank. The next day you shared your testimony with the group. I had never known that other people had been sexually abused. Then you shared about Jesus. I had never heard about salvation, let alone a personal relationship with Him.

I went home that afternoon and felt like something was gnawing inside of me. At the urging of a friend, I went back to speak with you to feel better. What an afternoon! At first, I actually refused to talk with you until you told me that Jesus loved me and gave His life for me. That afternoon I shared about the sexual and emotional abuse of my childhood and was delivered of the anger and hatred that I held so deep within me. You had me forgive those who had abused me and led me in the sinner's prayer. I gave my life to Jesus, and I remember the overwhelming peace that came over me. You even commented that lines disappeared from my face. I was supernaturally healed! A few months later you introduced two books on the Holy Spirit, which led to the experience of the baptism of the Holy Spirit.

The Lord showed me what He can do in a life devoted to Him—peace, joy and love not only for my students at school but also for my family. I was even worse with my family and asked them to forgive me. They said that I changed so much. At school, parents called to compliment me.

The next year I joined my husband in the Middle East where he had been working for almost four years without me (I was not going to go over there.) There I was to carry on with the Lord's work with many unforgettable experiences for ten years. And all because of God putting you in my life at His right time!

I pray that the Lord will continue to use you in showing what He can do in a person's life.

I love you very much,
Lorrie

Memories

I had seen her roaming the neighborhood since she was a very small kitten. Her beautiful calico coat of many colors was hard to miss. My eight- and nine-year-old children and I had discussed the young feline, and so far I had managed to avoid getting involved with her. However, one day in desperation she cleverly staged a dramatic catfight in front of my children. They promptly rescued her and then ran into the house with arms filled with the now-grown cat. She looked lost and hopelessly destitute. With great passion they pleaded their case, "Oh, Mom, pleeeease can we keep her? She neeeeeds us!"

Within the hour, they had acquired cat food and a pet named Patches. Within a few weeks, she repaid their kindness by blessing them with five irresistible, adorable kittens. They were spellbound as they watched new life being birthed, and they marveled at the new mother's instinctive ability to care for her family. They watched the new babies nurse and sleep and creep around with blind eyes that slowly opened to the world around them. They witnessed the kittens' first wobbly steps and their first attempts to play with their siblings. They were tiny miracles unfolding before my children's eyes everyday, and it was so much fun for them to watch this furry mass of growing delight.

However, each passing day sadly drew the kittens to the end of their stay with us. One day, as we stood watching this little family sleep peacefully with their mother, I asked my young son to go into the house and get the camera so that we could take some pictures. I knew this might be the last time we would ever see this little family cuddled together again. When my son did not quickly respond, I looked down at the little boy whose rigid back and tight muscles kept him frozen, unable to respond. His wide, blue eyes held back a well of tears and his top lip was neatly tucked under his bottom lip, a character trait he developed as a toddler when unhappy. Finally, in a voice as sad as the look on his face, he whispered, "Oh, Mom, please don't take any more pictures."

Surprised by his request, I asked him why. "Because, Mom, memories are so painful." He quietly sobbed as I pulled him close to me. His blonde head nestled under my arm as tears spilled down fair, rosy cheeks. Mother and son were transfixed in a capsule of time as emotions mingled together, each understanding the other's quiet, unspoken thoughts and grief.

Memories are like that, I thought. Indelibly printed in the recesses of our minds like acid burning, burning, burning—they never, ever go away. They are like a movie camera clicking off frame after frame and never allowing us to forget—the happy, the sad, the good, the bad. I did not want to remember either, because if I remembered, then I would have to feel, and I did not want to feel.

"Yes, my son, sometimes memories are very painful."

Chapter 1

Could Death Be More Confronting Than This?

The foreboding sound of heavy metal doors closing behind me blazingly defined my life in that cruel moment of shame. One of the night nurses on 3E of the adult psychiatric ward selected a key from the silver chain around her wrist and locked the now silent door behind me and my husband. Jake and I exchanged glances. There was no need for words. After a few moments of instructions, Jake was told that he would have to leave. Soft lights cast eerie shadows in the deadly silence of this unfamiliar place as strangers quietly began to rummage through my hastily packed bag.

"I will be okay," I whispered as I tiptoed to kiss tightly drawn lips. Without warning, I felt the warm security of strong arms around me, holding me tightly, not wanting to let me go. I could see the reflection of pain in Jake's clear, glassy blue eyes—eyes that possessed so much love and concern for the woman he held in such great esteem. Sensing his feeling of complete helplessness, I was unable to reach within myself and find the strength to comfort him. There was simply nothing left. With the exception of my shallow breath, there seemed to be no life within me. I silently wondered if death could be any more confronting than this.

Once again the portentous sound of the impenetrable door disturbed the quietness of the evening, this time putting a wall of separation between us that we both chose not to remove. Like a small abandoned child, I stood with my face pressed against the narrow window of the door and watched as my mate of twenty-two years disappeared into the elevator. I wanted to cry, but there were no tears. I wanted to scream, but there was no voice. I wanted to run, but there was no place to go. The reality of our decision began to sink in as my heart said good-bye. Methodically, I turned from the door and watched my few possessions being taken away and locked up. I was told that this was for my own protection and the protection of others.

I was too numb to care and wondered if the survivor that lived within me would be able to rescue me this time. There had been so many times before when I thought I would go to that place of no return, over the edge, but I had always managed to come back, to hold on and to survive just one more time. But no more! This was it! There was no turning back, and I would either find the answers I needed to do more than just survive—to get well—or I would die. Silently I cried out, "Oh God, will I survive? Will my family survive? How will we ever get through this? Please help us! Please, God, help me!" In that woeful moment the One to whom I cried out, the One who had been there so many times before, seemed so far away.

The barrage of instructions tossed at me went barely noticed until stern words caught my attention. "As of now, you are on a seventy-two-hour suicide watch which means that you cannot leave the unit for anything. You will have all of your meals on the unit. You may not have any visitors or phone calls. Your room will be checked every fifteen minutes during the night and throughout the day." I started to protest that I was not suicidal, but the nurse quickly explained, "This is standard procedure for everyone who checks into this hospital. You have no choice."

Suppressed anger rose to my temples and throbbed in sync with my pounding heart. It grasped at my clinched muscles. Veiled anger turned inward, deepening the numbness I felt. It anesthetized my mind and emotions and sent shock waves of pain throughout my body. These were the rules, and I had to follow them. I wanted to yell at these people and tell them to please stop—to please just lock me up and leave me alone. I sighed and reluctantly, yet obediently, turned to find my assigned room. If only I could stop the pain . . .

*　　*　　*

Dear Reader, I have just painted the first stroke on the canvas of my life story for you. I believe that every minute detail of our existence somehow fits onto a very large canvas that we call life. Our history continually portrays an immense picture that often remains obscure until one day we stand back, look at our canvas, and begin to see the genuine character of our emerging painting. Just like an artist who knows that his mistakes will often add character and depth to a painting, we who have struggled to survive also know that our life's canvas would not be complete without the shadows of pain.

Over thirty years ago that still small voice, which I believe to be God's spirit within, began to speak to me about writing my story. Although the seeds were planted many years ago, I could never have imagined in my wildest dreams just where those seeds would sprout up and take root. Eventually, that small voice became louder and louder until finally I spent an entire day searching through two large boxes full of notes and untold pages of previously written events about my life. The task was overwhelming to the point that I just stopped digging, went to my computer, and began once again to write my story.

Before I continue, there are a few things that are important for you to know about me. First of all, I am an *abused adult/child (AAC)*.[1] In other words my dignity, my power and my God-given rights as a human being were stolen from me as a small, innocent child. As an adult, I bear the scars of those atrocious violations. By God's grace I have experienced incredible healing, but my abused child will always

---

[1]　Abused Adult/Child (AAC): an adult within whom lives an abused child.

be with me. She will always carry the memory of the wounds of abuse. She will always live in my skin.

Almost everything about an abused adult/child's life is confusing, and as you read this book, you may sometimes find my story confusing as well. If this happens, then I have succeeded in giving you insights into the life of an abused child who must eventually survive in an adult world. And even though I do refer to this book as my story, you are actually reading an experience, which is defined as the accumulation of knowledge that results from the direct participation in events. My knowledge is neither black nor white, but has many variables. The life of an abused adult/child is often inconsistent, changeable, uncertain and often unexplainable. It is what it is! Some of my thoughts may seem repetitive, but there is a reason for the repetition. More often than not, we must hear an idea over and over before we finally understand it. And I really do want you to understand. Also as you read, it is important for you to keep in mind the venue from which the experience is written, a psychiatric hospital. Now, please stop and *read this paragraph again* and remember what I have said, so that when you do stop and scratch your head and say, "What?" you will recall that I warned you. The life of an abused adult/child in most instances is very confusing and difficult to comprehend.

It is important for you to know that I have absolutely no need to talk about or dwell on my past for my own sake. My past is behind me, and I do not need to go back. Therapeutic writing was done years ago. I do, however, feel that I have been called to open the doors of my life for others who are stuck in their pain. It is my heart's desire they might find the courage to open the locked doors of their own lives to find hope and ultimately to find wholeness.

Secondly, I have an unrelenting desire to honor God and to give glory to Him for all that He has done in my life through Jesus Christ and His Holy Spirit. To bear the title of Christian is a great privilege, but to be a Christ-follower, one must go beyond the privilege of simply bearing His identity. Jesus proclaimed that He came for the sick, the brokenhearted, the sinner. He came to set the captives free. As a

Christ-follower, I have been called to a life dedicated to bringing hope to a hurting humanity. I am to open my heart and pave the way for others to know this immeasurable love that is so strong and powerful and yet so gentle that human words fall short in defining it. To *know* that *I know* the God who *knows me* is a gift that is to be guarded and protected. It is sacred. It is a gift that every Christ-follower should earnestly pray for every human on earth to possess. We are limited by the boundaries of our humanness to fully understand it or explain it, but we can experience it, live it and share it. It is for this, the gift of knowing God's great love for me and all of mankind, that I have been called. To tell my story, my experience, is my gift back to God and to His wounded children.

Thirdly, my husband has encouraged me, and my three children have consistently begged me to write my story. Even Zoe, my daughter-in-law, pleaded that I owe it to our family to tell my story. "Yours is a great story of faith, and who knows what future generations will have to face. They need to know your story!" I agree with her because I strongly believe that America, as I have known it, is slowly passing away. I often shudder to think what my grandchildren and the children that come after them may have to endure. Perhaps someday an aged, worn book discovered on a dusty shelf, or found in a long-forgotten, old trunk stored away in an attic, will find its way into the hands of one who has lost all hope. Perhaps it will bring renewed faith in the God of a faithful, ancient grandparent. I sincerely pray that God's story in me will live on for many generations to come.

And finally, it was the harsh, never-ceasing cries of all abused children past, present and yet to come, that kept calling my name. *Enough.org* reported the following statistics: From the *National Center for Missing and Exploited Children*, research indicates that one in four girls, and one in six boys will be sexually victimized before reaching adulthood. The same website reported from the *American Journal of Preventive Medicine, 2005,* that one in four women reported sexual childhood abuse. They also reported that the magnitude of sexual childhood abuse is overwhelming and largely unrecognized and under reported. There is an unimaginable world of statistics about every kind of abuse on the Internet, and I encourage you to do your own research. The unbelievable, ever-increasing, sick exploitations of babies, toddlers and young children on the Internet and the trafficking of innocent boys and girls rattled my brain and tore at my heart. They forced me to face my overpowering fears and find the courage to tell my story. But before that was possible, there were paths for me to follow and lessons for me to learn so that I could remove the sackcloth of mourning and exchange it for pure, God-breathed redemption. I fervently pray that many will read my story, hear God's voice, and find His pathway to wholeness for themselves.

It is also my hope that many who have crossed over that sacred line and become abusers of children will read my story and will finally understand the devastating consequences of their actions. It is my prayer that my story will persuade abusers to be repentant and seek help—before it's too late—before they make the decision to abuse another child. What we fail to comprehend is that for every statistic recorded on the sexual abuse of children . . . there are predators to match those statistics. (Please see additional information about abuse in the Guidelines section at the end of the book.)

It is not easy to be open and honest about the deep, innermost realm of self. Vulnerability scares the heebie-jeebies right into the very core of my being, but I know that I must take whatever risk confronts me. If just one tormented, hopelessly defeated child of God (and we are *all* children of God) finds freedom, finds peace, finds joy, finds healing, then I find value in my own sufferings. Most importantly, if one finds God through my journey of unbearable pain, bereaved sorrow, unintentional mistakes and invaluable lessons learned, it gives meaning to my life. I must dare to be vulnerable.

I write to family members, friends, therapists, ministers, Christians, and non-Christians who are touched in some way by one like me in the hope that they will gain new insights. The abused adult/child is deeply misunderstood. Their sometimes-erratic behavior is the result of wounded, fragmented and sometimes-split personalities that are desperately screaming out for those closest to them to understand and to love them unconditionally. However, the abused adult/child is not always able to receive nor reciprocate the love and acceptance they themselves crave. Figuratively speaking, I want so very much for you to crawl into my skin so that you can better understand what I am attempting to communicate. Realistically, I know you will never fully understand the heart and soul of a child who has been abused and who will *someday live* in the skin of an adult, or the abused child who *now lives* in the skin of an adult.

I invite you to look inside my world where severe depression, suicidal depression, alcoholism, divorce, pornography and confused sexuality tormented the abused adult/child. You will begin to understand why she trusted no one and struggled with relationships. You will see what caused her to have severe panic attacks, forcing her to find dark places in her mind to hide when she was afraid and felt unsafe.

I will unmask what it means to be exposed to pornography as a child and the evils that lurk in porn's deadly pathway. I pray that you will grasp the devastating, lingering effects that pornography will have on anyone who is lured into its deception.

You will feel this mother's painful journey with her two terminally ill children. And you will rejoice with her in her many victories. It is my expectant hope that at this book's end, you will look at the world around you through the clearer eyes of understanding, acceptance, compassion, forgiveness, love, faith and hope.

Sadly, I am compelled to address the Church, the Body of Christ, and how it responds or does not respond to wounded souls. I had to give serious thought to this portion of my life's story and the impact that it had on me. It has been said that if you don't like something, change it; but if you can't change it, then change the way you look at it. I had to change the preconceived ways that I looked at the religion I embraced because the *religion* of Christianity, more times than we want to admit, fails the cause of Christ. Unfortunately, God is the one who gets blamed for our shortcomings. I hope my story will cause you to look anew at your own walk of faith, your relationship with God and your relationship with others. Please understand that I wrestled long and hard before and during the writing of my church experience. There were times when I literally paced the floor and wrung my hands, crying out to God for direction. I felt that I could not move forward. I struggled with the information that I was putting forth and feared its negative impact. But then, I would feel God's Holy Spirit pulling me back into my story and whispering, "Just keep writing. I am with you." Within my church experience, you will find my wounded abused child trying desperately to survive in an adult world that should have brought healing, but instead caused the wounds of my childhood to fester.

Before concluding this brief introduction, I want to say that this book is about my life, but this story is really not about me. It is about something that is far beyond the one who writes it. Once again, please know, please understand the stories I share with you are simply my stories and a part of my life experiences. They impacted me greatly, and I believe many of them will impact you, the reader, as well. It will not be an easy book to read, but I promise you, it will give any soap opera a run for its money. I believe you will be captivated by the redemptive drama charted by the choices of the characters depicted on the pages. Above all else, it is my sincere desire to ultimately bring good and in no way, with any intention, do I write to offend or to bring harm. Finally, as you read my story, I ask you not to judge me. I warn you, there may be times when you will be tempted to do so. You may even be tempted to stop reading. However, I beg you to persevere to the end. I promise it will be worth it.

In most instances, I have used fictional names especially for doctors, ministers, therapists, etc. For the most part, I have avoided using specific names of organizations and groups of people. I have used first names of family and close friends. It is my desire to be as sensitive as possible without losing the authenticity of my story.

It is time to move on! Grab a cup of hot tea—with three lumps of sugar and clotted cream—and a can of Pringles, or whatever excessive indulgences you occasionally desire. Let us gather up pens for sketching, plump tubes filled with an assortment of alluring colors and several good paintbrushes. Come along with me as I begin to paint an amazing picture of my life for you. Better still, let's do it together! Embrace me, cry with me, rejoice with me, ponder with me, grow with me, and experience the events of my life with me as we wash across the pages of time. I will sketch in the outline, and then together we will paint in dark shadows where we will occasionally add shades of light. At times, we will stand back and examine my unfinished painting. Then we will begin again until all the brilliant colors of my life unfold the power of my story.

Chapter 2

Facing the Roaring Lion

My blank canvas, like my story, must begin with sketches. Before we can begin to paint, I must come up with a plan that will lead us through this extraordinary maze of trials, errors, and successes. Let me first draw a few characters into the background where my story begins. For clarification purposes, know that I entered into the adult psychiatric hospital in July 1990, at the age of forty-six, for the purpose of working on issues surrounding sexual child abuse. However, the final downward spiral into this seemingly bottomless pit in which I found myself began in September 1989.

My husband's father, who was in his seventies, had undergone major heart surgery. Subsequently, he developed a syndrome that affected the use of his legs and was faced with a long rehabilitation. My mother-in-law, who was also in her seventies, had the effervescence of a thirty-year-old. Pausing to take care of her husband added undue stress to her very active life. In the meantime, Jake's youngest sister left her teenage son with us so that she could return to Michigan to finalize some personal matters. While there, she had a severe pancreatic attack which almost took her life. Because of the situation with Jake's parents, I gladly made myself available to help out during my sister-in-law's recovery after she was well enough to return to Texas. At the time our two older children were away at college and our twelve-year-old was, of course, still at home. By the time Christmas morning rolled around, everyone was out of the hospital, and in spite of all the stress, we managed to make Christmas the traditional all-day event that we cherished. My father-in-law continued rehab as an outpatient, and Jake's sister was scheduled for additional surgery after the first of the year.

The chills of January 1990 crossed over into February's dreariness, as life seemed to be getting back to normal. I was getting caught up on housework, laundry and a neglected pre-teen when I decided to attend a workshop for survivors of abuse which Clark, a therapist in our church, had recommended. He and I had briefly discussed childhood issues, and he thought that it might be beneficial for me to attend the rather expensive three-day event. The workshop unexpectedly opened Pandora's Box for me. I was just beginning to absorb the impact of the long weekend sessions when once again, storm clouds began to roll my way as my phone rang.

The frantic voice on the other end of the line belonged to my sister. "You have got to come and get Mother. I can't take care of both of them!" Our eighty-year-old mother had suffered a severe asthma attack several days earlier, and typically, instead of getting her to a doctor, my sister was just going to let our mother ride it out. Instinctively, I knew Mom was critical. I tried to give my sister some slack because her second husband was very ill with cancer. Sis had already lost one husband to cancer, and I knew this was a difficult time for her. I will get into family dynamics later, but the forty-minute trip across town gave me plenty of time to inwardly build up a storehouse full of anger toward my sister.

I pulled our large silver-and-blue Suburban into the driveway of the small, gray frame house where my sister had lived for forty years. The very sight of the house triggered off flashbacks of images that were not welcome to entertain me. I deliberately pushed them away and denied them access into my already-grumbling spirit. Heaviness filled my legs as I stepped onto the concrete porch, opened the wooden front door of the house and walked inside. Immediately, icy terror struck me in the pit of my stomach when I saw my petite, white-haired mother gasping for air. She was inhaling small amounts of oxygen and barely able to exhale. Carbon dioxide was building up in her body, and she was swollen to almost twice her size. She was incoherent to the point that she hardly recognized me, the youngest of her five children. I turned to my sister and asked her why she had not called me sooner. My tone of voice did not give way to the anger I was feeling. Giving neither of them a choice, I turned to my mother and told her I was taking her to an emergency room. For once, neither of them challenged me. In retrospect, I cringe to think of the decision that I made to drive back across town to a hospital closer to my own home. I wanted my mother away from my sister's influence, and selfishly I wanted her closer to me so that I could take care of her while not neglecting my own family. The trip was agonizing and seemed eternal. I kept begging, pleading with God to please help my mom breathe.

Emergency room attendants wasted no time tending to my mother and quickly assessed her need to be on a life-support system. Even as ill as Mom was, when she heard the words life-support, she raised her head and shouted, "No!" For some reason my mother had a huge fear of being kept alive and had frequently instructed me never to allow anyone to put her on life-support. She was moved to the intensive care unit of the hospital where a lung specialist informed me that he was not sure if he would be able to pull her through this attack.

I knew it was going to be a long night as I stood by her bed watching her struggle for each breath, unconsciously trying to breathe for her. How many times had she been through a similar scenario since my father had died in 1980 from the horrible effects of sixty-plus years of smoking? I could never understand how she could continue to smoke after spending a lifetime standing over him, trying to revive him as he lay on the floor choking and turning blue. I would get hysterical and be banished from the room. Smoking had become a source of contention between me and my family. Not only had my parents smoked, but all of my siblings smoked as well. They did not respect my personal space when it came to smoking, and I resented their attitudes. I was beginning to experience health issues, which I felt were directly related to my being around secondhand smoke all of my life.

Family members came in and out of the ICU throughout the evening. I think everyone was silently feeling they had come to say good-bye. Visiting hours came to an end, and I was left alone to watch and to wait, unaware that I was there for a divine appointment. During the sleepless, quiet, dark hours of night, I tried to comfort my frail, strong-willed mother as she fought the restraints that dug into her tender skin. "Mom, please try not to fight. You need to stay calm so that you can breathe."

Her white hair, tinged with hints of yellow nicotine, was drenched in sweat. The few lines in her face appeared uncharacteristically deep. "Let me go! I want to go!"

I reached out and gently touched the clammy hand of this woman who stirred so many mixed emotions within me. I tiptoed to reach over the bed rail, stretching so that I could whisper into her ear, "Mom, where do you want to go?"

Her voice became strong and determined, "I want to cross over the river."

I prodded, "What river?"

Feeble, shaking hands attempted to point toward the ceiling. "That river, the one right there! I can see Grandma and Grandpa, and there is Mama, too. Please let me go. I want to go over to the other side of the river."

I did not understand the true significance of my words back to her that night. I wanted to tell her that it was okay to go, but instead I pleaded, "Mother, you can't go yet. I need for you to stay with me just a little while longer. Please, stay with me just a little while longer."

To everyone's surprise, except perhaps mine, a week later I took Mother home with me to recuperate. I knew it would not be easy, but I did not care. I really wanted to take care of her. Consequently, our time together became the best memory that I have with my mother. I would not buy cigarettes for her, and for a change she was getting ample amounts of oxygen to her brain. I made sure she had regular healthy snacks and good meals. Her blood sugar levels remained steady, which kept depression and mood swings in check. She was healthier than I had seen her in a long time, and the sweet, good-natured side of her that I had occasionally glimpsed slowly began to emerge. We laughed, we joked, we hugged, and for the first time in my life I felt close to my mother. But it did not last. I had to let her go. She returned home to her cigarettes, and we returned to life as we had known it before she had tried to cross over the river.

February with its winter mix gently waved good-bye as March came in like a lamb, and as the old saying goes, we expected March to go out like a lion. And it did! On my son's nineteenth birthday, our golden retriever's restlessness told me that it was her time. Unbelievably, Chewy produced twelve huge, golden puppies within just a few hours. When puppy number ten was only halfway born, she decided that she had had enough and stopped pushing. Take-charge caretaker that I am, I quickly delivered Angel. When stimulation failed to produce life-giving breath, I put my mouth over hers and breathed life into her lungs. She squealed, I praised God and Chewy reluctantly lay back and gave birth to two more babies. As exhaustingly joyous as the whole event had been, somehow I just knew that a litter of twelve might not be such a good thing. At the advice of a local golden retriever club, I rotated these delightful, fluffy darlings every two hours for several weeks. Chewy only had ten places at the dinner table, so to speak, and I needed to make sure they all got their fair share.

Weeks of rotating puppies night and day, months of helping with Jake's family, trying to meet the needs of my own family and taking care of Mom for six weeks, were at best difficult. If the weekly trips across town to bathe, clean and shop for mom were not enough, let's add into the mix the death of my sister's second husband, Jake losing his job and the kids coming home from college for the summer. And, oh yes, I was just beginning to think about and feel the burden of my tumultuous forty-six-year secret life.

As spring turned into summer, an almost irreversible physical toll began to take over my body. The Texas summer heat encouraged my sleeplessness. I found myself getting up in the middle of the night and staring into a place of void for long hours at a time—unable to think, unable to focus, unable to deny previously dormant, unwanted images that had only recently began to flash across my mind. Depression resurrected a new wave of despair over me as its shrewd, black hole began to crack open and suck me into its grip, depleting my mind, body and spirit of hope.

I had danced with this fickle intruder of spirit since I was sixteen years old, but this trespasser had suddenly changed and was somehow different. I felt strangely numb, and for the first time in my life I could not function. I mentioned to Jake that I was struggling, and we agreed I probably needed to get some help. I sought out a therapist that our COBRA insurance would pay for and made an appointment. With hair and makeup in place and a smile on my face, I walked into this man's office and simply related the events of the past few months. He agreed that I had been under a lot of stress and that I probably needed to be on medication. He gave me the name of a psychiatrist.

A week later, dressed and groomed as though I had stepped out of a magazine, I met Dr. Kamen coming out of his office. We spoke briefly as he invited me inside, offering that he would return in a few moments. To this day I cannot tell you what really happened during my time with this doctor. Did I see trust in him, or was I just desperate to trust? Did he see a void in my eyes or hear emptiness in my voice? Did he sense shameful and sometimes forever-silent secrets and desperate unspoken cries? Had I offered to him more than my usual, "I was abused, I am depressed," response when I mentioned the workshop that I had recently attended? Had God opened a tiny window that allowed this perceptive stranger to look into my child-soul, or had this simply been another divine appointment?

"Nola, you are really scaring me! I met you an hour ago in the hallway and you looked as though you did not have a care in the world. I would never have guessed what you are carrying inside of you. How much longer do you think you can do this?" His words were unrelenting.

I drew my lips tighter as tears threatened to roll off my cheeks onto my neatly folded hands. My voice barely audible, I whispered, "I don't know." I was unable to raise my head and look into the doctor's concerned dark eyes.

He continued, "I don't normally recommend hospitalization the first time I see someone, but I suggest you go to the phone, call your husband, and have him meet you at the psychiatric facility near the hospital."

I sat in stunned silence, not wanting to breathe. To breathe meant to live, and it was just too hard to live. How could I tell anyone that I did not want to live, especially my husband and my children, when I had so very much to live for? But no! I wasn't suicidal! I did not want to die! I just wanted the pain to stop. I just wanted the perpetual, never-ending, all-consuming, secret pain to go away.

If I had been able to feel, I am sure I would have felt terror at the thought of actually going into a psychiatric hospital. If I had been able to reason, I would have made excuses that I could not leave my family for the proposed three week hospital stay. If I had been able to feel shame, I would have turned away and run for my life. I was an expert at minimizing and denying the power of my own experiences. But this course, this divine appointment, had already been set in motion for me in February when I had attended the survivors' workshop designed for adults who had been abused as children.

The workshop had been led by a well-known woman who had a highly successful treatment center in another state. This experienced lady quickly assessed that there was a very broken, damaged and vulnerable child living within me, but I was neither ready to talk about her nor capable of talking about her. For the first time in my life, I was told that there was a precious child living inside of me, and she was worthy of love and protection. Furthermore, a simple test revealed I had no boundaries. Anyone could walk into my space, and I would not retreat or object. Repeatedly she asked me, "Who took care of you?" I would just shake my head and say nothing as the distant voice of my aunt, my mother's unmarried sister, reminded me, "You weren't raised. You just grew up." I was clueless to the clues that were being given to me.

During the workshop, it did not take long for this gentle and wise lady to evaluate my fragile state of mind, although every outward appearance indicated that I was anything but fragile. The facade I had created for myself and wore diligently would prove to be a curse/blessing. A blessing because it helped me to survive by giving me a way to hide from the unthinkable secrets that picked away at the very core of my being; a curse because I was inadvertently as sick as my secrets the facade hid. By keeping my secrets hidden, I was doomed to inwardly relive them over and over. The disguise I wore kept people out, the abused child locked in, and everyone around me confused. This highly skilled professional told Clark, who had attended the weekend event with me, that she would do very little work with me during the sessions. She also cautioned that if he did any therapy work with me at all, he needed to be very careful. At the end of the workshop, she met with both of us privately and strongly recommended that I check myself into a hospital where I could safely deal with my troubling childhood issues. I was unable to comprehend the magnitude of what she was saying about me, or to me, and I came away with feelings of both resolve and restraint. Resolve, that someone had looked beyond the many masks I wore and dared to give me honest direction; restraint, because I was deathly afraid of removing them. I came away from the workshop feeling drained, confused and helpless as I went back to doing life as usual.

Little did I know then that the cold winds of February that had ushered in the gentle lamb of March would ultimately turn into the huge roaring lion that I now faced. The time had come for me to face this roaring lion. I took a deep breath and raised my head. My eyes locked into the steady gaze of Dr. Kamen's unyielding perception, and with resignation in my voice, I agreed to call my husband.

With my emotions back in control, the doctor led me to a private phone where I called Jake. Without emotion, I told him what the doctor had advised, but I was much too responsible to just drop out of life on such short notice. Since it was late Friday afternoon, we decided that I would return home and not check into the hospital until late Sunday evening. I needed time to prepare my children, get the house in order, and meet with a cousin I had previously agreed to see on Sunday. We had never met before. Otherwise, the timing was perfect for me to get away for three weeks. The older children would be busy with their summer jobs. My youngest was visiting a friend in Denver, and Jake would be home to stay with his daughter upon her return in two weeks. I can't begin to imagine what I must have put my family through initially. The children had never heard me talk about the depression or the abuse, but like their father, they loved me and supported my decision to go into the hospital.

Chapter 3

Unit 3E—There Is Nothing Shameful about Finding Answers

I don't remember very much about my first seventy-two hours in the hospital. I could not sleep and since I seldom took medication for anything, it did not occur to me that I could ask for something to help me sleep. My body became more and more tense, and the physical pain that I felt was unbearable. Dr. Kamen prescribed an antidepressant, and after a few days of taking it, I might as well have put my finger into an electrical outlet. When I finally complained, I was given something to counteract the negative effect of the antidepressant. Eventually, I began to level out somewhere between a high-wire performer and a zombie.

Rules on 3E were very strict, and the routine became extremely demanding for me after I was taken off the suicide watch. Up for meds, off to breakfast, back to the meeting room, down to the gym for physical activity, finally to lunch and then the fun began. Meetings, meetings and more meetings: cognitive therapy, occupational therapy, group meetings, therapy sessions, doctor's meeting, psychological testing, art therapy, music therapy, optional spiritual therapy, but worst of all was Barb, the psychologist who probed and prodded for information about my past.

I was allowed to have visitors after dinner each evening before the final meeting of the day in the meeting room. Then it was off to the dreaded bed for a dreaded night of dreaded tossing and turning and dreaded thinking, thinking and more thinking. I could not shut off my brain, and the black hole of depression continued its never-ceasing attempt to steal my life from me. I wanted out—out of my skin, out of my brain, out of this box that I lived in. But no matter how hard I tried, I couldn't find my way out. My mind was caught in a prison of despair that twisted my ability to be in touch with reality. I knew where I was, but I could not understand how or why life had managed to lock *me* up, whoever *me* was. And for the first time in my life, I questioned my identity. I was a wife, a mother. I was a daughter, a sister, a friend—but really, who was I? Resistant surrender began to settle on my raw emotions like a strong, black hawk covering its prey. My will to fight had slipped away. My will to survive was waning. But my will to live had not succumbed to the dark powers that wanted to defeat me. My silent pleas to God were continual, "Oh God, help me! Please, God, help me!" If only I could cry . . . would morning ever come?

*   *   *

My first encounter in the meeting room was ominous to say the least. I was oblivious to the fact that I was meeting my new temporary family. Michael, who was an attractive, exuberant young man with a thin mustache, magnetic smile and caring eyes, was in charge of the third floor unit. He also led the twice daily gatherings of all patients on 3E in the meeting room. With protective authority, he began the morning ritual, "State your name, tell how long you have been here, why you are here, and what your goal is for the day."

My thoughts did flip-flops all around the inside of my head, "What? I have to speak! Goals for the day? Are you kidding me?" I wanted to bolt from my chair and run to—a locked door. Oh great! With my legs crossed, foot swinging, muscles taut, poised, I sat like a stone statue with my hands gripping the seat of my chair. And I listened. I listened to snippets of tangled lives, much like my own. The nurturing, sensitive side of me emerged just long enough to give me a reason to set aside my own agenda and fears. I had always been called Nola, but in this setting, I made the decision to use my full name. Symbolically, Nola had been the part of me that had always been very strong, but now was also very tired and needed a break. If there was indeed a precious child within me, her name was Nola Katherine, and I had come there to find her. "My name is Nola Katherine, and I am depressed. I was admitted last evening, and my goal is just to get through this day."

*　　*　　*

I have had countless, unexpected encounters with people who briefly brought varied and diverse attributes to my life, but the memories of some on Unit 3E remain with me. Their many colors added new dimensions to my life's canvas as I watched their own stories slowly unfold before me. They came from many different walks of life. They were all very fine people, intelligent men and women who were more often than not highly educated. Through getting to hear their stories, I began to realize that I was not alone. Perhaps there were some who could understand the depths of my pain and not judge me if I dared to tell my story.

More importantly, I realized that like my new impermanent family, I was neither mentally ill nor insane, and there was *nothing shameful about wanting to find answers*. We all lived in crazy, mixed-up worlds and were just trying to figure out the why of it all. We wanted to learn how to do more than just survive. We wanted to live. Let me introduce you to some of these precious ones. Depression was epidemic. Just know that we were all depressed, so I don't have to repeat the obvious.

Bill was in his twenties and very tall and slender. Thick, black eyelashes made you look twice at his beautiful, dark eyes. He was kind and polite, but he was already well into the disease of alcoholism. He had lost his job and his girlfriend. Jimmy was overweight, and his low self-esteem was heightened by his father's abuse. Becky, mid-forties, was an attractive, blonde executive whose husband had divorced her five years earlier. She could not move on. Cheryl was a lawyer whose marriage was crumbling. Sue's brain had been damaged due to an incorrect prescription medication. She cried all of the time. Jean had been sexually abused as a child. John, mid-twenties, was gay and had been sexually abused by his mother. He could not cope with the confusion he felt. Gary had AIDS and was trying to cope with the devastating diagnosis. Jane's very successful fifty-something husband left her and her children for a younger woman. Jody had attempted suicide after the birth of her fifth child. The one we secretly called Barbie had a nine-month-old baby she could not bond with; she did not want to be a mother. Jack, who once had an extremely high IQ, worked for a large corporation doing detailed analysis. He was struck by a car while riding his bicycle. His head injury left him with an IQ of one hundred and fifty, and he was having a very difficult time trying to accept his *disability*. Suzanne, a single mother and business woman, was drugged and assaulted by business associates while on a business trip. There were many horror stories of abuse. There were many who came in and out of the doors of 3E for short stays. There were three who impacted me greatly.

My first night in the hospital, a slender, personable strawberry blonde walked up to me and said, "Hi! I'm Sharon. I've already been here six weeks." She then put her index finger to her temple and twisted her hand back and forth to signify that she was *crazy*, tilted her head, crossed her eyes, and offered me a contagious laugh. "And I am gay! Now that we have that out of the way, I'll show you around." In one of the darkest hours of my life, Sharon made me laugh. My entire family loved and embraced Sharon. In time she trusted me with her secrets, horrific secrets that she was unable to tell the staff or her small group, not even her doctor. I will always believe that it was Sharon's inability to talk that eventually enabled me to talk about my own deep, dark secrets. I saw the absolute confusion, terror, shame and fear that was trapped beneath a quick smile, a warm heart and a witty sense of humor. When Sharon's insurance would no longer pay for her stay, she was released from the hospital. She went into a county hospital, and upon being released from that hospital, she took a gun and blew out her brains all while talking to her mother on the phone and while policemen were throwing tear gas into the windows of her home. She was so alone and so desperately lonely. She needed more from this life than anyone could possibly give to her. I was heartbroken for this precious child of God whose life was destroyed by wicked, sexual child predators. Yet through it all, Sharon wrote beautiful poetry and believed in Jesus. Based upon what Sharon told me, I do not believe that she was actually gay; she feared men. This was her way of avoiding intimacy with them. Sharon was wounded. She is now healed, now set free, now with Jesus.

Julie came onto our unit like a bull in a china closet, immediately getting everyone's attention. If we met her coming down the hall, we would literally hug the wall opposite her. And for sure no one wanted to make eye contact with her. We would rather have died than talk to her. She appeared to be very rough, and everything about her screamed, "Don't mess with me!" Honestly, I was scared to death of her. But I will never forget this stout, robust young woman with large deep-set eyes and a wide, square jaw. One day, I was working at a table near Julie in art therapy. She had been working on an incredible drawing of a large city skyline. I thought it was amazing and felt compelled to compliment her artwork. Much to my surprise, Julie looked at me with soft eyes and graciously thanked me. From that moment on, I had a new friend. Julie was bipolar. In all my life I have never seen anyone so misunderstood, so judged. When I looked behind her mask, I found a dear, loving, talented person who just wanted to be loved unconditionally. I don't know what has happened to Julie, but I still get tears in my eyes when I think of her.

And then there was Joe, who came in and out of our lives in a flash. I talked with him when he first arrived on 3E and saw the all-familiar depths of depression with which he struggled. I was shocked when in just a matter of days he appeared completely recovered. He convinced his doctor to release him. The day following his release, we were called into the meeting room only to be told that Joe had left the hospital, driven to a nearby lake, and shot himself in the head. During my next session with Dr. Kamen, I told him that I had seen myself in Joe. I needed for him to know that I was just as capable as Joe of convincing everyone in the hospital that I was perfectly okay. I begged him to please not release me until we all knew for sure that I had made sufficient strides toward recovery. I really believe that was the day when I looked denial in the face and began to accept the truth about my fragile state of being. God had put me there for a reason, and I needed to pay close attention. I had a lot of work to do.

Chapter 4

Family History—You Have to Take What You Get

It has only been in retrospect that I have come to realize how important it is for us to find out as much as we can about our history of origin. My family history will become the wash or the background for my life painting. When working with oil or acrylic paints, sometimes before actually beginning a painting, an artist will cover the canvas with a small amount of paint mixed with water. When a wash is applied to a blank canvas, you never really know how it is going to turn out because water mixed with paint, whether gingerly or randomly applied, can take on a mind of its own, much like our family history. Sometimes it's good, sometimes it's not so good, but you just have to take what you get. My work really began when Barb, the psychologist, appeared in my room with pen and notepad in hand. She had come to help me pick up my paintbrush and begin the difficult and demanding process of washing through distant spaces of time with the hope of revealing untapped memories, unspoken truths and stowed-away secrets. There were many years of crucial information to explore and to sift through. It is time for you to pick up your brushes and work with me. Our task will not be easy.

In search of a quiet, out-of-the-way place to work, we settled into burgundy chairs positioned in front of a window at the end of a long hallway. The hot July sun peeking through the window gave welcome relief from the cold, air-conditioned building. I was always cold. As usual, I crossed my legs, and my foot began its anxious swing. I wasn't sure just what she meant by history and was a bit uneasy about our meeting. Barb, professionally poised with pen in hand and ready to listen, asked me to tell her about my father. In spite of my shut-down emotions, my knack for organizing detail could easily and methodically state the facts. I began . . .

Dad was born in 1899. He was forty years old when I was born, and he always seemed like an old man to me. He had a very hard life. He was one of nine children, being the third from the youngest. His mother died shortly after giving birth to the last baby. The baby died too. Dad was only three years old at the time, and he had a younger brother, Ben. They lived on a farm in Oklahoma, and I have been told that my grandmother walked to town to buy food and hemorrhaged to death. My grandfather was a heavy drinker and alleged to be a womanizer, so who knows where he was when my grandmother needed him. I have been told that all of Dad's brothers were heavy drinkers too, but thankfully my father was not.

I am amazed that Dad even survived childhood. He was born with a severe cleft palate and cleft lip. My grandfather refused to have his son's deformity corrected because, according to my mother, my grandfather boasted that no woman would ever have my dad looking like *that.* Apparently, my grandfather wanted to be assured he would always have someone to take care of him when he got old. By the time Dad turned eighteen, he had worked and saved enough money to have corrective surgery. The surgeon did an amazing job because I wasn't even aware of his condition until my mother told me about it when I was a senior in high school.

There was only one girl born in this family of boys. Her name was Eva, and she became a victim of incest. She had two babies, both girls, by her own father, my grandfather. Yes, you read that correctly—my grandfather raped his only daughter. One of the girls, Ruby Ellen, has been lost to the family.[1] No one knows what happened to her. The other girl Beulah, whom we call Billye, was sold for four hundred dollars and some land to a man in his forties. She was only thirteen years old at the time. Family members told my mother they heard Billye screaming all night long their first night together. She gave birth to two children by this man, and when she was nineteen years old she took her children and ran away. The father of the children found Billye and stole her children away from her. She never saw them again. They were only three and four years of age at the time.

Billye made her way to California where some nuns helped her to get on her feet. Eventually she became a companion to an elderly lady who had no heirs. She left her estate to Billye, who opened up a business, became actively involved in her community and married a prominent businessman. Her new husband tried to find Billye's children for her, but was not successful. He was able to trace them to Canada, but that is where the trail died. I grieve to think what those poor children had to suffer, and I cannot even imagine the pain of never knowing what happened to them. Billye was named Woman of the Year by the governor of California in the 1950s. I think she has always feared her past would surface and would destroy the image she worked so hard to achieve. Understandably so, considering everything she has been through. I admire her very much.

I was recently contacted by a genealogist investigator who was looking for my father's family, but more specifically the family of his youngest brother, Ben. Apparently, Ben had an illegitimate daughter, and this daughter was looking for her birth family. Ruth, who is now in her sixties, had been adopted as an

---

[1]   Before my book went into print, Ruby Ellen's granddaughter miraculously found me. It was an amazing reunion where many missing pieces were put in place.

infant. The adoption had been sealed, but when Ruth's daughter developed a heart condition, she was able to get her adoption files opened, and consequently that is how she found me. Her father, Ben, had died of the exact same heart condition shortly before his only legitimate child was born in 1942. I met with Ruth on the Sunday I checked into this hospital. No one else she had contacted would talk to her. The legal documents she brought for me to review left no doubt that Ruth is my cousin. I noticed she even looked a bit like Billye, who is both our cousin and our aunt. (Try to figure that one out!) I took Ruth to meet my mother, who would not acknowledge that she knew anything about her. I suspected otherwise. Mom was very quiet that day, and my mother is seldom quiet, except when it comes to family secrets. Ben was actually engaged to be married to someone else when Ruth was conceived, and Ruth's birth mother was married to a man who was in prison. Ruth eventually found her birth mother, who confirmed everything Ruth had found out about her father. In spite of all the craziness of the story, it was really neat to watch Ruth as she saw pictures of her handsome father for the first time.

I wasn't sure how Ruth was going to take some of the family history I told her about or the fact that this new-found cousin was checking herself into a hospital. However, Ruth and her daughter were very loving and gracious. She just wanted to find out about her family, and I was very happy to find out about her. *I couldn't help but wonder about the timing of Ruth's coming into my life, just when I too was searching for answers about my own past.*

Dad's mother was of Cherokee Indian descent and a schoolteacher. After her death, my grandfather sold the Oklahoma farm, put his family in a covered wagon and moved to New Mexico Territory. Mom says that he arrived with a lot of money in his pocket but handed most of it over to booze and gambling. He did buy some farmland where they lived in a dugout, which is a large hole dug into the ground and is covered with hay and who knows what else, to make a roof. I really can't imagine what life must have been like for my father. He didn't talk about it. I really think you could say they were dirt-poor.

I told my father's story with no emotion. They were just facts. Barb persisted that I had not told her anything about me and my father. Uncertainty tapped on my shoulders. I wasn't sure where this session was going to take me.

Well, there isn't much I can tell you, Barb. I really didn't know my father. He died in 1980, and I know it sounds odd, but it was after he died that I developed a relationship with him. Daddy was a quiet and distant person who had lived his life withdrawn into himself. I can't remember ever having a real conversation with him when I was growing up. He just didn't talk. He was a good man, but he just wasn't involved in my life. Considering his own childhood, I am actually surprised that he did not become an alcoholic or worse. I really do believe that he loved me and my siblings. He just didn't know how to show it.

After Dad's death, I went into therapy for the first time. I had been plagued with depression since I was a kid, and for some reason after he died, I got much worse. Because of those few months of therapy, I began to realize that Daddy did the best he could do with us kids. If you think about it, he had no mother to hold him and nurture him or tell him he was loved, and I seriously doubt that he got anything positive from his father. And then to live with the handicap he had. I just can't even imagine all he had to deal with as a child. My mother was always telling me that Dad never wanted children. In my young mind, I translated that as *Dad didn't want me*! In reality, I think he was afraid of having a deformed child, or maybe he just didn't want to bring children into this troubled world. I no longer believe that he didn't want me.

I was always concerned about my dad's salvation. He became a Mason as a young man, and the Masons became his religion.

Once when I asked him about it, I was shocked to hear him say that salvation came through the rebuilding of Solomon's Temple. Prior to that, he told me he had been saved—had a conversion experience through Jesus—when he was a boy, but he seldom went to church and he certainly did not rear his own kids in the Christian faith. Mom told me that Dad's father read the Bible a lot and that he had joined a church. That bit of information was always confusing to me considering my grandfather's alcoholism and his history of being an abuser. He must have had a conversion experience when he got older, and perhaps he took my dad to church with him. I don't really know. Anyway I was timid about talking to Dad about anything, so I didn't confront the issue of salvation with him.

Toward the end of his life, Dad was in and out of the hospital a lot. I would go and sit with him and read from the Bible. At night, when he could not sleep, I would take his hand and we would pray together. A few good hours of sleep would follow. One day as he was lying in bed, he began to quote from the Old Testament. Masons seem to know a lot of Old Testament text. Anyway, he said something like, "I will give you a plumb line in the wilderness. From dust you were made and to dust you will return." I had only seen my father cry once in my whole life, and that was when his last brother died. But that day in the hospital he sobbed, and the fear embedded on his face broke my heart. I asked him if he was afraid and he said, "Yes, I'm afraid."

Drawing close to his side, I picked up his soft, aged hand and said, "Oh, Daddy, don't you see that Jesus is the plumb line in the wilderness that God gave us to get through this life, the one who directs our path to God and to life eternal? Can't you see you have nothing to fear if you believe in Him?"

An eerie, peaceful silence followed, and the unmistakable presence of Christ filled the hospital room. My father slowly shook his head in determined affirmation and whispered back to me, "Yes, I guess that I do." I watched as this incredible peace settled upon my dad, a peace that never left him from that day on. I walked over to the water fountain, got a handful of water and baptized my dad. All his fears vanished, and whenever I visited him I could feel God's presence there with him.

When death became imminent, I was called to his bedside. For some reason when I walked into his hospital room everyone left us alone. Without hesitation, I picked up his limp hand and began to pray softly in the Spirit. The head of his bed was raised to an angle so that his head hung to one side. He drooled on his pillow. Although he was very thin and very frail, his skin had a youthful glow and few wrinkles. Whippets of snow-white hair embraced his balding head. I felt a tug at my hand, and when I opened my eyes they met his clear, blue gaze. "Daddy, what do you need?" There was no reply, just the gentle tug at my hand. I know it must have taken every ounce of his strength as he struggled to pull both of our hands to his moist mouth. Finally, he firmly pressed his lips against the back of my hand, seeking to touch the heart and soul of his distant, youngest child. My hand fell from his grip, and he quietly slipped back into himself.

This was a man who did not know how to say "I love you" and seldom showed affection, even toward his wife. He was a man who, not by choice but because of his own father, had been a detached parent. Yet in that one, brief final kiss, my father said to his cherished child what he could not speak with his words. It is only in retrospect that I fully appreciate and understand that precious God-given moment with my father.

It has been ten years since the day we buried my daddy. It seems like yesterday. I will always remember that it was bitter cold and snowing because he always hated the snow. I've wondered if it was because there was never enough heat or clothing to keep him warm as a child, but not on that day. I knew that he was in the warm, loving arms of his Creator.

I had felt no real grief when my father died. How do you grieve for someone you don't really know? I cried only because I saw my children crying, and I felt their sorrow. Yet there was emptiness, a sense of loss, repressed grief that was buried deep inside of me, which I carried for several years before finally seeking help.

It was during my first experience with counseling that I was offered the opportunity to role-play. David, the therapist, explained that he would take on the role of my father, which would allow me the opportunity to say things to my father that I could not say to him when he was alive. After I agreed to his suggestion, he asked, "What would you say to your father if he were here right now?"

It was many long minutes before I actually opened my mouth to speak and to muster every ounce of courage I could find to finally reply back to him. "Why weren't you there to protect me when I was being abused?" *Though my words were few that day, the act of actually speaking them paved the way for a time such as this, for the abused adult/child, almost ten years later.*

Through the voice of this wise counselor, I heard all of the things I had needed to hear from Dad as a child, but never did. "I am so sorry you were hurt as a child. I am so sorry that I was not there for you. If I had known, I would have protected you. Please forgive me. I love you. I appreciate the person you have become." Those loving responses enabled me to take three baby steps that I did not even know that I needed to take. I accepted that he probably did not know what was happening to me when I was a child. I forgave him for not being there to protect me, and I accepted that he truly did love me. He did the best he could do, considering his own circumstances. *The therapeutic value of this exercise was priceless to the abused adult/child even though she did not understand it at the time.*

I stayed in therapy for only a short time, never disclosing much information past saying that I had been abused as a child. But this discerning man knew there was much more that I was not saying. During my last session with David, he told me a story about Shamrocks. "My wife and I were once given a basket full of potted Shamrocks. It was absolutely full of beautiful blooms, and we loved it. One morning we got up only to discover that our two-year-old son had taken his toy bat and had beaten all of the blooms off our lovely plant, except for one lonely bloom. We were disappointed, but in time the Shamrocks came back to life and thrived wonderfully. Nola, you remind me of those Shamrocks. You have been beaten down and beaten down, over and over, again and again. And now you only have one bloom left standing. I believe that someday you will come back in full bloom, more beautiful than ever." The story of the Shamrocks has lingered in the soil of my soul. *David had planted seeds of hope in the heart of the abused/adult child.*

It was just after the role-playing session that I began having dreams about being with Dad in old familiar places—like sitting on the bank of a river for hours on end with a cane fishing pole in his hands just waiting for a fish to bob on his cork, or gathering food from his garden, or walking toward the house after he got off from work, or sitting at the kitchen table playing dominoes. In my dreams instead of just watching him from afar, I fished with him, worked in the garden with him, ran to meet him after a day of hard work on the railroad and played dominoes with him. We talked and laughed and hugged. He became so real to me that I began to have a sense of knowing him and having a relationship with him. And eventually, I began to grieve for him. The slightest memory would trigger tears. It was Kim, my youngest daughter, who helped me to move through that period of grief.

Dad was seventy-eight years old when his last grandchild was born. He and Kim had a surprising and very special connection with each other. One day when he was watching her toddle around on the floor in front of him, he began to shake his head and laugh. When I asked him what he was laughing about, he said, "Well, you have got two of the best kids I have ever seen (he was speaking of my two older children and had just given me the only compliment that I could ever recall receiving from him), but I don't know about that Kim!" Shaking his head, he laughed again. I can still hear him in my head. I really wasn't sure what he meant about Kim, but I am sure it was prophetic. She would prove to be my whimsical, capricious, lighthearted child.

When he died, I told Kim the part of Granddaddy we loved had gone to Heaven to be with Jesus, and we needed to tell the part of him we knew (his body) good-bye. She was only two years old. When I walked up to his casket, with her in my arms, she did what she always did. She stretched out her arms to give her granddaddy's neck a big hug and promptly fell into the casket with him. I will never forget the shocked look on her innocent face when she touched his cold, dead skin. She looked at him and looked at me, drew herself back into my arms, crossed her arms across her chest, and never said another word.

Several years later, we were walking down the candy aisle of the grocery store when she suddenly stopped and picked up a bag of orange peanut-shaped candy. I recognized them immediately and quietly knelt beside her as she thoughtfully caressed the bag. "I used to sit on the bed with Granddaddy and eat these." I was totally surprised that she remembered. She continued, "And I will tell you something else, Grandmother really misses Granddaddy." When I asked her where her Granddaddy was, she confirmed that he was in Heaven with Jesus.

When we said prayers together at bedtime, it was Kim who would cry when she put her small arms around me and tell me she missed her granddaddy. It was Kim who cried with me when she noticed that the flowers on the dining room table reminded her of Granddaddy's funeral. It was this tenacious little one who taught me to love my father, through the eyes of his loving grandchild, and it was she who ultimately helped me to let him go. A child's perception of reality is a precious gift, too often overlooked. I don't think we should ever underestimate the simple faith of a child.

One night Daddy came to me in a dream. He told me that he had come to say good-bye. He also told me I needed to talk to my mother, warning me that she would not be with me much longer.

The dreams promptly ended. I never dreamed of him again. I miss my dad.

For the first time since I had entered the hospital, I felt something more than physical pain. A teardrop searching for relief surprised me as it gently slid down my cheek. Barb was not going to let me slip away from the moment so easily. She asked me why my father was warning me to talk to my mother.

I quickly took control of my emotions and stuffed them into my stomach, my head and my legs, just anywhere to keep them hidden. The momentary expression of grief was lost in my now-rigid body, and I began to ache all over, again. My doctor had expressed great concern over my ability to feel physical pain but not emotional pain. I didn't understand it either. We would talk about my mother another day.

Chapter 5

I Always Hate Personality Tests—
I Never Know the Answers

In spite of the demanding hospital schedule, I was given much-needed time to myself, time to process and to reflect. The busyness of life had enabled me to avoid confronting the issues of my past, but I had suddenly been given the rare opportunity to walk away from the responsibilities of daily living. For the first time ever, I gave myself permission to pause and seriously look at the canvas of my life. If changes were to be made, now was the time for me to give conscious, diligent thought to what those changes might be. Let's put down our brushes for a while and just look.

I had walked through the first weeks on 3E very much in a daze. In the beginning, I resented the camaraderie of the patients who had been there for a while. Their laughter and joking irritated me. I judged them by wondering how they could possibly understand or relate to me in any way. All that I wanted was to be left alone, and I made that quite clear to everyone right off the bat. But time has a way of changing things. My peers had also figured out how to hide behind locked doors where shame and pain crouched in distant corners, begging to be found, hoping to stay lost. I embraced their pain and eventually let my guard down. Friendships formed, and reluctantly I began to feel that I was in a safe place.

The staff worked persistently to get their patients back into life as quickly as possible, but in those first few weeks, I found concentrating almost hopeless. Something that I could not wrap my thoughts around seemed to resist progress. I sat through countless training classes wondering what in the world these trained professionals were trying to show me. There were days that were torturous for me. Trying not to remember caused me to remember. Remembering caused me to try not to remember. I kept hiding and surfacing, surfacing and hiding, never knowing just who was hiding or who was surfacing. Denial was my game. Confusion was its name. How would I ever sort *me* out of these massive, tangled threads of information that I had forbidden my emotions and my mind to confront for over forty years? There were times when I thought I really might go mad, but I had to keep trying. Every day that I hung in there, each day that I worked hard and stretched beyond my limits, I found my hopelessness grabbing onto the golden threads of hope that dangled before me.

As I began to see that the circumstances of my life were anything but normal, reality slowly fell into place. Emotional chaos had been normal for me, but living in and with chaos is not normal, not what God has created for any of His children. I began to understand that these threads of knowledge represented my life, and they desperately needed to be rearranged. The very thought that I might be able to begin again gave me hope. Ever so slowly, I methodically began to untangle the strands of my life that would ultimately enable me to open locked doors where hopelessness and hope held hands.

The first of many doors that I opened centered on the confusing signals and messages I sometimes radiated to those around me. Either those who crossed my path pretended not to notice, or no one cared enough about me to notice, or simply no one knew what to do with the confusion. Probably all of the above could apply, but more importantly, *I* didn't know what to do with the confusion. If I was going to change, I had to look inside. I had to dig as deep as possible so that I could understand who lived inside of *me*. In the solitude of my hospital room, I allowed my thoughts to revisit worrisome memories in an attempt to establish the cause of my sometimes troubling patterns of behavior.

I was almost always in the kitchen when my husband came home from work, but on this one particular day, I recall being in the family room when he stepped into the entryway of our home. I don't recall exactly what I was doing, but Jake immediately stopped dead in his tracks, looked at me, and asked, "What happened to you today?" I looked up at him and simply replied, "Nothing!" I can still recall the puzzled matter-of-fact tone in his voice, "Well, you're not the same person you were when I left here this morning!" *He walked away, and I was left wondering what he meant. How many times had he and others been greeted by this unsuspecting stranger that mysteriously appeared and disappeared?*

Another incident came to my mind. My oldest daughter was only five years old when one day she suddenly turned to me with tears in her eyes and with tiny hands perched on slender hips asked, "Mommy, what happened? You were so happy a minute ago." *How many times had my moods turned on a dime, leaving my children feeling dismayed, confused and hurt?*

Even my handwriting gave way to confusion. One morning when I was a teenager, I left a note for my mother telling her I had gone to a friend's house. Later, she asked me who had written the note. When I told her I had written the note, she looked shocked and told me that I could not possibly have written the note because it was not my handwriting. However, I *knew* I had written the note. After that incident, I started to become very much aware that my penmanship seemed to change drastically from time to time. Some days it was hardly legible while at other times the very style of my writing took on different characteristics. *Why did this strange phenomenon suddenly begin in my teens? What were these drastic changes in my handwriting trying to tell me? And why do these frustrating changes continue to haunt me?*

As a cheerleader in high school, I recalled having the feeling that I was sitting in the stands watching rather than being on the football field performing. The same strange occurrence happened if I was standing in front of my class giving a book report or playing my clarinet in band competition or anytime that I was the center of attention. I just seemed to go somewhere else, and then a kind of darkness would engulf the space around me. It seemed that whenever I felt unsafe or threatened or scared I just faded into the background. *Why am I afraid of drawing attention to myself? Where is this dark place that I go to hide? And what is this overshadowing darkness I feel? Why do I feel so unsafe? Why do I want to hide? Why do I sometimes dance with the darkness? I have so many questions!*

Sometimes when someone is standing over me, watching me do something, I get fearful and my mind shuts down. I can't think clearly. Sometimes I feel so alone and lonely—deserted. *Why do these feelings of panic assault me when people are too close to me, watching? And why do I sometimes feel abandoned?*

Once when I was setting the dinner table for my mother-in-law, she commented that I was setting the table properly, for a change. When I replied back to her that I always set it correctly, she was quick to inform me that I seldom did. I was baffled and angry because I just knew I always set her table the exact same way. *Why did I sometimes do things and then deny that I did them? Why was I always changing horses in the middle of a stream? What compulsion fueled this strange behavior? Did my confusing mannerisms create the many issues that I had with my husband, his family and others?*

Occasionally, someone will comment about something I supposedly said that was totally out of character for me. I would think, "But I would not, and did not, say that!" Statements were even occasionally made about how I felt about something, and I would think, "But I don't feel that way!" I would actually get angry at people for making up things about me and would wonder what in the heck their problem was. *Anger! It seems to come from nowhere, unexpectedly, unexplainable, unbridled. Why? And why the confusing messages? What is wrong with me?*

Some people seem to love and respect me while others reject me. Some have walked away from me. I have walked away from many. Had I built walls of protection around myself so that no one could get inside? But then I am told I have no boundaries at all, I don't protect myself! *I am so confused. I don't understand. Why?*

I have often felt deserted, unloved and suspicious of others, unable to trust. *Why does the bad so often overshadow the good? And why do I not trust?*

Sometimes I have made such inappropriate, unwise choices that simply made no sense to me. Sometimes evil danced all around me, and sometimes I danced with the evil. I had no control. *Why am I so powerless?*

Jake once asked me if I knew that occasionally (at least ten times) I asked him if he wanted a divorce. I was bewildered because I did not understand why I would even ask him such a question. *Did I fear that he would leave me or stop loving me? Or did I feel so unworthy that I needed reassurance? Or did the abused adult/child just want to run away?*

If Jake and I argued, I would either go into a rage to defend myself or else I would bow my head, like a child being scolded, and turn childish emotions inward. Not always, but sometimes, if I was in a group discussion where someone challenged me or something was said that made me perceive that I was unsafe, unappreciated or devalued, I would actually feel myself becoming childlike—powerless. I am certain my outward demeanor would change as I withdrew into myself. More often than not, I would snap out of it and carry on, but at other times I would sink into depression that would last for days or even weeks. *Why did I feel so fragmented? And why did I sometimes disassociate from reality and feel detached? And why did I hide in the darkness of depression? Why did I always see the negative side of everything and why was I always on the lookout for danger?*

I have been called a perfectionist. It is true, except sometimes it isn't true. I will work for endless hours trying to make something be just perfect—my house, a painting, a project or the way I look. I expected my kids to be perfect. In my mind everything has to be perfect, but I can never make anything *be* perfect. Even unimportant things can control me. I will write a letter over and over trying to get my handwriting to look right. I get angry when things are not perfect. This is where I get into trouble because I will find something in disarray and get mad because "someone" has messed up my space, all the time knowing that I was the guilty one. *Why was I at war with myself? Why do I put so much pressure on myself, my family and those around me? Why do I strive for perfection and then fall short of my own expectations? Why do I have such unrealistic expectations of others and then find fault when others disappoint me? Why can't I just be me and let others be who they are? Why am I so angry?*

But wait! There is so much evidence to challenge or take exception to all of the above. There is a totally different side to me. A side that I know and some know to be calm, stable, strong and wise. One who is hardworking with determined values, quietly confident, dedicated, kind, loving, thoughtful and good at heart. One who loves God and desires to serve Him. One who deeply loves her husband, her children and people in general. And one who is optimistic, positive and strong in her faith. Doesn't this define who I really am? *Or is this troubled one the one I keep hearing about? I have been told there is a wounded child that lives within me. Has this wounded child been screaming at me for all these years hoping to get my attention, hoping that I would feel her pain? Is she the one causing all of this confusing conflict? I am trying so hard to find her, but is she trying to find me too? And who is holding us together? Who am I?*

Shades of tenderness, clouds of sadness, lights of joy, shadows of darkness, great moments of peace, rages of anger—what were they trying to tell me? *God, help me to understand. Please, help me to understand.*

I always hate personality tests. I never know the answers.

Chapter 6

Child Abuse Is What?

It was in this secular hospital environment that I began to embrace the psycho-analytical terms that were being introduced to me: dysfunctional family, codependency, lack of boundaries, disassociation, fragmented personality, denial, anger, latent development, abandonment, wounded child and history of origin. The therapeutic meaning of these words would prove to be invaluable to me as they slowly unveiled understanding to me about the abused adult/child.

Growing up, the term *abused* was not used as freely as it is today. In fact, I had only heard the term used once, and that was when I overheard my mother talking about a classmate of mine who had almost been attacked by a man as she was walking home from school. This was in the mid 1950s. I was very young at the time, but I remember making a personal connection with the word in my mind. I was seventeen years old when I actually first spoke the words, "I was abused!" I don't really know how I knew what had happened to me was abuse, but I suppose there are some things that do not need to be defined for us, even as children. We just know. But now I needed not just to *know* that I was abused; I needed to *understand* that I was abused.

Understanding the abuse was my missing link, and the missing link was held by the wounded child I was trying so hard to comprehend. Perhaps if I could understand her, I would then be able to find my

43

precious child! Days and weeks and hours were spent in my pursuit of the wounded child. I listened; I took notes. I answered questions, filled in blanks, charted my history, wrote endlessly, and I cried out to my God constantly. Slowly, powerfully, the voice of reason began to take my hand and gently lead me toward awareness of my precious child's wounds. *The abused adult/child was beginning to pay attention to what she was being told. She took detailed notes and studied them diligently.*[1]

The precious child—that innocent one, born with the expectation of being loved, nurtured and protected, lives within. The precious child is God-breathed into each one of us. We come packaged in magical yet vulnerable, playful gaiety. But, when the precious child's trust is broken by neglect and/or by sexual, physical, emotional or spiritual abuse, the little child will find many ways to compensate for the shame that has stolen her/his innocence. The resulting powerlessness will lead the abused adult/child into a life of varied, often destructive, unmanageable behaviors.

A **dysfunctional family** is created when unfavorable conditions interfere with the healthy structure of a family unit. There will always be periods of time when function is impaired by stressful circumstances. However, healthy families will return to normal within a reasonable amount of time after a traumatic event. But for a dysfunctional family, unresolved issues become monsters that refuse to go away. These monsters have long-term effects upon the children who come from dysfunctional families where any one of the following abusive conditions has occurred:

When children are *disrespected* and/or *shamed*, instead of feeling valuable, the child feels worthless and insecure and, as an adult, becomes controlling of others. When *unprotected*, children will learn

---

[1] The information that follows is my compilation and interpretation of notes taken while in the hospital, in various counseling situations and workshops. I have no direct reference for this material. There appears to be many variations to the definition of abuse available on the Internet.

they have no boundaries. Anyone can do anything to them, and they will remain silent. But as adults, they often become filled with rage, anger and resentments. When *goodness is stolen*, children believe they are bad and, as adults, will often become rebellious and live in a world of denial. Reality becomes skewed. When their *needs and wants are denied*, they may become either anti-dependent or overly dependent, often developing addiction issues or physical and mental illness. They will constantly be searching for love and acceptance. And *when innocence is thwarted*, maturity is often latent; emotional development progresses very slowly. They will either exert no control of their lives, or they will try to control every facet of their life, or they may even exhibit both of these traits simultaneously. True intimacy will elude them, no matter what.

Sexual abuse happens when a child is expected to fulfill or participate in anyone's sexual or emotional needs. It is *never* the child's responsibility to sexually satisfy anyone, ever! When any person, whether it is an adult or a child, coerces, forces, tricks or threatens a child into having any kind of sexual contact with him or her, that person is guilty of sexual abuse. Touching the private parts of a child or having intercourse with a child is abuse. Exposing a child to pornographic pictures or films, telling sexual jokes or explicit sexual stories or taking sexually explicit pictures of a child, is abuse.

Sexually abused children may either totally shut down, and their sexual development become latent or, because pleasure is associated with the abuse, they may become extremely promiscuous. It is important to note that God created us as sexual beings for the purpose of procreation. He gave us a bonus by making it pleasurable. Pleasure is the normal response to sex, and an abused child or an abused adult/child should never feel guilty or shameful for feeling sexual pleasure. However, when guilt and shame are associated with the pleasure of sex, I believe that is God's red flag trying to reveal that something is very wrong. Promiscuity, addictions to sex, masturbation, gender confusion and pornography will often be the result of childhood sexual abuse—all of which lead to feelings of guilt and shame. There is no stone left unturned for sexually abused children. They are forever changed, and *every* aspect of their lives *will be* affected.

Neglect is when a parent fails to feed, protect, nurture or provide the basic necessities for a child. Leaving a child unattended when he or she is not yet ready to care for himself or herself puts the child in potentially dangerous situations. This is child abuse. Substance abusive parents are often neglectful of their children's needs.

Physical abuse is when a child is slapped, pushed, burned, punched or beaten by a person of authority. Visible evidence of abuse may be scratches, burns, bruises, welts, broken bones and fractures. Intangible scars of physical abuse remain long after the bruises fade and the bones mend. Children are powerless to protect themselves from those who are entrusted to love and protect them.

Emotional abuse is ridicule, screaming or any verbally abusive attention directed at a child by an adult. When a child witnesses verbal abuse directed at others in the family unit, e. g., spousal fighting or harsh discipline of a sibling, this vicariously damages the emotional well-being of the child and is abuse. When parents ignore or do not take interest in a child, do not hug their child or are generally emotionally disconnected from their child, serious emotional scars result with devastating consequences for the child.

Spiritual abuse results anytime there is any kind of abuse toward an innocent child. Our Creator's greatest gift to humanity is that of a baby, a child. His intent for creating marriage and sexuality between one man and one woman was procreation and a continuation of life. Adults are given this precious gift to nurture and to pour love into one who will in turn someday nurture and pour love into another child. But when children are devalued to the point of feeling worthless, they will most likely devalue their own children. Out of that kind of behavior will be born a mistrust of even their Creator, God. All children born on this earth deserve the right to know their Creator, to know His love and to understand their worth in Him.

The vicious cycle of a **fragmented personality** overshadows the victims of child abuse. Abused adult/children are very *complex* *people*, and their thought processes do not flow down the same channel as those who are normal (those who are not victims of child abuse). Circumstances will dictate what part of their mind is going to do the reacting to any given situation. What was that again? Circumstances will dictate *what part of their mind* is going to do the reacting to any given situation. Hmmmm! Is it really possible that a mind can become fragmented, which means to be disconnected, disunited or even split? If the mind is suddenly forced to disconnect from reality because it cannot resolve conflicting and confusing circumstances, surely it is possible for unity of the mind to be altered, even destroyed.

There is a lot of interesting information on the Internet about personality disorders. In researching this topic, be sure to use discernment. If truth be known, I think we would find that most of us suffer from some form of personality dysfunction. However, because we are all uniquely different, I don't think everyone should be given the same label or put into the same category. Those with true multiple or split personalities are unaware of their erratic changes in behaviors. However, abused adult/ children who are fragmented usually know they are unpredictable; they are just clueless as to why they behave the way they do and clueless as to what to do about it. Those with fragmented personalities are extremely *ambivalent* which means, according to *Webster's Dictionary*, they have "simultaneous and contradictory attitudes or feelings toward an object, person or action" and are in "continual fluctuation (as between one thing and its opposite such as love/hate)." Abused adult/children can get angry at someone they love, but in that angry moment, they hate that person. Appropriate anger and inappropriate anger begin to war with each other, and this war can throw abused adult/children into inappropriate, ambivalent behavior, anxiety and depression. They want to die, but they want to live. They want to be good, but they do things that are bad. They love, they hate. They want sex, they hate sex. These types of conflicts lead to unbelievable confusion for abused adult/children and for those who live with them. They survive by *stuffing* their confusing conflicts deep inside where they cannot feel them and thereby deny the conflicts exist. **They will never deal with what they deny.**

Abused adult/children are *self-centered and self-absorbed*. They can only give complete attention to their own thoughts—even though they may, at times, be prone to think of others even before themselves. They remain fragmented and stay in the shadows and sidelines with their wounded child. Even though each person will handle things in unique and different ways, there are character traits and patterns that almost all abused adult/children tend to follow. Although they are "not normal," they are normal in the world of child abuse, and there are common threads they all share. It is very difficult for those who have not been abused to understand abused adult/children's often devastating patterns, because laced within those patterns are truly unique individuals who are capable of bringing many wonderful gifts into their relationships and into the lives they lead. They are called *survivors*—ones who have lived through affliction—because they have developed valuable skills that help get them through life. Abused adult/children are truly fine-tuned and are able to adapt to the stresses and changes of life. They tend to be empathetic toward others and successful in most anything they set out to do. But, in turn, abused adult/children have difficulty understanding the thought processes of a normal person. They don't understand that everyone does not think or process thoughts in the same way as they do. These misunderstandings always lead to conflict in relationships.

The secret underworld of the survivor is created by every type of abuse which leads to a variety of vicious cycles. Another of those vicious cycles is what many call *codependency*. There is a lot of information on the Internet about this subject, but it is generally defined as one whose tendency is to behave in inappropriate ways that have a negative impact on relationships. The core of codependency is when an individual's emotional stability depends upon the dependence of another. For example, "I feel personally validated because you depend on me to take care of you. When you become self-sufficient and no longer need me to support you, I will have to find someone else who needs me in order to feel good about me. I need to keep you under my thumb." If a codependent retards the growth patterns of another, it is detrimental to the relationship and to both parties. This is another form of abuse.

Abused adult/children have unrealistic expectations of others to meet their needs. The roots of abuse establish lifelong patterns that affect every area of their lives, and they hit the core of every relationship they encounter. Self-esteem does not come from within for abused adult/children, so they will look for ways to fill the pillaged spaces in their minds through their relations with others. That is why abused adult/children typically become controllers and/or caretakers. They deny their dysfunctional past and pain-filled feelings and the inability to be intimate. They have extreme issues with distrust and are hyper-vigilant, which means they are always on the lookout for possible danger, even though they will often deny the dangers they see. They are often physically ill.

Regrettably, abused adult/children are seldom able to celebrate the God-given uniqueness and beauty of their own existence. They can see only ugliness where self-loathing gives birth to the denial of anything good within. When unworthiness is reinforced over and over, a healthy concept of self-worth does not develop. In fact, it can not develop. Victims of child abuse are constantly trying to find a way to heal the secrets of their wounded child, but will stay stuck like glue in the deception of depression, suppressed anger, bitterness and the inability to forgive, until they can one day face the reality of their abuse. When they are finally able to face this reality, they must grieve over the loss of their precious, wounded child and acknowledge that not only does God love them, but they too love their wounded child, their precious child, and the survivor they have become.

When I was asked to answer the following questions to determine the effects my childhood had upon my personality, I was surprised by the results.

Do you consider yourself a perfectionist?
Does everything around you have to be perfect?
Do you seek approval from others to feel good about yourself?
Do you overdo for others while denying your own needs?
Do you go to extremes, either taking on too much responsibility, or
    do you avoid and ignore responsibilities? Do you do both?

Is it hard to trust others?

Are you other-focused or are you self-absorbed? Are you both?

Is it difficult to have intimate relationships?

Can you express your feelings, either negative or positive?

Do you feel lonely in a room full of people?

Is it impossible for you to tell others what you need from them?

Is it your tendency to migrate toward unhealthy relationships/ people?

Are you aware of others' needs more than your own?

Is it difficult to deal with anger and/or criticism?

Is it hard for you to respect authority?

Do you feel that you must give false impressions of who you are, socially or professionally?

Is it difficult to play and have fun?

Almost everyone can answer yes to a few of these questions. However, I was told that if I answered yes to half of them, I probably came from a dysfunctional family. If I answered yes to more than half of the questions, I probably had a personality disorder and needed help. I answered yes to all of them. The results were difficult for me to hear, but they were also eye-opening.

As surely as I knew the term *abuse* connected us (me: the survivor, the precious child, and the wounded child), I also knew it was God who connected our threads of hope. Over a period of weeks, I had been given tools to work with and knowledge to process. Now, I had to try to figure out what I was going to do with all of this information. I was totally overwhelmed. I knew I had a lot of work to do.

Eventually, I began to accept that I had a fragmented personality. What you are about to read is my perception of what happened to me and does not come from clinical studies or any other source. I believe our Creator has given children and adults a way to escape mentally from traumatic situations that are beyond their ability to cope. He has given us the ability to store unwanted experiences away in our minds so that we can survive, and for me it looks something like this:

I, the survivor, took my precious wounded child and mentally put her into a safe, well-guarded place of protection. The core of who I am, my soul, is the precious child within me, and she is the one who quietly held me together. The wounded child left the precious child in the safe place and joined the survivor, and eventually the abused adult/child emerged. The survivor then had a wounded child, a precious child and an adult living within her conscience. The problem came when the survivor did not know what to do with these seemingly "other entities" that kept popping in and out of her mind, causing much confusion about who she was.

I know you are now thinking this is really weird, but you will begin to see this scenario unfold as you read my story. The mind is a marvelous creation, and I believe it has astonishing abilities that we humans never really understand or tap into. Again, this explanation is just my way of understanding what happened to me, why I do the things I do and who I am.

Chapter 7

Teddy Bears—in Search of My Lost Little Girl—a Dog and a Rooster

Everyone thought it strange at first, but before long just about every patient had one—a teddy bear! I had actually brought two with me when I checked into the hospital. One was white and had been a Christmas present from my son. I tucked her in my bed each day because she symbolized the strong part of me that had struggled so hard to survive. She simply needed to rest. The soft, cuddly brown one begged to be held and became my symbolic wounded child. She went everywhere with me. We needed each other when sleepless nights found us walking the dimly lit hallways or sitting quietly in the meeting room where often another restless patient would join us. Sometimes we would stare into the night through a large window of the building that was quickly becoming the pathway to my past. One day during free time, the three of us curled up together on my stiff hospital bed in search of the lost little girl we longed to know . . .

"How does it all end?" The little girl pondered thoughtfully as she flipped through the pages of the large, old book. The smell of ages past lingered on the worn, yellowish brown pages. The once rich, brown leather cover was beginning to fall apart. This Bible had belonged to her dad's father whom she did not know because he died before she was born. She never saw anyone read it and wondered how it had gotten in such a state. The young girl with long, dark brown hair and blue eyes sensed the mystery of the ancient book as she felt its power drawing her deeper into its grasp. Her heart beat faster as she once again turned to the very last chapter of Revelation. She often went there, searching to understand how it was all going to end. How strange that one so young would be so concerned about the end of life when her life had just begun. It all sounded so weird, and she was never sure if she had gotten answers or just more questions. "If God is the beginning and the end, then where did it begin and where does it end? What was before the beginning and who made God? Where did He come from, and who made whoever made Him? How did it all get started? And I still don't know how it is going to end." Her desire to know God seemed insatiable.

There had been many West Texas hot summer days like this one spent on the screened-in porch of the yellow Santa Fe company house. Lying on her back, she paused to search the baby-blue sky with its cottony clouds to find dragons, bears and faraway places with kings and queens that would tell her stories of things past, present and yet to come. Leaving her imaginary friends in the sky, she returned to the book she embraced. "Why would God want to keep dogs out of the city anyway?" she mused as she read Revelation 22:14-15. "Now, murderers and those immoral guys, that's okay, but dogs!" She shook her head quizzically. Actually, the child was quite sure that God loved dogs and cats too. He was always sending stray cats for her to feed, and she knew that her dog, Lady, with her white coat and great black patches, was a gift from above. Lady Bug, as she was sometimes called, was her constant companion and soul-mate. She was the only living being that was allowed to enter the closed doors of her heart.

Sultry, summer nights would find the two of them sneaking into the living room in the wee hours of the morning to try to catch a few hours of cool sleep, away from the sweltering heat and buzzing, giant Texas mosquitoes. The only air that moved in the night came from the window cooler in the small living room. They managed to slip back into her room before dawn. By then, the bugs would be gone and the heat would miraculously rest for a spell. Peaceful sleep would finally come to both of them. Cold winter nights would find them snuggled together in her bed. The trip to the small space heater in the living room was just too far away.

A tattered, homemade quilt tossed on the grass in the front yard on clear, cloudless summer nights called the little girl to gaze up into the blackest of black skies where she would find billions and billions of brilliant stars. They beckoned her to imagine far beyond their limits until she would almost become frightened. Lady could have cared less, but the young girl yearned to know all about the mysteries that she could not see.

Mischief and adventure became twins to be shared and worthy of any consequence. They made kites out of flour paste, old newspapers and sticks. They walked the railroad tracks for hours on end and played in the enchanted forest of the nearby creek. The sight of a snake would send the child screaming (she hated snakes) with Lady chasing after her and wondering where in the world they were going in such a hurry.

A rarely possessed balloon would quickly turn into a water balloon, but you had to be very careful what you did with a water balloon in such a small town. Your sins would be sure to find you out! A trip to the gas station down the road for a five-cent Coke was a rare treat, and if you were really lucky, you might be able to buy a bag of Tom's peanuts to pour into the bottle of Coke. Mmmm! Along the way they might find a great, giant anthill in the middle of a dusty road where they would stop and disturb the red six-legged bugs with a long stick. She found strange delight in standing over them and watching them scurry around in a panicked state of confusion. She wondered if they were afraid of the dark, ominous shadows that lurked over them, disturbing their peace. And she wondered why she wondered. There were times when she also felt a dark presence standing over her, and sometimes she was afraid. If they couldn't find ants to torment, they would surely find a small horny toad to play with. She loved these adorable, ugly little creatures. They brought out the tender side of the child as she would turn them over on their backs and gently rub their tummies until they trustingly fell asleep in her hand. The little girl somehow knew that she too was gently held in the palm of a trusting hand.

In their circle of friends were the piglets and baby chicks. She and Lady would stand on the slats of the pigpen and giggle (actually she would giggle, Lady would bark) as the pink, bald babies would wallow in the red mud and squeal with delight. Together they marveled when wet, fluffy yellow balls of feathers emerged from white shells and almost before their eyes became great big white chickens. But there was always a price to pay for stolen moments of happiness. Slaughter day for the pigs would find Lady and her forever friend taking a very long walk as far away as possible to avoid the final squeals of their entertainers. And then, almost every Sunday morning, they were faced with the ungodly sight of headless hens hopping all over the yard after bare hands had wrung their necks. The two friends would hide on the other side of the big yellow house until a cold, wet nose pressed against a moist cheek signaled that the dastardly deed was over. A huge pot of boiling hot water waited in the kitchen where the hens were dunked, plucked and singed. She memorized the smell and the crackling sound of burning chicken fuzz as the now limp, headless hens were held over the open flame of the gas stove. "Life is just too hard to understand," she would tell Lady with a sigh. It was disturbing to watch those once cute little chicks come to such a dreadful end, but she knew that she was powerless to change what is. The child felt strangely powerless to change anything in her life.

The finale to all of this much-ado-about-nothing was, of course, sitting down at the dinner table to a huge plate of golden fried chicken or fried pork chops while Lady waited patiently for the leftover bones to be fed to her under the table. Suddenly, the horrors of it all would get lost between grief and lustful hunger. The little girl always stuffed her emotions deep inside, right along with the delicious meal that sat before her.

Then there was the time when she learned, with no help from her black-and-white friend, that roosters have absolutely no sense of humor! The old wooden chicken coop was home to a bunch of hens, but only one great, majestic, colorful rooster. Every morning sunrise would find the little girl standing on the front porch mocking that silly old rooster. As he strutted around with his head held high and his chest stuck out, the competition would begin. He would crow and then she would crow, each turn getting louder. The girl could tell that she was really "getting his goat" and would double over with laughter when she heard him flapping his wings in frustration. A distant voice would warn, "You better stop that! Someday that old boy is going to get you!" Well, one day when she was only about six years old, she decided that she was going to gather the eggs. She called her friend to join her as she skipped across the yard past the vegetable garden and the now-empty pigpen and finally to the tin-roofed chicken coop. An old, dented metal bucket used for gathering eggs hung high from a rusty nail just outside of the henhouse gate. It was almost out of her reach, and when she finally stretched tall enough to tip the bucket off the nail, it came crashing down on her head, creating a bit of a stir among her feathered friends and a bump on the top of her head. Perhaps this should have been a warning to leave well enough alone, but the stubborn side to this child never wanted to listen to the voice of reason. Lady sat by quietly watching with a guarded look in her eyes. Her tail twitched in anticipation. The girl unlatched the gate, picked the bucket up off the ground, and confidently stepped inside the smelly chicken pen. She immediately turned around to place the latch securely back in its place because she was, after all, wise enough to know that escaping chickens would not be a good thing. Picking up the bucket again, she cheerfully turned around only to find the joy of the moment, doing a grown-up's job, suddenly snatched right out of her head. With her full body suddenly plastered against the locked door, she found herself staring eyeball to eyeball with—*the . . . rooster*! Beady eyes looked vengeful as his mass of colored, ruffled feathers hovered over her, his wings spread wide. There was no time to retreat.

She was trapped. The very first peck on the top of her already-aching head told her that she had done gone and gotten herself into a heap of trouble this time. The chase began! With eyes as big as saucers, she ran as fast as those little legs could carry her. That old codger was hot on her heels. Around and around and around that old henhouse they went. Hens cackled, wings flopped wildly and feathers flew all over the place. Her desperate screams were triumphantly muffled by yucky, flying feathers attacking the child's mouth and being sucked all the way to the back of her tonsils! Lady joined in on the fun by encouraging more chaos with her fun-filled barking. Before too much damage had been done (the hens probably didn't lay eggs for a week), her father quietly rescued her from her perilous plight. The child was done with eggs and roosters, but her adventurous, strong-willed, rebellious spirit stuck to her like flour paste on a stick and would prove to be both her strength and her weakness. The child wondered where her mother was. She needed a hug.

As the years passed, neither of them sought the adventures of the past. Lady Bug was content to dream of chasing rabbits while the growing child found new friendship in a little blue parakeet. As surely as Lady had given her the gift of love and companionship, Dickey Bird would lead her to the threshold of faith.

The knock at the door was intrusive. I did not want the little girl who had come to visit us to leave. I wanted more of her, but then there were so few good memories. I could hardly find my parents anywhere in my brain, especially my mother. Who had been there to teach me, protect me, or wipe my tears when I cried? I began to think seriously about the question I kept being asked, "Who took care of you?" *The abused adult/child did not remember being taken care of.*

Barb had been the one who had interrupted my childhood adventure. When she entered my hospital room, I knew she had come for more information. We decided to continue my family history in the sunshine, at the end of the hallway.

Chapter 8

Who Took Care of You?

O nce again, I eagerly welcomed the warmth of the hot sun coming through the window at the end of the deserted hallway. Texas summers get progressively brutal, but for me, inside the cold air-conditioned building was just as harsh. I snuggled into the soft, familiar chair with my arms securely wrapped around my little brown bear. She had become like a security blanket for me to hold on to when long days brought conflicting emotions and feelings. The protective arms of 3E continued to do their magic as I slowly allowed myself to peek over the walls that I had built around me. I continued to talk only in generalities when it came to my being abused as a child. Details of the abuse remained locked away inside of me. I knew they were there. I had memories, many memories, but I would not, could not talk about them. My doctor and my therapist wisely understood my inability to talk. For now, they were patiently waiting for me to trust them. Trust did not come easily for me, but I was beginning to process . . .

Barb settled into the chair across from me, and once again, with pad and pen in place, she came prepared to press on. She repeated her question from our last session. I had not wanted to answer her then, but perhaps now . . . "Why do you think your father was warning you to talk to your mother in your dream?" I sat pensively as I thought about the last dream that I had of my father. I was still in a great deal of physical pain, and my emotions remained numb. It took great effort to think, to respond, but I knew that I had to keep pushing. I began once again to try to give Barb the answers she sought from me. I was beginning to stand in front of my locked doors and to look at them through different eyes. Let's pick up our brushes and continue with the wash, the background for my painting.

Barb, I will always believe God was speaking to me through that dream because He knew I needed answers, and my mother was the only one who could give them to me. David, the therapist I saw after Dad died, had encouraged me to talk to her about my being sexually abused as a child. I have always felt she knew about the abuse, but did nothing to stop it. I'm a mother. I would know if that were happening to my child. Especially a very young child—she had to know and she did nothing. I am very angry at her. *My voice was flat and void of any emotion.*

About five years ago, I finally did confront her. I really do not like talking to my mother, so this was very difficult for me. She appeared totally shocked and denied any knowledge of my ever having been abused. She sternly forbade me to talk about it to anyone else in my family. She was more concerned about the pain I would cause than the pain that I was in. I was certain that another in my family knew my secret. David had warned me that Mother's response might be negative, so I was somewhat prepared, but it still made me angry. It still hurt. However, it was a beginning, and I did get some valuable information from her that helped me begin to understand my mother. Mother admitted to me that one of her older brothers had raped her when she was fifteen years old. I strongly suspect that I am the only person she had ever talked to about it, and she was close to being eighty years old at the time. She later admitted that he had been abusing her since she was a young girl. I cannot believe she held that in for all of those years. *My own words began to speak back to me about my own secrets—the ones*

I protected and guarded, the ones I had a death grip on. The ones I refused to talk about . . .

I suppose that is why my mother has always been sick. I can hardly recall a time when she wasn't. She always seemed to be angry and bitter about something. I know that underneath all of her pain there is a really sweet and loving person because I caught glimpses of this as I grew up. However, the fact remains I don't really know my mother any better than I knew my father. *I was beginning to see that perhaps I was just as complex and perplexing as my mother. The abused adult/child wanted to deny the similarities that were surfacing.*

My mother's attitude about God has always been so confusing to me. She was reared in the church, but she talks about church with such bitterness. Every time her brother's name was mentioned, she made a snide remark about him being a hypocrite because he was a big deacon in the church. My uncle never came to my mother to ask for forgiveness, and I have a big problem with that. My mother's mother was in her mid-fifties when she died rather suddenly. Apparently, she dragged all six of her kids to church every time the doors were open, but at home she acted like anything but a Christian. My grandmother was perceived as having a mean streak. I found this out from a cousin, because my mother never really talked about her mother. Actually, now that I think about it, Mom has a mean streak, too. *It had never occurred to me to question why my mother never talked about her own mother. Did she too blame her mother for not protecting her? And what had happened to my grandmother that made her so confusing and harsh? Strange, yet familiar parallels were beginning to emerge—and I wondered about the three of us. Had my mother somehow twisted her own mother's actions and that of her brother's around God and church until they became a monster in her mind? Was the abused adult/child's judgment of her own mother unjust?*

Mom's father eventually moved to California and married Georgia, who became the only grandmother I knew. She was what they once called a "hard-shelled Baptist" who loved Jesus and loved wrestling. She was the first person I called when I was finally baptized because she always talked to me about God, and I know she prayed for me. Grandad, who lived to be in his nineties, was always just a sweet old man in my eyes, but it appears that was not always the case. He was a farmer and apparently very strict on all of his kids. One of my aunts died at the age of sixteen from a heat stroke. She had not been allowed to come in out of the heat while chopping cotton, even though she had complained about not feeling well. I am sure that my mother probably had to work very hard as she was growing up, and I find it amusing that she seldom cleaned our house when I was living at home. I started cleaning for her when I was very young. After I started to school, I would spend every Saturday cleaning. I couldn't stand the mess. I resent her terribly for that. Now every time I have to go over and clean her house, it just makes me angry all over again. If only she would just halfway try to pick up after herself. *My voice remained steady with no hint of the underlying anger the abused adult/child was feeling.*

Somewhere along the way my mother started going to fortune-tellers and reading her horoscope, and that is where she put her faith. It is dangerous to fool around with those practices, and I suspect her involvement with them is just part of what kept her and her family in spiritual bondage. She was not at all happy about my becoming a Christian. When I begged to be baptized, she flatly forbade it, refusing to give me an answer when I asked her why. I didn't understand then and I don't understand now. I am still angry at her over that one.

She was always saying things to hurt or embarrass me in front of people, especially my friends. One Christmas Eve, my brother, who had come home from college, started giving me spiked eggnog. I was only fifteen. My mother knew I had plans to go to a midnight

Mass with a friend and did nothing to intervene. We had just moved to the town we lived in, so this was a new friend to me. Anyway, my mother thought it was really funny that I went to church drunk. She later told the story to the parents of a boy that I was dating. I was so embarrassed, and I just could not understand why she would do that to me. I could never understand why my mother did not like me. I never wanted my friends to come over to my house. *The tone of my voice never changed. I just continued to state the facts.*

About a year ago, I confronted her again about the sexual abuse. I had actually gone to her house to find pictures of me when I was a child. I had been trying to find some connection to my childhood. I was hoping that looking at pictures would trigger some memories that would help me make some sense of my life. I noticed that our family looked so normal in all of the pictures. Everyone smiled, except me. I seldom had a smile on my face. I don't think that I was a very happy child. *Will the innocent face of a child lie? Was I beginning to face facts?*

I was determined to get answers. I pushed against my fears until my mother finally began to talk. I kept telling her that not only did I have actual memories of abuse, I also had physical and emotional memories that I could not connect to reality. One of the feelings I had was extreme defiance, and I associated it with my birth. She reluctantly told me that when she was pregnant with me, Dad's oldest brother lived with them. My father traveled with his job and was gone most of the time. The anger she harbored for all of those years snapped within her, "He was after me all of the time. The whole time I was pregnant with you I had to fight him off me. Every night I had to push my dresser up against the door to keep him out of my room." As soon as the words tumbled out of her mouth, I remembered . . . this same uncle had molested me. I told my mother. She sternly asked, "Why didn't you ever tell me all of this was going on?" My voice remained determined as I replied, "And why didn't you ever tell anyone about your brother raping you?" Without hesitation she flatly said, "Well, no one would have believed me!" The moment of truth had arrived because she understood that no one would have believed me either. My mother just looked at me with defeated resignation, finally giving me permission to talk to the other family member that I felt I needed to confront. However, the thought of ever actually doing so was very frightening and felt very unsafe for me. *I wondered if the emotions felt by my mother's defiance of my uncle could actually have been transferred to her unborn child. If so, I wondered what other emotions I might have sensed from her. I allowed myself to dig deeper as I dared to ask myself, "Had my mother, at the age of thirty-four, wanted a fifth child? Had I, from the womb, felt unwanted? Is this why I felt so detached from her? And where was my sister when Mom locked my uncle out of her room? The abused adult/child's heart sank at the realization that her poor sister would have been twelve at the time and very vulnerable and defenseless!*

Previously talking to my mother had paved the way, but talking about my mother was now allowing me to force my way through those locked doors where my precious, wounded child remained hidden. It was also giving me the courage to face the secrets that had caused her to hide in the first place. For the first time, I truly realized my mother was not unlike me, and I had to face the fact that she was in just as much pain as I was. We had each controlled our lives in unhealthy yet different ways in order to survive. I flashed back to a dream, a river and the pleading words of my father, "You need to talk to your mother." And my own pleading words to my mother, "I need for you to stay with me—for just a little while longer." Barb listened intently and watched with eager anticipation as the mask of denial slowly began to fade. I continued to tell her my story. She had earned my trust. *The abused adult/child could feel the hand of God leading her, step by step. Without Him, she knew she would not have been able to continue on. The darkness was just too dark, and she was so frightened.*

Since my mother had used sickness as a way of escape, and since she had actually confessed to me that she was always sick in bed, I wanted to know who took care of me when my thirteen-year-old sister was away at school. I had constantly been reminded of the responsibilities that my sister had been forced to carry, as just a child herself. A strange kind of laughter came from my mother as she told me that there were days when I went the entire day without getting my diaper changed because she was just too sick to take care of me. (This was long before disposable diapers and special creams for diaper rash.) I felt ill at the thought and could not bring myself to ask for any more details. I wanted to know how I got fed. I knew that I was not nursed. The fact that I constantly cried from earaches tells me that I was probably not held, but laid down with a bottle propped against something. It slowly became apparent to me that I was probably not nurtured as an infant, a baby or a toddler. What teenager could possibly handle all of the responsibilities of a household, a sick mother, school, a younger brother and a crying infant too? *I wanted to know who comforted me when my diaper needed to be changed, or when I needed to be fed or when I just wanted to know that I was not alone. Who picked me up when I cried? I could not bear to linger with those thoughts for very long. I wanted to weep for my precious wounded child.*

The emotional and physical memories haunt me. Once, when I was keeping a friend's toddler while she was at work, I had a sudden overwhelming urge to shake the child. I literally wanted to hurt her. I physically forced myself to back away from her and to leave the room where she was playing with my own toddler. It scared me so badly that I immediately told the mother that I could no longer keep her sweet little girl. I had no idea what it was about this child that had brought such horrific rage out in me, but I strongly feel that it was the result of something that had happened to me as a child. Like I said, what young girl can handle such stress? What ill mother can handle a screaming child with an earache? Something dreadful had happened to me that I cannot remember. I just know it.

Barb suggested that I might want to explore abandonment and physical abuse issues. I had never thought about those being issues for me. She questioned me about the safety of my own children.

As a parent I have been a very strong disciplinarian and did spank my children, but thankfully, I never physically abused them when they were young. In fact, I was a very protective mother, a good mother. I hardly ever let them cry. I picked them up the minute they whimpered. And I was quick to feed them and change them. I even changed their beds every single day. I could never harm or neglect a small child. *My words once again echoed in my head, and I began to wonder if the inner anger that I was learning about had unknowingly spilled over to my precious children and if my spankings had been much too quick and much too harsh. They were such good children and not deserving of anything but kindness from me. I recalled finding a stash of wooden spoons hidden behind some bookcases. Had I been so out of control they had to hide my weapons of punishment? The reality was unbearable for me hold on to. I had to move on. The abused adult/ child was stricken with sorrow. She could never harm a child, never! Or could she?*

Last year when I went to Mother's house to look through her pictures, I came across a picture of my brother and me with some young men who worked for my dad. I flung the picture in front of my mother and asked, "How do you know if one of these guys didn't abuse me?" I had heard Mom talk about the fact that I had learned to speak Spanish before I spoke English because I was always around these guys. She seemed to see nothing wrong with the fact that these men were allowed to take me and my brother, almost five years older than me, to town and buy us candy and stuff. With no emotion, my mother told me that one day she heard me screaming, and when she went to see about me, she found one of the men abusing me. When I asked her what she did, she simply said she told the man to get away from the house and not to come back. I then asked her what Daddy did when she told him about me being abused. I wanted to know. "Well, Daddy would have killed the man if I had told him!" She flatly stated her case.

In a flash, the monotonous tone of my voice changed as I almost shouted my disbelief at Barb. The stark reality of what had happened was like a sharp slap across my face. I continued with angry energy in my voice . . .

If it had been my child, I would have done serious harm to the man myself. I was a toddler, still in diapers and running around outside with all of these strange men, while my mother was in bed and didn't care enough to watch after me, and then she protected the jerk! *Putting my voice to my mother's confessions pushed denial away; reality intervened. I had to face the fact that what I had been told, and what I was telling Barb, really did happen, and this is not normal. It is unacceptable behavior.*

I am beginning to wonder just how many times something like that had happened to me. I have vivid memories of my bottom hurting and burning and itching. These are just part of the physical memories that I have—but I don't remember what caused these pain-filled memories. My first memories are of my being five or six years of age, and I can pinpoint those ages only because I can remember the surroundings and the house I lived in at the time. I remember having repetitive dreams about being in these long tunnels, looking for a place to hide. I just have this knowing about something, but I don't know what it is that I know. I do recall one incident when my mother was changing my clothes. I was about six and was ill. I can still remember the strange, troubled look on her face when she commented that my "private" area was red and swollen. I recall that part of me being like that a lot. *Openly reciting the memory of my mother's words was confirming to the abused adult/child that her emotional and physical memories were very real, as were the "real" memories that she constantly tried to deny.*

Typically, I would bypass anger, head straight into disbelief and settle into denial, but not on this day, during this session. The magnitude of what I had just told Barb went so deep that I can't find words to describe the rumblings of rage that slinked just below the surface of the strong armor that had kept me from exploding for all those many years. Even though I had been imploding all of my life, I was still not capable of outwardly facing the anger, not yet. There was nothing else that I wanted to say about my mother. Wisely, Barb did not press me further but instead shifted the interview to my siblings.

Jack, my oldest brother, ran away from home just after I was born. He was only fifteen. He never wanted to talk about his childhood, but finally one day he confessed to me that he never felt wanted or loved. Jack was often beaten with a razor strap for things he did not do because his sister, just two years younger, always blamed everything on him. I always knew that he held deep resentments toward her, but I never knew why, and I think there is more to the story that I don't know. Jack told me the last time Daddy beat him, he grabbed the belt out of Dad's hand, threw it in the fireplace, and ran out of the house. He came back home after everyone went to bed. Dad never touched him again. I have no doubt my father was beaten as a child, and that was the only way he knew to discipline. *I was beginning to understand that adults often repeat their parents' behavior and that children are so vulnerable, so easily molded into both good and bad behavior.*

One summer my brother and a cousin made their way to Arizona to work. When the summer was over, both he and the cousin wrote to their parents and asked if they would send money for them to come home. His cousin's parents promptly wired money to their son. I can still see the shattered look of disappointment and hurt on my brother's face all those years later when he told me he never even heard a word from Mother or Daddy. Shortly afterward, Jack left home and joined the Merchant Marines. Eventually, he ended up in the army and fought in the Korean War where he was injured and received a medical discharge. That happened the same year that Mother suffered a stroke that left her temporarily paralyzed on one side of her body. She was only forty years old, and I was about six. When I asked him what he remembered most about our mother, he just said that she was always sick in bed. Jack is an alcoholic and has twice been divorced from the mother of his three children. I have always been very close to Jack and his family.

I was only two when Sis, as she is called, ran away from home and married a man who was only nineteen. I think they lied to get their marriage certificate because she was just a child herself at fifteen. Mother constantly reminded me that my sister had to take care of everything and everybody. I guess I really can't blame her for wanting to get away. I've had a difficult time feeling close to my sister. We are different in the same way my mother and I are so different. She never stopped trying to be a mother figure to me, and I resent her for it because, in many ways, she is just like my mother. Sis can also be a very sweet, loving person. I think I subconsciously put a huge wall between us because I believed she knew about the abuse and did nothing to protect me either.

Sis lives in the same town with my mom and won't let anyone else help take care of her, but then my sister complains because she has to do everything for our mother. My sister's first husband died with cancer, and her second husband recently died with the same awful disease. I feel sad for her. I know her life has not been easy. Her son is only six years younger than I, and her daughter is only ten years younger. They are more like a brother and a sister to me, and I love them very much. *Confusion flashed through my mind as similar, ambivalent feelings for my sister paralleled those I had for my mother. I loved her. I didn't love her. She had been my caretaker and then she left me behind. She abandoned me. I needed her. She did not protect me. I resented her. Feelings were atrociously jumbled up in the mind of the abused adult/child . . . and now confirmation that her sister had probably been abused by her uncle stirred up additional mixed emotions.*

Alice Ann was the third child born to my parents. She was only twenty months old when she died. I have been told that my dad was devastated by her death. I have always wondered if they both resisted getting close to me because of losing Alice Ann. I wish she had lived, Barb. Then maybe I would not have been born.

Perry is almost five years older than me. We have mostly had a very close relationship. He, too, is an alcoholic. He stopped drinking for a while after his middle child was killed in an awful car accident. He is divorced from the mother of his three boys. Perry's youngest son became a father at the age of sixteen, and needless to say, he and his young son have had a really tough time. I really love those boys and have prayed diligently for them. My brother does not believe in God and has traveled down some very dark roads. I grieve for my brother for many reasons.

Perry is my mother's favorite. A close family friend, who took me under her wing, once told me she scolded my mother because all she ever talked about was my brother, "No one even knows you exist." I don't think the friend meant to be unkind, but her words hurt deeply. I knew what she said to be true. I was about twelve at the time. I don't fault Perry for being the favorite. It was not his choice to make.

After Jake and I were married, he wrote to the hospital where I was born and requested a copy of my birth certificate. When we received it, we were surprised to see that I was a twin. Jake asked my mother about it, and she told him she did not know what he was talking about. He wrote a letter to the hospital, and they sent the certificate back. The word *twin* had been removed from the document. I think my mother would have told me if a twin had died, but I am not so sure she would have confessed to giving up one of her children. For some reason, I have never wanted to open that door, but sometimes . . . I wonder.

I know I only have tidbits of information about my family history, but it is enough to make me question what was really going on. I wonder just how many secrets my siblings have that they don't want to talk about either. I have been told by a reliable family source that I was not the only one in my family who has been a victim of incest. After realizing my sister's vulnerability, I have no doubts about it. And what about the secrets both my parents kept to themselves and their parents before them? Where does it stop? I can account for two generations of incest, and I am beginning to believe it has been a long, generational sin that has plagued this family.

I will probably never really know all the reasons why my oldest brother and sister ran away from home at such early ages. I have heard my mother say that when I was born, she told my father she had made a mess of the first two, so he could raise the other two. I suppose that is when she washed her hands of raising me. My mother's sister, who often came to visit us, would tell me that I was not raised, I just grew up. I don't think any of us were raised. We all just grew up, just like our parents before us, and I suspect their parents before them. *I sat quietly, choosing not to speak any more about my family. For the first time, the abused/adult child felt her family's pain. And really, who took care of any of us?*

A feeling of sadness had fallen over me, and once again I was emotionally drained. Every muscle in my body was shrieking at me. I physically hurt all over. It had been a very long and difficult day. Since I had been on 3E, I kept hearing about shame. Shame! I just could not wrap my mind around the emotion of shame. What did it mean to feel shame? Another defining moment emerged as Barb's invasive question rolled the cold stone of shame away from those who had stolen it from me and allowed its sting of conviction to speak to me. Barb dared to probe once again, "Nola Katherine, who else abused you? What did you tell your mother that you are not telling me?"

My chin resting on my chest and my eyes cast downward, I whispered, "There are nine that I know about." I could not, would not, say anything more and the session ended. I was not ready to deal with the underlying shame I was beginning to feel.

Chapter 9

Facing a Fear, Comic Relief,
a Special Friend and an Angel

Visitation time, gym time, mealtime and free time became treasured moments for all of us on 3E. We each had grueling sessions that drained our resources, and we desperately needed respites. The medications I was taking began to punch pinholes of light through the black veil of depression. Consequently I was able to embrace shared laughter and fun. "Come on, Sharon, it's time for someone to hold the door open for *you*!" We giggled as I grabbed the slender, freckled arm of my new friend and pulled her into the long cafeteria line. Sharon was always holding the door open for the rest of us, while at the same time tossing morsels of dry humor our way to make us laugh and to help us momentarily forget where we were and why we were there. I really think her humor was more for her own benefit than for the rest of us. We all loved her and cherished her ability to bring light into our cloudy spaces.

I was always blessed to have visitors in the evening. Sharon never had any guests and would always manage to drop by my room, not staying long, but just long enough to make us smile and perhaps feel like she too was part of a family . . . of friends. Jake brought her a bouquet of flowers. To Sharon, it was a pot of gold.

Sharon had several thick books with volumes of poetry in them that she had written. I felt honored when she told me she wanted to show them to me. One day we went into her room and closed the door because she did not want to risk having anyone else enter into her private world. Sharon had started to trust me and had begun to tell me, as much as her wounded child would allow, about her childhood. I was horrified at the stories she told me and was overwhelmed by the look of stark terror that hung relentlessly in the windows of her soul. Anyway, I got so flippin' mad when one of the staff nurses threw open the door! I suppose she was expecting Sharon and me to be engaged in some despicable act (remember that Sharon professed to be gay). What she found was Sharon stretched out facedown across her bed, and I was sitting cross-legged on the floor covered with books. With unpremeditated anger, I let the nurse know in no uncertain terms that she was way off base. We were never bothered again, but this too became a defining moment for me.

When I returned to my room that day I questioned why I had been so defensive when I had absolutely nothing to be defensive about. Or did I? Sharon was wounded, and in her pain she reached out to women for intimacy. I could not blame her, considering the cruel and inhumane treatment of her precious child by men. In her mind, being gay protected her from ever being bothered by a man again. I could no longer deny that my own story was much like Sharon's. Had I stuffed my own confusing sexuality so deep inside that I could not see how the sexual abuse imposed upon me as an innocent child had become a predator too? Abusers leave, they go away, but the effects of their abuse stay with the victim forever. It confuses sexuality and then compounds it and stuffs its shame and guilt into dark, forbidden places. This was a door that I did not want to open, but I knew I had no choice if I was going to find *all* the answers to *all* of my secrets.

* * *

Once again my two companions and I curled up on my never-soft bed and relived one of the most cherished times of my life. It was a time when a small corner of my child-soul was healed, and it was a place that I needed to revisit and process questions that I had previously dared not ask. It is time to begin adding some color to our painting. Splashes of yellow, lavender, purple and pink will begin to bring illuminations of pure pleasure to the canvas of my life. Select your best paintbrush and paint with me. This will be fun, as we learn many lessons along the way.

After graduating from business school, I moved to the Dallas area to look for a job. I moved in with my sister and her family and eventually went to work in the accounting department for the same company where my sister's husband worked. Jo Ann came to work there about the time my first marriage (I'll tell you about that later) came to a traumatic end. We quickly became inseparable friends. Jo Ann owned a little house that rested on five acres of land outside of Dallas, and occasionally we would go out on weekends and ride horses around a nearby lake. Sometimes we would detour through the grounds of a monastery not far from her property. I would always get a rather strange, mysterious feeling as we rode our horses through the unfinished chapel. The wall-less shelter with its concrete floor, large square pillars and finished roof offered shade from the intense sun. We always felt a sweet, cool breeze sweeping through. There was a small quaint building where we discovered a quiet, inviting chapel adjacent to the living quarters for resident monks. A larger, more modern structure designed for meetings nestled under large trees. The entire complex was a beautiful, peaceful place for religious seclusion.

It was the gift of laughter Jo Ann gave me that I cherished the most. Laughter was just one of the many missing links in my childhood experience, and to discover its healing power was truly divine. Probably for the first time (as an adult), I allowed the abused adult/ child to play.

Each summer Jo Ann's father led the famous Old Chisholm Trail Ride from Dallas to Saint Jo, Texas, near the Oklahoma border. She asked her father if I could go on the trail ride with her, of course convincing him that I was an experienced rider, which I was not, but oh well! I was always up for an adventure. I can still hear her mischievous chuckle as she asked me if I wanted to go along. Like her father, Jo Ann loved to have fun, usually at another's expense. She knew that she was in for the time of her life watching me stay on a horse for three days. And I didn't disappoint her. Jo Ann made arrangements for me to ride her mother's horse, Pam, and before I could even think about changing my mind, I found myself packed and ready to go. It was June 1967.

Proud, reddish brown and really big describes Pam well. And oh yes, I forgot smart—much too smart for a greenhorn like me. The first morning out on the trail, she bloated out her belly when we put the saddle on her so that it wouldn't be so tight. I didn't know that I was supposed to check the saddle before I got on her. Just before we crossed a long, steep, narrow dam, this mass of long hairy legs began a swift gallop together as one. In other words, the whole herd of horses took off running at neck-breaking speed at the exact same time. I tried to hold Pam back because I didn't like swift gallops. I liked slow gallops. But there was no holding her back. Instinctively she wanted to keep up with the rest of the herd and so off she went—and off I went—literally! If only Lady could have seen me. I would have taken a mad rooster in a henhouse over this anytime. And this was only the first day!

The saddle slipped sideways, and I slipped sideways with it, shooting off Pam faster than a bullet out of a gun. I looked like a tumbleweed in a sandstorm, not so eloquently rolling across the vast Texas plains. When the dust settled and air returned to my lungs, I slowly lifted my head and opened my eyes. There was Pam nonchalantly returning my gaze while casually chewing on a blade of grass. I am sure that I saw a smug grin on her face. Gutsy thing that I was, or maybe I was just in denial, I had no choice but to "buck up," dust off, and get on that horse and let her catch up with the rest of the herd. With eyes wide and mouth run dry, I stuck myself to that animal like a fly sticks to honey. I was never short on stubborn determination when I really needed it!

Considering all else, the first day wasn't so bad. As I moseyed along with the other thirty or so participants, the endless, cloudless skies stretched for limitless miles and miles ahead of us. The scorching June sun parched my lips even under my straw cowboy hat, and the back of my hands slowly turned blood-red. I forgot to bring gloves. But it did not matter. My entire being came to life as this new adventure captivated my imagination and carried me back in time. I tried to relive the unmistakable hardships that my ancestors must have endured as they migrated by covered wagon from Georgia, Mississippi and Oklahoma to settle in Texas and New Mexico Territory. Whole clans traveled together, which I supposed accounted for the fact that both sets of my grandparents were married to cousins. As hard as I tried, I could not really conceive of living in such a time, and I wondered how many never reached their destinations.

As I guided Pam beside the now-paved road, I imagined buffalo wandering the prairie land around us and Indians hunting them. Had this once been a path where they too rode their horses? I wondered if any of my Cherokee ancestors had walked the Trail of Tears. Had they been driven from their land and their homes burned? Were some unjustly murdered? I could almost feel their sorrow as I thought about the native Indian blood that runs through my veins. I wished that I could hear their forever-lost stories.

The sun was beginning to close in on the western horizon as the trail riders came to a stop just ahead of me. I was suddenly famished. Oh well, at least we didn't have to find our own food and water. I was thankful for the chuck wagon that followed along with us. It was full of delectable country vittles and cold water.

We rode forty-one miles the first day and camped near an old cotton gin. That night I had no trouble falling asleep under a star-studded sky that briefly reminded me of long-ago summer nights spent lying on an old tattered quilt, wondering about the mysteries of God. I was so tired that I didn't even think about what might be crawling around on the ground beside me. (I hate snakes!)

The dawning of a new day immediately told me that this carefree escapade might not have been such a good idea. I could hardly move. And this was only the second day! My bowed legs didn't want to walk, every muscle in my poor body yelled at me, and to make matters worse, my right knee, which had hit the ground just after my chin the day before, was swollen. A kindhearted retired cowboy came to my rescue. He bathed and massaged my swollen knee with liniment and told me that I was doing fine and that I looked like I had been born in a saddle. Oh, yeah! That was all the encouragement I needed, and after riding with the chuck wagon gang for a spell, I wanted to get back in the saddle again. I had noticed that Jo Ann hadn't laughed much since my big splash on the ground the day before. We traveled only thirty-eight miles the second day.

By God's grace I made it all the way to Saint Jo where the local cowboys immediately began throwing all of us dirty, sweaty cowgirls into the horse troughs located around the old town square. We had traveled a total of ninety-two miles in three days, and water from any source for our sun baked skin was more than welcome. It was an unforgettable experience and so much fun, mostly because wherever you found Jo Ann, laughter was sure to be lurking close by. For instance, just after we arrived, the people of Saint Jo provided a huge barbecue for the trail riders. Jo Ann and I piled our plates high with food and sat on the grass Indian style across from each other. Somebody upwind from us unthinkingly started to brush their horse, and at the exact same time, we discovered there was something rather strange about the food on our forks that we were about to put into our mouths. We looked down at our plates only to find that our food was totally covered with coarse, red horsehair. We just looked up at each other and burst into uncontrollable, unquenchable laughter. But that is the way it was when we were together. Everything and anything became an excuse to laugh. These were stories that I would indeed someday tell my grandchildren. Surely, our trip to Washington, DC in the fall would not be nearly so adventurous! Or would it?

We were a conspicuous pair. Jo Ann is taller than I, lanky and a natural blonde. I am petite with contrasting short black hair and am solid, not weighty, just solid. We had looked forward to our trip from Dallas to DC for months. We borrowed her mother's camper pickup truck and set out with a number two wash tub, a Coleman cook stove, lots of food, sleep gear and just enough clothing for the ten-day trip. In the 1960s, it seemed a reasonable and safe thing for two young gals in their early twenties to do.

We were giddy with excitement as we drove out of Dallas toward the District of Columbia. It was September 1967. We stopped at every historical place we could find, read every piece of historical literature we picked up, and jabbered nonstop the entire way. I was mesmerized by the beauty of the southern states and the incredible history they held. Jo Ann's ability to tell stories made the Old South come to life as we traveled. Grave markers along the roadsides beckoned for us to stop and visit. We could not resist. It all seemed impossibly different from where I grew up on the flat plains of Texas, where there was nothing but miles and miles of nothing but miles and miles. Texas was a place where strong winds frequently tossed its red dirt into the spacious sky, changing daylight into darkness, breathing into wheezing and people into the salt of the earth.

Our visit to our nation's capital was absolutely awesome to me. I stood captivated by the majestic capital buildings and monuments. We ate peanut butter sandwiches on a bench inside the immense Smithsonian Institute. I wished for more time to spend there. I was moved to tears, frozen in disbelief and bewilderment, as the perfectly lined white crosses in Arlington Cemetery shocked my senses. I tried to understand the thousands of lives that wars had claimed for my freedom. I found no peace there.

I mourned that fateful day in Dallas as I stood near the Eternal Flame of our fallen president, John F. Kennedy. Grief still fresh, I reconstructed for Jo Ann a precious gift that life had given to me just moments before the tragic shots were fired. I had walked with a co-worker to within a few blocks of Dealey Plaza where President and Mrs. Kennedy's motorcade was to travel. I was close enough to reach out and touch the leader of our country as their open limousine slowly crept down the noisy street where people clapped and cheered for them. This handsome, charismatic man and his beautiful wife were both looking my direction smiling, waving and appearing so very happy and safe. That one precious glimpse hangs framed on a space in the corridor of my mind. As they passed on, we turned and began our short walk back to our office. On the way we heard the sirens, not giving them much thought. The deadly news greeted us as we walked into the office building. Skepticism, doubt, disbelief, denial—they all swirled in the air around us. The President had been shot. I recalled the deadly silence of the city those next few days. The city had stopped breathing. That same eerie silence lingered around the tomb of John F. Kennedy that day in Washington, DC, and for a moment, I stopped breathing too. Our time in the capital city was much too short.

On our way back home, we managed to get lost on Mount Mitchell in North Carolina. It is the highest point east of the Rocky Mountains. At first, we didn't know we were lost, but eventually we realized we were getting higher and higher as it kept getting darker and darker and colder and colder. We definitely were not prepared for cold weather! We didn't have a clue where we were or where we were going. So far, we had been very good at getting to campsites before dark, but now we didn't know if we were even near one. We were beginning to get a little anxious when suddenly, from out of nowhere, appeared what we at first thought was a mirage. But there in the bend of the road and in the black of night was a small log cabin. Jo Ann brought the truck to a stop, and we sat there for a long while just looking at the wooden structure. There was not a soul in sight. After a while, we cautiously got out of the truck to investigate. For once, we didn't find anything funny about our predicament. We slowly opened the cabin door and stepped into the soft glow of a small space heater. Its welcoming warmth invited us in and directed us to hot, running water and public showers. The place was spotlessly clean. After bathing in a wash tub in the back of a truck for over a week, we didn't even hesitate. Without a word, we just grinned real big at each other and ran back to the truck for soap and towels—thanking God all the way! Refreshed and warm, we climbed into the back of the unheated camper and piled everything that we could find on top of us. We slept like babies. I think we skipped supper.

The next morning, we awoke to a cloudy, overcast sky. The obscure, quaint cabin seemed to smile back at us as we peered at it from inside the frigid camper. It had not been a mirage after all, and the mystery of it still lingers with me. As far as we could tell, we were the only living creatures around.

We found our way off the beautiful, magnificent mountain and continued our trek homeward, making as many stops as possible. Consequently, we failed to reach the campground where we had planned to stay before it got dark. Back then, campsites were very primitive and had no lighting at all. As we drove into the pitch-black campground, once again, there was not a soul in sight. Jo Ann parked the camper truck parallel to a picnic table where we quickly began to set up for a camp supper, which we had anticipated all day long. There is absolutely nothing better than a can of pork and beans cooked over a Coleman stove on a cool night in a national forest—if you are really hungry.

Because it was dark, we lit a candle and put it on the table beside the Coleman stove, which was low on fuel. Jo Ann looked for a paper cup while I retrieved a plastic milk jug from the camp box. The milk jug was more than half full of fuel. We were quietly enjoying the peaceful evening as I poured the white liquid into the paper cup that Jo Ann held in her hand. Without warning, the fuel splashed out of the cup and hit the lighted candle. In a flash, my hand along with the fuel-filled milk jug was covered with fire, as was the cup, the stove, the table, and *oh no*—her mother's truck was next to the table! We looked at each other in total shock and disbelief. Jo Ann sternly instructed me to quickly walk as far away as possible, to set the jug down and to run away from it. For once in my life, being obedient was not a problem.

And then the most unbelievable, amazing thing happened. A man with a fire extinguisher walked out of the woods and casually put out the fire. When he had accomplished his mission, he calmly looked at us and said, "Good night, ladies" and disappeared back into the woods. I think that we ate cold beans that night . . . in complete silence.

When daylight peeked through the clouds the next morning, we quickly dressed. We wanted to thank the man who saved us, the national forest, and Jo Ann's mother's truck. But there was no man to thank. We saw no one. We devoured a tasty country breakfast, packed up, and pulled out of the campground and still we never saw a soul. I will always believe the man who visited us that night was an angel sent by God to watch over us. And occasionally, I wonder . . . if we went back to Mount Mitchell, would we find a heated cabin sitting in a bend in the road with a fiery heater, hot running water, and clean showers? And one other thing . . . I forgot to mention . . . there was not even a red mark left on my hand by the fire.

Jo Ann made my small world so much bigger and happier. She gave me so much, but in retrospect, I feel I gave her so little in return. I was such a needy person. She was probably the first person in my life that I really loved. But there were limits to my ability to love and to be loved, and our relationship scared me. Even though there was never even a hint of anything physical between us, I did not understand the unspeakable, conflicting sexual issues that were a result of my childhood. We pulled away from each other, and we both began to date again. God had a perfect plan for each of us, which has included our lasting friendship.

The soft tap on my hospital door beckoned me to return from my introspective thoughts. I opened my eyes and found that Sharon had come to remind me of the time. I had never before noticed that her smile, her personality and her sense of humor reminded me a bit of Jo Ann. I smiled back at her, hugged my teddy bears and then looked at my clock. Indeed, it was time for me to see my therapist, and after that, I had another session with Barb. I wasn't sure what or if I would tell either of them about my visit with my forever friend. There were extenuating circumstances in my life that I was not ready to face just yet, but I was beginning to process—beginning to think. I was continuing to rearrange the threads of understanding and hope that I was finding along the way, in this place, where God was calling me to trust Him as I had never trusted Him before. Once again memories of my special friend had brought joy to my very sad world, and for just a moment I felt a twinge of happiness.

Chapter 10

So What Does a Little Bird
Have to Do with Faith?

My psychiatrist was beginning to push me. It had been almost three weeks since I had given myself permission to allow total strangers into my private world, but I was not really telling them what they wanted to hear. I could get into everybody else's stuff, but not my own. In my small group I was the attentive listener, the comforter, the friend. I could even encourage others to talk, but I would share only in generalities about my own stuff, never really allowing the vulnerability of honesty to be exposed. I sincerely wanted to move forward. I had begun to make progress as I talked with Barb, but I still could not bear to look her in the face and tell her, or anyone else, about the wounded child I protected.

To make matters worse, my therapist's silence felt like fingernails scratching on a blackboard. During my sessions with him, he would just sit there, usually looking at the floor or the ceiling, waiting for me to say something—to talk. If I sidetracked, he would just put me on the spot and ask me why I needed to talk about something else instead of myself. I resented his behavior and his mannerisms, but eventually his silence became his gift to me. I was always relieved when our sessions ended.

*   *   *

Barb and I were back at the sunlit window. This time she wanted me to talk about my marriage. As I admitted to her that this was actually my second marriage, I began to feel the dreaded pain that kept my emotions numb and my feelings crammed down inside of me. Before bringing Jake into the picture, we would have to visit those years leading up to my first marriage, and I really did not want to go there. However, I would let Barb travel with me down roads paved with pain, where God's tender mercy and grace miraculously found their way into the deep ruts of my treasured anguish. For this part of our canvas, dark shadows must fill empty spaces where strokes of purest white will expose the bright light of hope. Today, perseverance will guide our brushes.

My dad worked for the railroad, so we moved around West Texas quite a bit. When I was in the second grade, we moved to a small town near Abilene. This is where most of the abuse that I can remember happened. Ironically, this is also where I found God. Mrs. Gray, whose husband worked for my dad, had a life-changing effect upon my life, and I will always be grateful to her. I loved going next door to what we called the bunkhouse with its great, long concrete porch, to play with her son. Wayne was a year younger than me, and we spent hours together pretending to be lost in imaginary worlds. But mostly, I loved being with Mrs. Gray because she was always so sweet to me. Her house was always clean, and mouth-watering smells invited me to sit at her table and listen as she talked to me about a man named Jesus. *Had this precious Saint of God looked into the soul of the abused child and seen her great need for love, for God? Had she sensed the child was deeply troubled?*

I don't really recall how old I was when Mrs. Gray began to take me to church with her and her son, but I loved going to the small white church on Sunday mornings and evenings. I loved Sunday school and singing the hymns. I loved the peace I found there and the people who freely gave me hugs. I listened intently to the preacher, not always understanding, but clinging to the words he spoke. He did not know he was tossing out lifelines for a wounded child to grab on to.

Although pinpointing exact dates is sometimes difficult for me, I think I was around nine years old when the words of the songs we were singing spoke to my tender spirit and beckoned me to go into the loving arms of Jesus. "Just as I am without one plea, but that thy blood was shed for me . . . Have thine own way Lord, have thine own way. Thou art the potter, I am the clay. Mold me and make me after thy will . . . Softly and tenderly Jesus is calling, calling for you and for me, come home, come home . . ." I can still remember how I felt on that Sunday morning as I slipped out of the long, wooden pew, walked to the front of the peaceful church and knelt at the altar. Before my knees barely touched the floor, it seemed that the entire congregation was on their knees around me, soaking me in prayer. The pastor's wife wrapped her arms around me and began to weep and pray fervently over me. She asked me if wanted to invite Jesus to be in my life, to be saved, to be born again. I eagerly whispered, "Yes." That day, I committed my life to God not really knowing or understanding the full impact of my decision or the tears that wrenched from somewhere deep within me. I remember sobbing so hard and feeling, at prayer's end, that I was somehow different. I had been born again, not in flesh, but in *spirit* as God's Holy Spirit came to live within me.[1] In retrospect, I just know God commissioned special angels to watch over me because He knew there would be many spiritual battles fought over the life of this, His wounded child.

Several weeks later, when the pastor called for the recently saved to come to the altar for additional prayer, I was compelled to go forward. In some churches, this additional prayer is called a

---

[1] In John 3:3 Jesus declared, "I tell you the truth, no one can see the kingdom of God unless he is born again." John 3:6 says, "Flesh gives birth to the flesh, but the Spirit gives birth to the spirit" (NIV).

second touch or consecration, but in that little church, it is called sanctification—all of which is a prayer for the anointing work of the Holy Spirit to be upon the life of a believer in Jesus.[2] It didn't matter to me what it was called. As a young girl, I just knew I wanted whatever God had for me, and I wanted to be prayed for again because I absolutely loved being prayed for. I will always be thankful to Mrs. Gray and the small body of believers who prayed me into the mystery of a transformed life through Jesus Christ. *The spirit of the precious child had been reborn, transformed, but the transformation of her wounded child was far from complete. This was just the beginning. God knew change would not come easily.*

My intimate relationship with God really began when He used a small bird to seal my faith. A beautiful, blue parakeet had been given to me as a Christmas present from my sister. Dickie Bird quickly became my new best friend, and whenever I was at home, he was almost always on my shoulder. He would stop at nothing to get my attention. If I was attempting to study, he would be chewing on the corners of my schoolbook. If I was writing, he was on my hand trying to take away my pencil. If my record player was on, he would jump on the record and try to go for a ride on the spinning record. It was such a hoot to watch him go sailing off the record, flapping his wings wildly. If all else failed, he would waddle over to my dish of jacks and drop them one by one over the edge of my dresser. Once the dish was empty and the jacks had been scattered all over the hardwood floor, he would peer over the edge of the dresser, turn his head toward me, and stare intently until I got up and put them back in the dish so that he could do it all over again. We kissed and whistled and talked to each other like any friends would. And like Lady, he filled an empty place in my little girl world.

My greatest fear was that someday I would forget about my little buddy and walk outside with him on my shoulder. Sure enough,

---

[2]   In John 17:17, Jesus prayed for his disciples, "Sanctify [set apart, dedicate, make pure] them through your truth" (NIV).

one day it happened. When I went out the back door to hang laundry on the clothesline to dry, I heard Dickie's wings flutter in my ear and then he was gone. I screamed in horror as I ran back into the house to tell my mother, seeking her help. She casually looked up from reading her newspaper and suggested that he might have headed for the trees down at the creek, which was about a hundred yards from our house. *Emotions! Confusing emotions! Why didn't she go with me? I'm a mother. I would have gone with my child to help find her bird. The abused child did not understand then, and the abused adult/child did not understand it now as she told her story.*

In West Texas, trees are sparse, leaving lots of wide open spaces where a little bird can get lost. I rushed out of the house sobbing so hard, I could hardly see. Terror ran to my heart, causing it to pound against my chest as the blistering summer sun mingled sweat with my tears. I sprinted down the long dusty path in search of my companion, and for the first time in my life, I cried out to God for help. In panicked desperation I pleaded, I prayed, "Please, God, please help me find my bird!" When I reached the tree line of the creek, I stopped and looked into the forest of mesquite trees and wondered how I would ever find him. I called his name, and then I heard his strong reply. "Hello, my name's Dickie Bird—(wolf whistle)—whatcha doin?" I looked up, and there he was sitting calmly on a limb, looking down at me and chatting away. Immediately, he flew down on my shoulder, and I wrapped my small hands around his hot, panting body. And then, I thanked my God over and over and over for helping me to find my bird. It was on that day that indefinable faith was born in my heart. I knew, that I knew, that God hears and answers my prayers. *The precious child did not know it then, but the direction of her life had been changed forever. The wounded child did not know that such faith would surely be tested.*

If my life experiences from years one to five defined who I was to become, then the years from five to nine must surely have revealed something about those earlier years. When I look back, I can see the confusing roles I played. I was a good kid and sweet, a shy kind of a girl that most everyone liked. I always had friends, but I was constantly changing friends, never really staying close to anyone for very long. I rebelled against authority and often found myself in trouble at school.

I recall being told not to go over and play on the playground with the big kids. What did I do? I went over and played with the big kids. I was also late getting back to my class, but I didn't seem to care. If I was told not to talk in study hall, I talked. In fact, I was always getting in trouble for talking and passing notes in class. Once when the teacher left the room, all of the boys started throwing erasers. Guess who was the only girl in the room who got into trouble right along with the boys? And guess who, just once, got lined up with the guys and got a paddling with a wooden board with holes in it? Ouch! But this time there was another girl involved, so it wasn't so bad. During recess, I played baseball with the boys (girls weren't supposed to play ball with boys), but that is how I learned to hit a hard, straight ball. One day, I got hit right smack in the middle of my tummy with one of those hard fastballs. I thought I was going to die and decided it was time to find something else to do. I liked to put gum in my mouth before class just because it was against the rules. If I was careful, I could get by with it. Of course, I had to steal the gum out of the Five and Dime store because I never had any money of my own. By today's standards, these are not serious infractions, but back then they were shameful acts. For me, they were symptoms. I had no shame, and I was left to my own devices. There was no one there to pull me aside and help me be any different. *The wounded child seemed predestined for larger offenses, more painful failures.*

There was never an incentive to learn, so I did what I had to do to get by. No one had ever read to me, or even tried to teach me that learning was a good thing. I recall when I learned to spell *envelope.* I went around the house all day saying, "e-n-v-e-l-o-p-e." It was such a big word, and I was so proud of myself; but no one stopped to listen, no one patted me on the head, no one said, "Good job." To this day, I remember having an overshadowing sense of disappointing sadness.

Another defining moment happened when my fourth grade math teacher towered over me in front of the whole class and chastised me for not making a one hundred on a test. I think I missed only a couple of problems. She announced to everyone in the room that she had taught my brother math, and he was a whiz. "I know that you can do better than this. You are just freezing up on tests!" she demanded. As all eyes were focused upon me, the space around me turned dark, and I seemed to disappear into the darkness. From that moment on, I hated math. For some reason the actions of this woman caused me to sink further into myself. I strongly believe that single incident caused me ultimately to just sail along with the wind when it came to my education. I had a very "I don't care" attitude, but I really don't understand why. *The precious child had no power and often retreated. The wounded child turned anger inward because she knew that adults have all the power.*

I clearly had a talent for music and art. But even those gifts were not seen as anything special or important, kind of like me—not special or important. For years, I had begged for a piano, but my mother told me that my dad, who played the fiddle by ear, would not allow a piano in the house. I now wonder if that was really true. Anyway, when I didn't get one for my thirteenth birthday, I was so disappointed I refused to ever look forward to birthdays again. After I graduated from high school, a teacher told me I was a big disappointment to him because I had done nothing with my artistic talent. He told me that I was one of the best artists he had ever seen. I was so surprised because no one had ever told me I was talented, and I was not capable of seeing it in myself. *Why was there never anyone there to encourage the precious child? Why could the wounded child never see that she had value? Why was she so shut down?*

(Testing done while in the hospital indicated that I was on the high side of intelligence. Keep in mind, these tests were done while I was depressed and in an awful state of mind. Up until then, I never believed that I might actually have a brain in my head. It is also interesting to note that during testing I was connected to a machine which monitored my heart rate. When I was asked to do math problems, my intense anxiety about math tripled my heart rate. I could not verbally solve even simple equations.)

Small towns can be difficult places to grow up, especially if you think you are different. But they can also be a place where lifelong friendships and memories are born. After I asked Jesus into my life, I began to see changes in my behavior and my attitude. My Christian family and friends meant everything to me, and I especially cherish the memories that I have of Wayne, Iona, Patty and Nelda. We all came from low-income families, but we had the ability to create our own fun, and we all loved Jesus. We shared joy, in spite of what life handed us. I read from the old Bible I found tucked away in a cabinet, and I thought about God a lot. I was in church every time I could get a ride because my parents did not attend church. There are good memories to be found in the heart of the precious child, but they are overshadowed by so many bad ones. The years between the ages of nine and fourteen ultimately defined the survivor I became. *Within those very early years, the abused child often felt confusion and shifts in her personality. She fit in, she didn't fit in. She was sweet, she was angry. She was good, she was bad. She just wanted to be good, not ever bad! She had been crying out for help all of her young life, but those who needed to hear were not listening. They were not paying attention. But clearly, Jesus was watching this wounded child.*

We moved away from the security of my church family at the end of my freshman year in high school. Friends gave me a small white Bible and signed their names on the inside cover with a gold pen. I was heartbroken at the very thought of moving away from my church and my friends. A sense of foreboding began to settle upon me, even before my final good-byes were said. I was fourteen years old.

Chapter 11

Secrets Are like Ducks—They Will Bite Off Your Nose if You Are Not Careful

*   *   *

*S**ecrets! Unconsciously, I buried them right along with the fear of having them exposed. It has been said that if it looks like a duck, walks like a duck and quacks like a duck, then it is a duck. Secrets quack like ducks in unexpected places, at unexpected times, in unexpected ways. You don't even know they are there. They torment, confuse, confound and perplex everyone who hears them. Your quacks are rejected and judged and ridiculed, but you don't even know that you are quacking. You wonder what is wrong, because you can't hear the secret quacks calling out to you and those around you. You don't understand, because no one will tell you about them. No one will stop and help you hear them, so the quacks just keep going on and on and on. They control you, but you don't know they are controlling you, because you can't hear them. Sometimes they become silent and no one hears them . . . and then all those around you begin to wonder why they are no longer hearing your quacks. Now everyone is confused. And, if that all sounds confusing, and you are confused, then I have succeeded in helping those who hear the quacks understand the confusion that* *surrounds the abused adult/child. Watch carefully as they emerge, and be careful. Ducks will try to bite off your nose if you hold them too close to your face!*

*   *   *

My Session with Barb continued . . .

The town we moved to was small like the one we left behind, but different in ways that would change me. Summer Saturday nights would find the back two rows of the drive-in theater full of drunken teenagers. After my first night out with a group of kids, I went home and wept. My first day in the new school was not much better, and a tug-of-war began within me. One side was warning me, pleading with me to hold on to my faith, while the other side pulled at me, encouraging me to let go. A spirit of doom began to surround me and grip me. It would not let go of me. I had no church family or Christian friends to support me, and there was no protection or guidance from my parents. *The abuses that had stolen the soft, tender, innocent soul of the precious, little child began to create a monster whose personality began to take control. She knew in her spirit that her life was going to change but was powerless to stop the changes from happening. There were tormenting demons hovering nearby.[1] They had their prey in sight. They had been lurking in the background, knowing that the abused child was like a stray sheep without a shepherd to guide or protect her and that she would be rendered incapable of making wise choices. The precious child began to disappear as the wounded, abused child took over.*

Subtle changes began to come over me as I managed to get through my sophomore year. During the summer, I went to Dallas

---

[1]   Ephesians 6:12, "For we wrestle not against flesh and blood, but against principalities, against powers, against the rulers of the darkness of this world, against spiritual wickedness in high places" (KJV).

94

and lived with my sister and her family so I could work and have money for the coming school year. I returned home to begin my junior year and quickly became part of the popular crowd, doing everything that the popular crowd did. Every success was dangled in front of me, and the principles of my faith slowly began to slip away.

Almost overnight I became uncharacteristically concerned with learning, and my grades drastically improved. I was even elected to the student council and became the recording secretary. I became a cheerleader and was elected football sweetheart my senior year. I joined the band and landed the solo clarinet position and was named to the state's All Star Band. I became an art editor for the school paper and the yearbook. And I even had a science project that was entered into state competition.

Everything about my life pointed to a well-balanced, happy teenager, but nothing could have been further from the truth. I lived in guarded fear that people would discover I was really bad and I was neither smart nor pretty nor any of the things I was trying to be. I told no one, not even my closest friends, about my past, my unhappiness or my struggles. I kept my secrets to myself. No one had a clue, and only the wise would have noticed my sometimes-strange behavior. Teachers surely must have turned their heads. *Guilt and shame laughed at the abused child around every corner as she began to dig deeper holes to bury them in. Why did no one notice? Why was there never anyone there for her? Her facade (that which conceals something unpleasant) was created as she put on her first mask, the mask of deception. The age of accountability had come. The abused adult/child was born.*

My junior year I began dating a popular football player who was also a junior. Everyone liked him, and I liked being associated with him. Dee's laughing eyes and quick smile earned him the title of Best All-Around Boy our senior year, and at the same time I was runner-up to the same title for girls. We had become one of the school's sweetheart couples, and my girlfriends always wanted to know when we were going to get married. From the very beginning of our relationship, I denied that Dee was already well into the disease of alcoholism. Since I was well into the disease of victimization, which I also denied, we were a deadly combination. I had learned as a child that I could not say no, and while under the influence of alcohol, I finally gave in to him sexually. When he asked me why I wasn't a virgin, I just told him that I had been abused. I had no choice but to tell him. It was the first time I had actually said the words out loud, the first time I had openly admitted it to anyone. I hated sex, but I was numb to the power it had over me. *By then, the black abyss of depression invited the demons of suicide to begin their voodoo dance in the mind of the abused adult/child. Their poisoned darts hit their target and almost claimed an innocent life. The private, raging war within turned to self-hatred, and behavior became erratic, bouncing like a ball from good to bad.*

The first signs of suicidal depression emerged when I was only sixteen years of age. I began to have thoughts of dying. I wanted to end the pain of living. One day, when I was at home alone, I decided to turn on the gas heater in the living room and put an end to my insane life. Just as I was reaching for the jet connection, Dee appeared at the front door and saw me through the window. The moment passed. He never knew what he had thwarted. *Or had God's angels brought him there to stop the abused adult/child?*

After graduating from high school, Dee went away to college and I attended a business college about seventy miles away from my home. When I graduated, I moved to the Dallas area and went to work for the same company where my sister's husband worked. A year later, Dee and I were married, and he enrolled in a local college. I knew I was making a mistake, but I had made my bed and thought I had to lie in it. We moved into an apartment close to my sister and her family, and I rode to work each day with my brother-in-law.

There were good times and there were bad times in my first marriage. I loved Dee's parents. His father worked on a very large ranch that was owned by a Texas senator. They were hardworking, kind, loving people. He had a younger brother who was mentally challenged, and they were totally devoted to him.

Shortly after Dee enrolled in college, he was asked to join a fraternity. He accepted the invitation, which unfortunately only became an open door that fueled his addiction to alcohol. His excessive drinking brought turbulence into our strained relationship, and each passing year his drinking became more and more progressive. Taking care of myself was so uncharacteristic for me, but for once I had the good sense to stop drinking. Not only was I seeing the negative effects it was having on Dee and our marriage, I was beginning to see the effects it was having on both of my brothers' lives as well. I wanted nothing to do with it. I had personally slept with the demon of alcoholism, and I was afraid to stay in bed with it because I wanted so badly just to go to sleep and never wake up. *God protected the abused adult/child from giving into this addiction that ran so freely in the veins of her family. She did not understand then that if she had chosen to drown her pain in alcohol's unforgiving comfort, it would have destroyed the precious child that lived within her.*

Dee began to come home late at night, feeling no obligation to account for his tardiness. We began to have awful fights, and once he threw his fist into a wall rather than into my face. Although I functioned in a deep state of depression and unhappiness, no one knew the personal hell that I lived in—not my family, not my coworkers, no one. But anger's boiling rage would sometimes fuel unexpected, unpredictable behavior that I am sure was not missed by those around me. *The abused adult/child was learning to wear her facade very well. Her mask, with its many faces, was becoming an intricate part of her identity.*

One Saturday night I went to a party with Dee. Slowly, I began to realize that I was at a party for gay people. Dee had been working part-time for a famous shoe store, and I had become suspicious of his male coworker. (This was long before people would ever openly confess to being gay.) That night I went into that dark place where I hid, except this time, I took something with me. I gave into the demon that chased me, and drowned my fears in a bottle of Southern Comfort, which I sorely regretted the next day. I had never allowed myself to drink to that extent before, but denial completely defeated me. Dee began to invite his co-worker to our apartment. Then he began to disappear for days at a time, again with no obligation to account for his whereabouts. I cried, I begged, I pleaded with him to stop drinking, but my words fell on indifferent ears. I could no longer live with his lies, his drinking and the unknown.

Finally, once again, I found the courage to take care of myself. I didn't know what he had gotten himself into, but whatever it was, it terrified me. I moved into an apartment without disclosing to Dee my address or my phone number. However, Dee was the type of person who could look you in the eyes and tell you a lie, and knowing full well that he was lying, you'd believe him anyway. For reasons that I still do not understand, he convinced someone in my family to give him my unlisted phone number. I never told them the real reasons for the separation.

I was pressured by my family to reconcile with my husband, so out of frustration and just to shut everyone up, I invited him to move into my apartment with me. The reunion was short-lived because on the first day back together, we got into a huge fight. I locked myself in the bathroom with every intention of slitting my wrists. I had never wanted out of life as badly as I did at that moment. Suicidal depression had no mercy upon me. Its evil voice told me that life was hopeless, and that there was no other way out of my marriage or the underlying effects of the secrets I carried. I was determined to end my life, and Dee knew it. He literally knocked down the door to get to me, to stop me. The one that kept pushing me over the edge was strangely the one that kept pulling me back from the edge. *Or had it been God's angels again?*

Later that evening my unlisted phone rang and Dee answered it. I heard him tell the person on the other end of the line that he would be right there. Dee then told me a friend had car trouble and needed some help and promised me that he would return shortly. The meal I had just prepared was waiting on the table. I offered to go with him, but he walked out literally closing the door in my face. There are no words to describe the rejection, the pain, the defeat, the aloneness, the hopelessness that I felt. The unseen forces I felt around me were powerful and frightening. They caused me to flee from them or else I knew I would be pulled into their unrelenting grip. Three days later, Dee called me at work, and I told him I was filing for a divorce. I was thankful that there were no children involved.

We had been two very immature kids who thought they were in love, but had no understanding or responsibility toward love. We were both in need, but not in love. We were each perishing in our own twisted search for significance, hoping to find it in each other but destroying each other in the process. I felt great pain for Dee's family. They deserved much better from both of us. (Dee has since remarried and has a daughter and grandchildren.)

Months later I stood in a courtroom full of people—alone. It seemed as though every ounce of blood drained from my body and spilled on the floor around me, as the harsh whack of the judge's gavel ended almost four years of marriage. Divorce is never good. It leaves its own bitter mark upon the soul. I felt exposed for the failure that I was, especially back then when being divorced labeled you as flawed. Strong-willed determination emerged, and hardness of soul walked with me as I left the cold, stone courthouse and walked back to my office. I held my head high. For the first time in many years, I felt I could breathe. I was strong. Nothing was going to break me. I would let no one ever hurt me again. *But deep within, the abused adult/child was dying from the pain . . . the never, never-ending pain. She would indeed remain strong, but she would have to be broken before finally understanding that true strength comes from God and not from self.*

The following three years were good years. I was successful in my accounting job. I discovered that not only was I good with numbers, I really loved the challenge of working with them. I even landed a position in the company I worked for that required an accounting degree, which I did not have. I bought lots of new clothes and a car, made new friends, dated, traveled, and just lived life. I began to have a deep longing for God in my life, and I began to return to the principles of my faith that I had walked away from as a teenager. They were well-deserved, peaceful years. It was during this time that God brought Jo Ann into my life.

It was also during this period of time that I was introduced to Ann, Janie, and Phylis. They were young, Christian women who needed a roommate. I wasn't at all sure if they would want a divorced woman living with them and was very nervous about meeting them and confessing my sin. My facade had probably never been thicker. They were clearly a part of God's plan for my life because we have enjoyed lasting friendships as we have each traveled down different paths. I will always be thankful to them for taking a chance with me, because their lives influenced me greatly. In them, I saw what I had abandoned. I began going to church and was finally, gloriously baptized. This is when God sent Jake into my life.

Barb had taken my hand and gently pulled me along as I struggled to unwind the threads of my life before her. I slowly began to accept what the staff had been trying to tell me for weeks. Sometimes my personality fragmented, and I often disassociated from reality. Simultaneous conflicting attitudes and emotions called after me, and I followed them as though I was running with a wild wind. I survived by hiding in my dark sanctuary, so that I would not have to see the unsafe world around me. I was beginning to understand my lack of boundaries and my inability to take care of myself. The victim role that I had walked in all my life was beginning to take form in my mind. I began to see that I was indeed a very complex person. When the wounded child within me would come out to fight, usually with another's wounded child within, life got really messy. While attempting to crawl out of the box of past behavior, I would sometimes fall back in, pulling others in with me. My wounded child acted out inappropriately in an effort to bring attention to the abuse and the devastating pain it caused her. She longed to find and to touch the core, the very essence of the abused adult/child . . . the precious child, which had been stolen from her. She wanted her precious child back. The wounded child's brokenness, her sadness, everything about her, was begging for the abused adult/child to please love her; but I could not hear her, and I did not know why.

The years between fourteen and twenty-three, when I was moved away from my church family until I was baptized, seemed lost and confusing to me. I honestly did not understand them. I didn't understand the person that I became during those years. It was confusing to me because when I initially received Jesus into my life, I was changed. I know that I was changed. The core of who I am was reborn, and I found the essence of who I am in Christ. But, there were these invisible forces that I seemed powerless to control. I did things I did not want to do and lived in the denial of doing the things I did—but why? I just could not understand. I tried to understand the path God had allowed me to travel, or maybe more truthfully, the path that I chose. Was He just *waiting on me* to respond to His great love for me, or were the effects of being an abused child so intricate that they crippled the god-child within? Or, did I truly wrestle with the evil powers and principalities of this world—those who seek to destroy the testimony of the children of God? Perhaps all of the above applied. The one thing I knew for sure is that the part of me that was strong and good and held me together came from God.

I had to keep unraveling the tangled strands of my life until I found the key to unlock the door of hope that would put them all back together again. I was so tired, so very tired. There were so many times when I just wanted to give up. But I couldn't! I had to make the duck stop its quacking.

Chapter 12

The Unlikely Love of My Life

B y now you can see that my painting is beginning to take on a form of its own. It may seem to be out of control, but don't worry. There is a plan. And isn't that just the way our lives are? Everything seems completely out of control, and then before we know it, we realize there was a plan in place all along. So, thank you for hanging in there with me. Soon you will begin to see where all of this work is taking us. More than ever before, I really need your support as my session continues with Barb. She knew that she had to be diligent or else I might stop talking.

"Tell me about your marriage to Jake. Surely this has not been an easy relationship." Just stating facts, I continued . . .

By the world's standards, this marriage should have failed years ago, but when trials come and tragedies strike, when passion wanes and differences arise, love does not walk out; true love walks in. Our love for each other, our love of God and His immeasurable grace sustains us.

We met at a party the day before Halloween, October 1967. My costume for the party was so out of character for me at the time, and even now I am a bit baffled by it. A friend had loaned me her long, black "fall," a hairpiece that fit at the top of my forehead, leaving my own dark bangs exposed. It looked very natural. I also borrowed my roommate's white majorette uniform, which was sleeveless, legless and covered with fringe that jiggled when I walked. The outfit embraced my 5'1", 102-pound frame just like the long, white gloves that covered my arms. Black high heels complemented my nylon hosiery, which had provocative black seams running down the back of my slender legs. I carried an empty champagne glass even though I was a teetotaler. I did not drink, nor did I do any of the other things that I was shamelessly putting out there. The extra makeup and long, fake, black eyelashes were the icing on the cake that caught the attention of every guy at the party. But it was Jake who took command of the night.

After the party was over, he walked me back to my apartment. I could not help but notice that he was really handsome, tall and trim with sandy blonde hair, blue eyes, fine skin and a beautiful smile. I really never expected to see him again. I perceived a quality about him that caused me secretly to think I was not good enough for him. He told me he really liked my hair . . . oh my! Much to my surprise, the following week he called and asked me to have dinner with him. I had to quickly borrow the hairpiece, again! This became a frantic process that continued until I finally got caught in my deceit when we were looking at pictures of my trip to DC. I had very short hair just one month before we met in October. By then, Jake had fallen in love with me and politely overlooked my indiscretion. *Unintentional deception followed the abused adult/ child like a lost puppy.*

Jake's phone calls continued as an almost supernatural chemistry began to form between us. He told me wonderful stories about his father's family history of lawyers. His great-grandfather had even been a senator, and there was a priestly lineage on his grandmother's side of the family. They owned farms in Iowa and had connections with a large land company in Louisiana. He seemed to be a never-ending fountain of information and was an entertaining storyteller.

If Jake had aimed to impress, I certainly obliged him. His family belonged to country clubs and took vacations to South Dakota, where his mother had been raised in a farming community, and to Iowa, where they visited relatives and the family farms. At one time, his father owned his own airplane and frequently flew his family across the country. Jake, being the oldest in his family, had endless childhood stories to tell about his two sisters, who were away at college, and his younger brother, who was still at home. I was quick to note that his family attended church regularly. I had been mesmerized by it all but scared to death at the same time. I felt that I was really out of my league.

On the other hand, I mostly listened. I had learned that if you ask intelligent questions, and keep people's focus on themselves, they won't focus on you. I offered Jake as little as possible about me or my family. I had small-town Southern roots, came from a low-income family, my parents were uneducated, only one of my siblings had attended college, and I had only graduated from a business college. We lived near the railroad tracks, and I was lucky to get a pair of new shoes once a year. I learned to sew when I was very young and made most of my clothes. We did not even have indoor bathrooms until I was in the first grade, and until then, we got a bath only once a week in a number two washtub in the kitchen. Thankfully, our basic needs were met, but there were no extras. Even to get a nickel for a Coke or a dime for the Saturday afternoon movies was a huge treat. A bag of popcorn was a delicacy. Christmas was celebrated on Christmas Eve, with no thought given for its reason. My family did not go to church. Gifts were few and Mother always made candy from scratch. There was always a lot of family around, and there was always a lot of good food. But I always secretly dreaded for Christmas to come. I kept family stories mostly to myself.

Our family dynamics were as different as the dialects we spoke. My thick Texas accent prompted Jake's mother to send his grandmother a book on how Texans talk so that she could understand me when we met. His grandmother lived in Chicago. Culturally, spiritually, emotionally and educationally we might as well have been raised on different planets. Jake was raised in the northern part of the country, having lived most of his life in Iowa. His family roots hinted of wealth and status, as he grew up in an educated, upper-middle class family. When he was in his teens, his family moved to Texas where they moved into a spacious house. They eventually added a large swimming pool, which seemed lost in their huge backyard. Dinner was served in the dining room with china, real silverware and cloth napkins held by your own personal napkin ring. Jake's father always sat at the head of the table, and his mother sat at the opposite end. When I was a guest, I was given a place of honor to his dad's right, a place that remained my own after we married. Jake had to instruct me on certain etiquette, such as never picking up my fork to eat until his mother picked up her fork first, and not helping in the kitchen because I was a guest. My southern roots reeled with shock because in the South, you would have been frowned upon if you didn't help. I wanted to belong to this perfect family, not understanding that there is no such thing as the perfect family.

Jake had lived a very sheltered life. At the age of twenty-five, he had a lot of growing up to do and was needy in his own way. Just as I had seen what I wanted to see in him, he saw in me what he wanted to see. In some respects, he only saw what I wanted him to see. Even when I tried in subtle ways to warn him that I might not be what he expected, he chose to see what I could not see in myself. He saw only the good. He had no idea who I really was, because I didn't even know who I really was. I had created an image for myself to live by that was far from my roots. I had learned to hold my head high and to walk with dignity, taking on an air of sophistication. I discovered that I had good taste in clothes and wore my choices well. My makeup and hair were always in place. Even his father once commented that I was a classy lady. I guarded every word that came out of my mouth.

When Jake discovered that going to church was important to me, we started attending the church where his family had attended for many years and where roots went deep. It was a sacramental, ritually oriented church that was light years away from my own childhood church experience, but a place where, in the beginning, I had been awe-stricken. In time, those differences would shockingly come to haunt us and almost destroy our marriage.

Eventually my divorce had to be discussed, and I briefly mentioned that I had been abused as a child. His response was difficult for me to believe or to accept: "I don't care about your past. I just care about you." I was most surprised when very early in our relationship this young man told me he loved me. My walls went up so fast it would make your head swim because I *thought* I knew his intentions. After all, I knew about men. When after weeks of dating he had not pressured me sexually, I began to let my guard down, and for the first time in my life I dared to trust a man. For as much as I was capable, I began to allow myself to fall in love with Jake. He respected me as a person, and sex before marriage was not an option. There was goodness about this easy-going young man. He had a quality about him that pulled at me like a magnet, and I wanted to be a part of him. I wanted the hope for a better life that he seemed to be offering to me.

However, disturbing family issues began to surface not long into our relationship. When we were invited to dinner at his parents' house, we were asked to be there in time for "happy hour." I mistakenly thought that Christians did not consume alcoholic beverages, but I quickly learned that in Jake's denomination, drinking was totally acceptable. I did not understand. I had a huge problem with this casual acceptance of drinking because of my own family's issues with alcoholism, and my own personal battle to defeat the demon that had chased me all of my life. I refused to allow it to get a grip on me because of what I had seen alcohol do to the people I cared about. Alcohol terrified me, and I did not want to bring children into a family where drinking was the norm. I came very close to breaking up with Jake over that one issue.

I knew I would have to be very strong to overcome my own insecurities about myself and my own family. Little did I know how strong I would have to be in order to deal with issues surrounding Jake and his family. I found that I had little in common with his family. They had difficulty understanding the world that I came from or the internal turmoil I lived with, even when I tried to explain it to them. Communication would become our Achilles' heel.

Because I had no real roots in any church denomination and I did not feel that I could ask Jake to let go of his, I buried my concerns over the church. I denied the inward warnings about the differences in our background, and the drinking. We were married just eight months after we met. Jake had won my heart.

The first six months of our marriage were heaven on earth for me. We were so very much in love. I kept my personal intimacy issues to myself and relished in the joy of being loved and respected. It was easy for me to return love back to Jake. After our small June wedding in his church, Jake whisked me away to the Virgin Islands. This small-town, country girl's breath was taken away by the beautiful blue-green waters of St. Croix where we swam and snorkeled. I had never seen anything that had so delighted my senses. We walked on white, sandy beaches, shopped for souvenirs in quaint shops and drove into the hills on narrow, shady, tree-lined lanes to visit old sugar mills that had long been abandoned. I felt like a princess living in a fairy tale, hoping never to wake up to find it was all a dream.

Shortly after returning home, we bought almost an acre of land in the country. On our property was a spacious three-bedroom, red-brick house with an attached double garage, and a second double garage on the other side of a large garden. The house came fully furnished, except for a television. We were very lucky that a co-worker of Jake's was building a new house and just needed to get rid of all of his furnishings. I fell in love with our new home, never dreaming that I would ever own such a beautiful place. We quickly acquired three cats to help keep the field mice out of the house and the two garages. Each day when Jake came home for lunch, the cats would escort us down to the end of the road to get our mail. My love for animals found so much pleasure in watching them chase bugs, tumble in the dirt together and roll over playfully in our paths, begging for a scratch on the tummy. I had more than I ever dreamed possible, more than what I thought I deserved. I was safe and happy and loved.

Eight months after we were married, I became pregnant. We were overjoyed when our first child was born in November of 1969. Our baby girl was a beautiful, chubby, blue-eyed doll with a head full of honey-blonde hair. I had not been raised around babies, so this was a totally new and awesome experience for me. I had never known that love could be so compelling, so consuming, and so strong. I vowed always to protect her, to never allow harm to come to her in any way—ever! It was a promise I would not be able to keep.

My blissful fairy-tale world shattered when our baby daughter was only eleven months old. After she became very ill, we were told that she had an incurable disease and would not live. I was already four months pregnant with our second child when our precious baby girl began chemotherapy for acute lymphocytic leukemia, a cancer that affects the blood. In 1970, the treatment for this type of cancer was very experimental, and the success rate was practically nil. We began an incredible journey with our daughter that would stretch our faith and our marriage to the limits. That was not all that we would face. Our son, who was born in March of 1971, became very ill just ten days before he turned two years old. He was diagnosed with bacterial spinal meningitis. We were told that our son would probably not survive, and if he did, he would be mentally and physically impaired. *The wounded child's faith was indeed tested.*

In February of 1977, I found out that I was expecting another child. Just two months later, Jake's twenty-four-year-old brother was tragically killed in a motorcycle accident. Kimberly's arrival the following November was just what this family needed. *God's grace was sufficient for the abused adult/child and her family. Blessings happened when we needed them the most.*

It has been twenty-two years since my marriage to Jake began, and no, it has not been an easy journey, but it has been well worth the trip. We have found something together that is far beyond the limits of human understanding—something supernatural. We have learned much as we have grown up together, pulling each other through the muck and mire of marriage and all that it entails—the good and the bad. We brought different strengths and weaknesses into our family, and where one has been weak, the other has been strong. We have laughed, and we have cried, and sometimes we have failed. Human love and respect sometimes tottered, but true love never failed us. We have loved our children. We have made many mistakes, but true love has not failed them either. This love, not of worldly understanding and not of human nature, came straight from the heart of Jesus. *God's true love did not fail the abused adult/child.*

Time had run out, and our session had to end. Barb closed her notebook and tucked her hands under her legs. She leaned forward and looked purposely into my eyes. She did not waver or mince her words. "Nola Katherine, I have spent a great deal of time pulling needed information from you because you needed to get a clear perspective about your life. I am very glad to see that you are beginning to understand that your life has been like being on an airplane that is out of control. You are all over the place, and now—today—you don't know where you are going, much less how you are going to get there. You have been given the tools. Now you must figure out what you are going to do with them. It is your choice. You will either remain stuck where you are, or you can choose to move on. You need to find a way to unlock the doors that you are guarding, because if you do not, you are going to crash."

Barb got up from her chair and gave me a caring, tender hug. And then, she told me that her job was finished. I wanted to run after her, but all I could do was to sit in silence with my small brown bear pressed tightly against my anxious heart. I wanted to stop. I wanted to go home. But I knew I could not. I had to keep going. I had to dig deeper. I had not told Barb the whole story. I had avoided important details, and she knew it. For weeks I had been telling my story in a methodical, monotone, factual manner. But that would have to change. I could not recite the secret parts of my life without emotion. Details for the period of my life that had impacted me and changed me so dramatically could not be treated with such dignity.

The weight of the burdens I carried fell hard upon me. Once again the ache began—that deep ache that will sometimes recede, but will never go away—that nothing will satisfy. The weight of deception—how many times had I unknowingly tried to deceive, not just those around me, but myself as well? Hiding behind every disguise that I could imagine in an attempt to cover up truth, in order to protect or deny the wounded child within me, but why? Why?

In this place of refuge where I had lived for such a short time, the many faces that I wore stared back at me from behind the facade and screamed, "Here I am! Please, look at me!" The face of denial, the face of insecurity, the face of fear, the face of panic, the face of abandonment, the face of deceit, the face of depression, the face of suicide, the face of disassociation, the face of sadness, the face of oppression, the face with no boundaries. All of these faces were hidden behind my masks so that others would not see the true face of abuse. Then there was the face of confusion that pulled all of the faces into a melting pot, reminding me that I also wore the face of tenderness, goodness, caring, mercy, wisdom, peace, joy, love—the face of Jesus. And finally, there was the face of the survivor that I was so very tired of wearing. Had I not declared when I came into this place that I did not want just to survive? I wanted to do more than just survive. I wanted to live!

But why was I so afraid to open this one door that I did not want to open and search for the face of the one that I did not understand—the angry one who mocked me and controlled me along with her companion twins, shame and guilt? Did the survivor hold the key that would unlock the door that would set all of us free? *The abused adult/child implored, "Please, God, give me courage."*

Chapter 13

Facing the Predator, Touched by a Song,
Set Free with a Bed and a Bat

Today will mark a turning point on our canvas. We will have to allow our paint to flow freely and our brushes to paint swiftly, or else we will not be able to capture the very heart and soul of my life canvas. Perhaps this will be both our most difficult and our most glorious session, where in the solitude of my hospital room, I face the worst of my perpetrators. He is the one who twisted in and out of my days and nights like an unrelenting, ferocious hurricane, with its reckless, raging winds seeking to devour my precious child. He is the one I protected. He is the one I pretended to be safe and trustworthy at every family gathering, and in his home where I sometimes lived, and at the office where we worked. (Please note that the following information contains graphic descriptions of child abuse.)

Through the eyes of my abused child, I—the survivor—picked up my pen and began to write a letter to my sister's husband, my brother-in-law . . .

August 6, 1990

You ruined my life. You took from me my innocence, my youth, my pride, my dignity, my virginity, my ability to give love or to receive love, my ability to be intimate, my joy, my laughter—the very essence of who I am. Your selfish acts made me hate sex and caused me to turn my anger inward to the point of wanting to destroy my own life. You threw me into the black hole of depression and covered my mind with your unforgiving darkness. I cannot see out of it. You have affected every area of my life, my relationships and my health. You gave me your shame and guilt, and I despise you for putting that on me. Did you have no shame or guilt about what you did? How could you be so shameless? How could you allow a little child to carry your guilt and shame? I am beginning to understand that you were a sick and evil person, and it makes me sick even to think about what you did to me—and maybe to other little girls. I am so glad that you died before you had a chance to hurt my children. I hate to think what I would have done to you if you had violated or even come anywhere near them. I struggle as I remember—I don't want to remember—those dark, lost years that are buried in my mind. I know they are there. I must think about those first memories of you. I must find you and find that little girl whose spirit you strangled to death. I do not like Christmas. Because of you, to this very day, I always dread Christmas. All of the family was home the first time that I remember you . . . I don't know how you got me out of the house alone. You drove to the elementary school and parked the car. I could barely see the school building as I tried to look out the car window. I was so little. It was very dark. If I close my eyes, I can still see us. I am beginning to feel afraid; afraid of what I will

113

see. My chest is tight. I feel the weight of your body on me; I cannot breathe. How did you get my underwear off? Did I not protest? Had you done this before? You were breathing heavily. I was afraid and I asked, "Why are you hurting me? What are you doing to me?" You did not answer. You just kept on hurting me, saying nothing. Your breath was hot and heavy above my head. Darkness—deep, deep, dark, black darkness—engulfed me, and I disappeared. I went somewhere else—somewhere far away from you. Was that when I disconnected from reality, or had I done that before too? I remember when you got off me. I felt this wet stuff run down my legs. I didn't know what it was, and I tried to wipe it off with my dress. It stuck to my hands. Blank! Everything goes blank! The next thing I know is that I ran into the living room and jumped into the bed that had been made up on the couch for me and my niece. I pulled the covers over me, curled up in a ball, and went to sleep. My niece was only two or three years old. I would have been . . . I must have been between seven and nine. Just a child! I don't remember the shame, but I know it was there. It had to be there, right along with my hatred of you. I don't remember that either. Where did you make me put them—the shame and hate? And, why did no one notice my wet dress when I walked in? Oh yes—now I remember—I was trying to hide. Why? Did you tell me not to tell, again? And, who washed my dress? Why didn't someone notice? Didn't anyone care? Has anyone ever cared that I was being hurt? Where was everyone? How many Christmases did you steal from me? I know, I really know that something had been going on long before this. I can remember pain and swelling and burning down there long before this happened. How dare you do this to me! How dare you! There are so many gaps! You always wanted me to go to the store or go for a ride with you. I never wanted to go, but your wife, my own sister, and my mother always insisted that I go with you. I was powerless! You could do anything to me. You had power, and I was just a little girl, and I had no power. And, when did you start showing me those awful pictures, and those cartoon drawings of people having sex? How old was I when you first exposed me to pornography? I can never get those images out of my mind—they haunt me, remind me. I hate them and I hate you. When we sat in your car and I looked at the pictures, you rubbed me with your finger and put it inside me. I don't remember feeling the shame, but I know it was there. Why couldn't I stop you? I remember one time, oh God! You were driving down a country road, and an older couple drove past us. I was sitting next to you and you had given me more pictures to look at. The couple looked suspiciously at us, and I ducked my head because I did not want to be seen. Where did my shame go? How old was I? Oh, dear God, even then those pictures had begun to take on a strange hold over my mind. What you were doing to me stirred no feelings—all that you had done to me totally shut me down—but what I saw did arouse me and I became powerless to pornography's evil. I gave my life to Jesus while you were putting this evil into me. I was so vulnerable. I did not know it was evil, but I was still powerless with you. I trusted you. Did my guilt and shame deepen each time you forced yourself on me? When I became a Christian, could I not face those emotions? Did I just bury them deeper and deeper until I denied that they existed and could no longer find them? When I was fourteen, we came to Dallas to visit your family. One day, I was left alone with you at your house. Why was I left alone with you? Why did I stay behind? I don't know. I never knew how you managed to take advantage of me. I don't know how you got me there, but my panties were off, and you had me on your bed with my legs spread apart. You told me that you were going to put it in. You were fully exposed and coming toward me. It was not the first time I had seen you. Oh, Lord God! I now recall that you made me touch you and hold you and rub you. I feel sick all over just thinking about it. You would spit in your hand and—oh, no! How young was I? It hurt so bad . . . Is that why you spit in your hand? To make it not hurt? The memory of it . . . I can't even go there! I didn't want to look at you. Something, thank God, snapped inside my brain, and I kicked you away and ran. All of the hate I had for you surfaced, and I told you that I would kill you if you ever touched me again, and I meant it. But you just never stopped, you were so sneaky. You began to harass me verbally. You called me an Indian giver, trying to make me feel responsible and that I owed you something. What manipulation! I really hate you for all that you did to me. You left me alone for a while, but then you got into photography; and every time I turned around, you had that damn camera staring me in the face. When I went to Dallas to work so that I could have money for school, oh dear God, I can't believe that I lived with you and your family. Why? I cannot explain why! Was it denial? I felt nothing! I was just so incapable of taking care of myself when it came to you. You bought nighties that you could see through and you persuaded me to put them on for you. Then you posed me and took pictures of me, all while my sister watched. Why? Why was I so disconnected from the guilt and shame and anger I know that I must have felt toward both of you? Why did I turn it all inward on myself? Where was my power? When I went to work for the same company that you worked for, men were always coming by my desk and talking to me. It made me so uncomfortable, and I did not understand, but now I wonder if you took those pictures to work. Did you show them to your friends? How shameful for me to now think about it! I hate you to this very day. How could you stoop so low? I feel sick all over. I wish I could throw up. All of this just makes me sick. You make me sick. You even had the nerve to ask me to pose in the nude for money after my divorce. Finally, I was able to tell you no and mean it! But until then, you just never stopped hitting on me, and I could never confront you and make you stop. You never gave up. Then you got a boat, and we started going to the lake to water-ski. Oh, dear God! I had forgotten. You always went out swimming when I went out swimming, and I could not get away from you. You pulled me up against you, and you held me, and your hands were all over me under the water. If I moved away, you always followed me, and your family and friends were right there—close by. Why couldn't anyone ever see what you were doing? What was wrong with everybody? What was wrong with me? Why didn't I scream and expose you? Oh, dear God in Heaven, help me! I feel such hate for you! Every time we got in the boat to ski, you always managed to get me alone, even though the rule was never to pull a skier alone, I could always feel your eyes on me. Those eyes—they still haunt me; there was so much lust in them. Your voice would change when you talked to me, and I could see your body change as you watched me. I disconnected—I could not stand it—I would always go to the dark place to hide from you. You said things to me that I did not want to hear. I can still now feel my whole body becoming rigid every time I was in that boat with you. Oh, how I hate you. You are the lowest of scum. You don't deserve any justice or mercy, and I hope you did not get any when you died. I wish you could be here right now so that I could give back to you all the pain that you gave me. You are a monster in my mind, and I want you to die. I want your haunting presence to leave me. I am going to find a way for this to happen, and I am not going to stop, even if it takes another month in this place. I am not going to stop until you are dead—completely dead; not until this power you have over me is broken. God, please help me, give me courage, stand beside me, and help me to let go. *This detestable pedophile was shameless, totally relentless in his pursuit of me, a defenseless child. His greedy, self-satisfying, self-seeking flaming desire was to overtake, capture and control my innocence. This stealer of my soul is the personification of evil.* **They all are.**

I stopped writing and laid the letter aside. I had to stop. I could no longer continue to force myself to go through the hell of facing any more of the crushing memories that had haunted me all my life. Every cell in my body had come to life, and it was just too much to bear. My tearless body shook uncontrollably as I pulled my faithful, comforting companions into my arms and curled up with them on my bed. I reached for the blanket lying at my feet and slowly pulled its warmth over us. I had clawed my way to a door that I had never wanted to open. I had dared to pull myself into the malignant, heinous, shockingly brutal pit of child abuse. I had looked squarely into the faces of shame and guilt, reliving them and their unthinkable deeds. And yet, it was still difficult to face the reality, to really believe that these cruel things had happened to me. But that was my problem. Denial! I had the memories. I had not imagined them. They were real. I had always had them. I just did not know what to do with them. Even worse, I minimized the value of my memories. I told myself it just happened; it could have been worse. The abuse from this man probably started shortly after he married my sister, who was in reality only a child herself. Perhaps, I was as young as two or three. What could be worse? And what about all of the other abuses that I remember. Would the pain ever go away? Would I ever stop remembering? I just wanted to stay under the covers and make it all go away. *The abused adult/child had to somehow accept the abuse as her truth and the fact that she was a victim and was not responsible for what others had done to her. She was getting so close; she had come too far to stop now. She had to keep moving forward. Her bed of anguish consumed her with sorrow for her precious child . . .*

The following day I read the letter to my psychiatrist. I showed no emotion. He wanted to know where my anger was, saying, "You are reading this as though you are reading a newspaper article." I told him that I did not know, and this is just what had happened. I read it to my therapist who had the same reaction. Their eyes gave way to their anxiety. When I read it to my small group, they were moved to tears, and I found myself comforting them. Several of them fell sobbing into my arms. When Jake came to visit, I read it to him. My husband was furious to the point of being speechless. I read it to a few of my friends who visited me. They were shocked, except for one, who proved not to be my friend. She judged me and has hardly spoken to me since. *The abused adult/child would have to discern when and where she could share her pain. There will always be those who will judge and not understand.*

I forced myself to read the letter over and over, again and again, until its words became raw reality, and until the relentless, raging fury that sat precariously below the surface of guilt and shame could find its rightful place. *There was yet another divine appointment waiting for the abused adult/child.*

*   *   *

I have always loved music because it almost always speaks to my spirit, but on this particular day it would speak to more than just my spirit. I was the last one to enter the large room where so many things took place on 3E. The weekly music therapy class was just beginning as I slipped quietly onto a chair near the door. The room was full. The instructor pushed the button on the cassette player, and an unfamiliar tune fell on my ears. The instrumental introduction began, and then without warning, the words to a song took my ruptured heart, laid it open, cleaned it out and put it back together again. It reached into the very soul of the abused adult/child.

Alone again in a crowded room
Cornered by the questions in my mind
It's so hard to understand
How the life that I had planned
Stole my joy and left me far behind.

Though all I have is lost it seems
In the shadow of a dream that used to be
I can look beyond the skies
Deep into the Father's eyes
And see that there is hope for one like me.

I can begin again
With the passion of a child
My heart has caught a vision
Of a life that's still worthwhile.

I can reach out again
Far beyond what I have done
Like a dreamer who's awakened
To a life that's yet to come
For new beginnings are not just for the young.

I face the dawn of each brand new day
Free from all the doubts that gripped my past
For I've found in trusting Him
That every day life starts again
As I look for the things of life that last.

I can begin again
With the passion of a child
My heart has caught a vision
Of a life that's still worthwhile

I can reach out again
Far beyond what I have done
Like a dreamer who's awakened
To a life that's yet to come
For new beginnings are not just for the young

New beginnings are not just for the young
New beginnings are not just for the young
Starting over again is not just for the young
No matter what you've been told
It's not just for the young
It's not just for the young[1]

The field of my soul had lain dormant, stricken, beaten down, but suddenly the long-ago promised hope of the Shamrock nurtured its soil. New life tugged at the root of the single, solitary bloom left standing alone within me, so many years ago. And, it began to grow once again. Words from the past reminded me, "Someday, I believe you will come back in full bloom, more beautiful than before." *Yes, the beauty that God had created for this child was indeed coming back, and when in full bloom, as David, her first therapist had predicted almost ten years before, she would be more beautiful than before.*

It had taken me three weeks of insoluble searching, resisting, denying and struggling to come to this crossroad, a place of surrender that would

---

[1] "I Can Begin Again" used with permission from award winning artist Larnelle Harris. To hear the song, visit www.larnelle.com.

ask me to choose a different path for my life. Unrestrained tears began to flow freely down my cheeks as the words of this powerful song came to life within me. Every face behind every mask that I wore, including my precious child—the very core of my being that had so stoically held the wounded child, the survivor, and the adult together—began to mesh in agreement that healing could now begin. God's Holy Spirit whispered, oh so softly and tenderly, "You *can* begin again!"

I knew, that I knew, that God had just shown me the way toward freedom from every dastardly act inflicted upon me as both a child and an adult. All I had to do was to walk in His way. The choice was mine to make. I could either stay stuck, or I could take back my power and move forward. Once again God was *waiting on me* to respond and to step into His will and purpose for my life. *The abused adult/child was empowered by the words of a song that was written into the spirit of another but intended for her on that day. She would never be the same. God had touched her. There were more divine appointments awaiting the abused adult/child.*

I had a prescheduled appointment with my therapist just after music therapy. I walked into the small room where he waited with my head held high and a new resolve in my voice. I was most surprised to see that my psychiatrist, Dr. Kaman, was waiting with my therapist. I did not give them time to comment. I told them about the words to the song I had just heard, and with deliberate determination, I told them I was ready to talk about the others who sexually abused me. Their eyes danced with anticipation as they listened.

There are simply no words to convey the shame of exposing my wounded child. She was now so vulnerable, bare and totally exposed for all to see. A huge part of me died when I was still just a baby. I wanted my precious baby to live again, and if that meant talking, then I would talk. The two professionals already knew about the man who worked for my father, my uncle, and my brother-in-law, but there were six more to add to the list. It hurt so much, and I cried and cried as I revealed the memory of them one by one.

I don't know at what age I was, probably pre-adolescent when my girlfriends, with whom I was spending the night, wanted to play mommy and daddy. They would tell me, "You can be the mommy, and I will be the daddy." I know this happened on three different occasions with three different girls. I remember, once again, becoming numb and disappearing into the darkness while they intimately explored my body. And now, I can't help but wonder what had been happening to those young girls. There was a teenage boy who forced me to participate in sexual activity with him. I recall that I felt absolutely nothing during those awful encounters and would just walk away, disappearing into the darkness. There was a neighbor who owned a gas station near my house. One day, I went to his station to put air in my bicycle tire. He cornered me inside the station and began to molest me. I think I was about twelve and big enough to fight him off before it went too far. There was a doctor, who, during a gynecological exam, began to touch me inappropriately. I was in my early twenties. I froze and went into that dark place where I hid. I could not move. I remember leaving the room and nothing else.

And finally, there was one whose abuse I carried with deep sorrow, and I desperately needed to get out of me the anguish that I felt. It seemed an eternity before I could actually open my mouth and finally talk about my mother's old-maid sister. She was the one who, in many ways, was more like a mother to me than my own mother. She helped take care of all us kids. I loved her visits. She always cleaned the house and would fix my breakfast each morning and play games with me and talk to me, but she also slept with me. I loved her so very much, but she had inappropriately used me to meet her own needs. I know that she loved me, but I was clearly beginning to understand that it was not my place or my responsibility to meet anyone's needs—ever! I found out long after her death that she had a malady that few in our family knew about. Nature had been unkind to her and gave her both male and female organs. I grieve to think of the personal hell that she had to endure, the struggles. She was a kind soul, a good and giving person who deserved better from this life. I have wept bitter tears of shame for her and my wounded child, but I had to get the confusing agony of her actions out of me. I needed for the session to end. I felt I had very little pride or dignity left. I had said all that I needed to say to them.

The repercussions from both male and female perpetrators rebounded in tormenting confusion. Dr. Kaman helped me finally grasp that the *only* thing wrong with me was that a very sacred part of my being had been horribly violated. None of the things that had happened to me were my fault, and under the circumstances, confusion was understandable. More importantly, I was not accountable for others' indiscretions, nor did God hold me accountable for others' sins. I was thankful for the wise, affirming feedback that I desperately needed to hear.

My counselors were two very happy men. I thought they were going to do cartwheels as we stepped out into the hallway. They had come prepared to push me into talking because Dr. Kaman, who remained true to his promise to not let me out of the hospital until I had made sufficient strides toward healing, wisely understood that it was imperative for me to disclose the details about the abuse and to expose all of my abusers. Otherwise, I would have stayed stuck in my pain, and that was not an option for any of us to accept. Instead, they witnessed God's undeniable grace that enabled me to make the choice to move forward. *The abused adult/child felt as though the weight of the world had been lifted from her shoulders. She had taken a giant leap of faith toward wholeness.*

Immediately after lunch, on that same day, the weekly spiritual growth group was scheduled to meet. I had come to trust the hospital chaplain who greeted us with pen and paper as we entered the room. At the top of the page were written three statements: (1) Write down the losses that you have experienced, (2) How did you feel about the losses then? (3) How do you feel about them now? Under the first column I wrote, "I lost my precious little girl." Under the second I wrote, "I felt nothing." And under the third I wrote, "I am angry!" I asked permission to read my letter, and as I recited the words, acquiescence set in, and for the first time I fully and completely believed it was *me* that I was reading about. *I was that little girl.* Uncontrollable sobs came with almost every sentence as birth was given to the magnitude of all that I had carried for so long. I began to mourn the loss of my little child, but more enormous than the grief itself was the untamed, unclaimed anger. The words in my letter, "How dare you do this to me!" screamed back at me, and I began to explode. I was finally accepting that over and over I had been used. I was a victim, a victim of others' sick, sinful lust and selfishness with no regard to the pain they were afflicting on another human being—a child—**ME**!

Once again truth lunged at me, but this time *I finally got it*! I finally really understood that the adults in my life had power over my precious child, and she was completely helpless and powerless to protect herself. The powerlessness spilled over into my adult life where Christian standards and Christian morals clashed unmercifully with the standards of those who abused me. I wanted to be morally and sexually pure more than anything, but in my mind I knew that I never was and never could be. Even though I had accepted God's gift of forgiveness, and had truly believed in and felt the powerful, cleansing blood that He had shed for me, there were voices inside my head that constantly nibbled away at the God-truths I had been given. They told me that I was bad and that I could *never* measure up, *never* be accepted, and I could *never* be worthy of all that God had done for me. And, I could *never* let anyone find out about me, and I could *never* allow anyone to get to know the real me. And, I could certainly *never* live up to the pedestal that some had put me on. And, I could *never* afford the luxury of allowing myself to be real. The voice of my wounded child had mistakenly been lying to me, as she had been lied to by the powers of darkness that sought to destroy this child of God. You will not know a lie until you know the truth. These lies were not our truth, not God's truth. *The door of understanding was being opened to the abused adult/child as healing continued to come to her.*

I carried the guilt of undeserved shame, others' shame, until that day, the day when I finally allowed God to speak healing into the soul of my wounded child. I would carry it no more! I believe that in my spirit I had sincerely forgiven my brother-in-law at a spiritual retreat I had attended years before. However, my wounded child was emotionally bound and had continued to carry not only his guilt and shame but also the guilt and shame of all the others who had violated me, resulting in suppressed anger, controlled rage. It was time for me to give back to all of them everything they had viciously imposed upon me. And it was time for me to take back that which they had stolen from me—my power! *The abused adult/child had found the survivor's key that she had been looking for; now she had to forever unlock the door that had kept her in bondage.*

To accomplish this feat, I went into rage therapy. This enabled me to safely deal with the raging anger that would rear its ugly head and then quickly disappear below the surface of my consciousness, staying hidden until another crippling opportunity arose. Here I could safely deal with those times when I would blindly explode and do and say crazy things that made no sense, even to me. I had been like a yo-yo, a Dr. Jekyll and Mr. Hyde, with periodic out-of-control moments that were crazily intertwined with kindness, love, joy and peace. For the first time, I was realistically acknowledging the anger that resulted from the abuse and the realization that I needed to feel the anger and then, to do something about it. This anger was not mine nor had it ever been mine. Like guilt and shame, it had been unjustly carved into my personality, and it was time for me to give it back to those who had created it in the first place.

I was given a small room, a bat and a bare bed. A small camera in the ceiling of the room monitored my actions. I took that bat and timidly, slowly at first, began to beat the stuffing out of that bed. The more anger I released, the more power I felt rising up within me, until that innermost realm of self that only God can heal was filled to overflowing. His all-consuming, overcoming power unlocked the door where the life-defeating, suppressed rage was finally unrestrained. I cried and screamed and raged, and yes, even cursed at those who had robbed me of every innocent, good and decent thing that was rightfully mine to possess. I don't know how long I was in that sterile room; but when tears were spent, anger quieted, and rage was no longer present, there came a serene moment when we were set free, my little girl and I. Free to breathe, to feel, to think, to run, to play, and yes, finally free to turn that corner and move on. God had been *waiting on me* to give Him the key that would unlock this door so that He could come in and heal me.

One of the staff persons who observed my transformation told me that I kept yelling, "Get it out! Get it out!" The little girl was finally given a voice denied her for so long. It was her way of finally being able to shout at her predators, "No, you can't do *this* to me! Not anymore! Never again!" All of my *why* questions were suddenly answered. The answer was simple—**because I had been abused as a child**. And I got my power back! *The abused adult/child, now empowered, could confidently finish what God had brought her there to do. There was still important work for her to accomplish. She had gone too far to stop now.*

Chapter 14

A Three-Hour Pass, a Long and Honest Talk, the Final Crossroad

At the end of my fourth week I received a well-deserved pass to go home for three hours. Dr. Kaman urged me to use this time to talk to Jake about what had been happening behind the locked doors of the hospital. Although somewhat anxious, I was happy to be free from the confinement and stress of the hospital environment, even if it was for just a short period of time. Riding home with Jake in the quietness of our car, I found a new appreciation for the many things I had always taken for granted. The greens of the grass seemed greener, and the multiple shades of leaves on the trees waved to the purest of white, scalloped clouds that were delicately poised over the bluest of blue skies. Late summer flowers' brilliant array of colors teased my eyes. As our car rounded the circle toward our house, our neighbor's giant maple tree standing tall and majestic took my breath away with its golden splendor. It was as though I had never seen it before. God's creation came to life before my eyes and touched my spirit as I sensed that something had awakened in me that had long been asleep. I could not recall when Texas was ever beautiful in August.

I walked through the front door of our modest, middle-class house with a hint of excitement. But just for a moment, I felt like a stranger in my own home. The silence that greeted me became a sad reminder that I had missed an entire summer with my children. The older kids had returned to college and our youngest was at school. At Dr. Kaman's request, we had engaged in several family sessions prior to everyone's returning to school. Those sessions had given my children the platform they needed in order to hear and to be heard. We were blessed with wonderful, understanding kids, and even though they had been shocked by the extent of their mother's abuse and its resulting effects, they had been totally supportive. They were, understandably so, spared details of the actual abuse.

Our thirteen-year-old was at a very vulnerable age and seemed to be affected the most by what was happening in her family. In retrospect, she claims the best thing that has ever happened to our family was my going into the hospital. She learned that it is okay to express herself and that it is important to have boundaries.

My son learned this lesson when he was about the age of ten. I had picked my children up from school one afternoon, and when he got into the car, I knew something was wrong. When pressed he clammed up. I had been watching the telltale signs of unhappiness for a while, and I knew that somehow I had to draw my son out of his shell. When we got home, I instructed the girls to go into the house and proceeded to tell my young son that we were not going to get out of the car until he told me what was going on. I vehemently proclaimed, "It is not healthy to hold things in! You need to tell me what is going on!" Slowly the dam broke as he told me of the unkind ways his peers were treating him. From that time on we were pals, and he told me everything. Well, almost everything! In retrospect, I have to chuckle at the irony of my wisdom, considering all that I was holding in at the time.

My oldest daughter was a different story. She is the one on whom I practiced my control issues the most. I was overprotective, overbearing and over-everything else that a mother can be. I could not allow life to be anything but perfect for her; therefore, she was not allowed to be anything but perfect. Unfortunately, those unrealistic expectations held devastating consequences for my beautiful daughter as she grew up.

To make things worse, when she was sixteen years old, she did some typical teenage thing, which I cannot now remember. I don't know why, but my pent-up rage lashed out at her, and I cornered her in the hallway and I began to hit her uncontrollably. I recall having to force myself to back away from her. We were both totally stunned! I had been a strict disciplinarian when it came to the kids, but up until that moment, I had never physically abused them. Emotions, for reasons far beyond my ability to comprehend at the time, resurfaced on my precious daughter. My perception is that we had a good, loving relationship up until that day. If I could take back any moment in my life, it would be that moment, because I put a wedge between us that would take many years to remove. It is heartbreaking for me even to think about. In many ways, she, like her mother, is a survivor too.

I loved my children more than the air that I breathed, and I would have done anything to protect them from ever going through what I had experienced. In spite of, or maybe because of, my own dysfunction, I gave them the one thing I knew would sustain them in this life, and that is the knowledge of God's immeasurable love for them through Jesus. I know that by God's grace I have been a good mother regardless of my own childhood circumstances. They know how much their mother loves them. *God proved Himself to be faithful to the children of the abused/ adult child. His love covered her mistakes.*

But this day was not to be about our kids, and no matter how much I wanted to avoid our issues, I knew we had to face them head-on. Jake and I spent the few hours we had talking about me, about him and about our relationship. There were some things that I could not bring myself to talk about to strangers. My dignity was teetering on a precarious line. In the privacy of our home, I told him about the other abuses and details that I had not disclosed to my therapist, my psychiatrist or anyone else. Some of my secrets would stay between me and God, and I was okay with that.

My husband needed to understand my confusing, conflicting personality. He needed to understand why from the very beginning of our marriage I had difficulty responding intimately. I had fallen in love with Jake because he did not see me just as a sex object but as a person whom he loved and respected. Because of this, I made myself available to him whenever he needed or wanted me. I made sure that his needs were always met regardless of how tired or secretly depressed I might be. It was my gift of love to him.

For some who are abused as children, promiscuity is fueled because pleasure is sometimes associated with the experience; but for others, the abuse causes them to shut down sexually. I fell into the latter category. Growing up, I did not experience a normal sexual metamorphosis, and I believe my emotional response to that resulted in just one more reason for the suppressed anger. Even during the adolescent and teen years, when all of my girlfriends were talking about sex and experimenting, I had no feelings about sex, and I only pretended to be on the same page with them. The truth is I hated sex and anything related to it.

Early on in our marriage, Jake discovered that bringing *Playboy* into our bedroom enhanced my response to him. As the years progressed and pornography became more open and explicit, so did our involvement in it. Because I had been exposed to these images at such a young age, those images became my sexual trigger. They changed my sexuality. They became my partner. That is the evil power of pornography. It grips the mind, the body and the soul. It will not let them go. Pornography changes who you are. It steals human intimacy. And don't be fooled. Addiction to porn is not limited to just men. Women fall into its clutches also, and children are especially helplessly vulnerable to its evil. Pornography *will* become your partner even if you do not wish it to be so. It is no respecter of persons. It became our partner.

Simultaneously, my spiritual journey exposed the entrapment of the human spirit for which pornography is designed. Once it becomes your sexual partner, your desire for it is insatiable, and personal intimacy alone is never enough to satisfy the addiction to pornography's power. Spiritually, I knew sexual response was God-given and holy. It was designed to bring a man and a woman together as one, for procreation. I also knew that sexual response is a sacred gift that when held in respect to God's provision can bring joy and contentment beyond our ability to define. However, when human beings step out of that provision, we open ourselves up to a dark spiritual world that will bring dishonor to ourselves and to our Creator. When we invite pornography into our lives, we invite strong, forceful powers of darkness to work in, through and against us and our families. As a child, this darkness had been superimposed upon me, and I was not accountable. But as an adult, I am accountable.

When you pause to consider the exposure to pornography, add unresolved sexual abuses by females and males, and then mix in my sincere desire to be a godly woman, you will indeed find one who is on an airplane that is always flying around out of control, always waiting to crash. *That was me.* This also describes thousands upon thousands of women and men just like me. My husband had no clue about the spiritual, emotional and sexual battles that had raged within me during our marriage because, like many other areas in our lives, we did not talk about them. And my thick facade concealed them. My struggles produced unbearable, consuming guilt. I heaped more and more anger upon already suppressed anger, which added fuel to the depression which had invaded my life as a child.

Long before these few precious hours spent with Jake, I had been freed from the addiction to pornography (I write about that later), and learning to be intimate without it was like trying to breathe without air. The battle was enormous. Jake had not yet felt the conviction of the Holy Spirit in this area, nor did he understand the demonic influences that came with the package. He had not yet fully realized his place as spiritual head of the family nor the impact of not assuming that responsibility. His family needed the spiritual covering that was his responsibility to provide us. These and other issues had to be dealt with once and for all.

During my recovery process, I encountered gay people who were depressed and unhappy—people who had found themselves in a dark place from which they desperately wanted to be free. Without exception, they had been abused as children. Like me they were sexually confused.

Even though I had never actually felt a physical attraction toward women, I secretly struggled with the idea that I might be gay simply because of my understandable lack of sexual response toward men. However, I was very wrong in my assumption, and my time on 3E definitively clarified for me that I was wounded, not gay. Jesus told the disciples that if they knew truth, they would be set free. I believe His words enlighten us. Knowledge and truth embrace one another. When it gets dark enough you can see the stars and the darker it gets, the more stars you will be able to see. In my darkest hours, when I finally acknowledged why I was so confused and was finally able to share the truth with my husband, I saw the truth and was truly set free from my confusion and fear, just as Jesus promised. [1] I believe there are no limits to God's mercy toward an abused child, especially a sexually abused child.

In many ways, our true journey together began on that day, perhaps because we began to choose a different path. For the first time in our married life, we actually talked about feelings and issues that had plagued us. God had been patiently *waiting on us* to find His pathway. He had long been holding the door open for us to walk through, and it was now up to us to take each other's hand and discover what He had there for us. With God's help, we would find our way together. There was much work yet for us to do. Life is all about choices.

My soul-mate, my husband, the father of my beautiful children, the only person in the world that I could trust to love me no matter what, held me close to his gentle heart, where he invited me to live as one with him. He had a better understanding now of what he had always understood. I was not a bad person, but bad things had happened to me. I was just beginning to understand that myself. Our tears washed away our pain. Jake's assurance, support and love returned me to the hospital where I could safely hide until it was safe for me to come back home. I had never loved my husband more than I did that day.

---

[1]   In John 8:32, Jesus said, "And you shall know the truth and the truth shall make you free" (NIV).

I was torn between my need to stay at home with my family and the gut-wrenching knot in my stomach that persuaded me to return to the hospital. I could not stop this rolling ball that seemed to be getting bigger and faster with each passing day, at least not just yet. Our insurance would pay for two more weeks, and I needed to take advantage of this time, time for myself that I knew I would never have again. I was no longer feeling the pangs of depression, and the many facets of my life had come into clear focus. There were two more mountains for me to climb. If I was ever going to get on the other side of those mountains and find the peaceful valley I sought, it had to be now, when I felt invulnerable. The first mountain would be the church where Jake and I had twenty-two years of history that I needed to sift through. The second mountain was my relationship with my sister. I loved my sister and yearned for both of us to be free from our past, to be healed.

Barb would not be able to guide me over these mountains where steep cliffs hid deep caves and where slippery rocks sat precariously on narrow pathways waiting to plunge me violently to the depths below. It would be so easy just to hide in the dark caves along the way or just to let go and slip over the edge and end my journey here. But no, I would not hide! I would not let go! I would trust in my God to lead me. Only He would be able to set my course and help me to find my own direction to the final destination where my healing would be brought to completion.

*　　*　　*

Dear Reader, we are now at the final crossroad. Let me speak for a moment to those of you who have never experienced child abuse or any other type of abuse, those of you whom I refer to as normal. Hopefully, by now you have a better understanding about what goes on in the mind of an abused adult/child. I don't want to rehash those complexities because I believe you are beginning to understand that for every abused child who survives, there is an adult walking around *trying to do life* with a wounded child living inside of them. You can believe me when I say to you that, at almost any given time, you are standing near at least one person who is like me. *We* are everywhere. Hopefully, you now understand why the abused adult/child acts out in so many different ways, most often contrary to the adult that you outwardly perceive her/him to be. Wounded adults have to find a way to appear to be normal. But as you can now see, they are "not normal" in the sense that they were abused as children, and abuse is *never ever* normal. As I have previously said, we who are abused are extremely complex people.

As you continue on my journey with me, please keep in mind *all that you know* about the secrets that the abused adult/child carried as she tried so hard to walk through life with her head held high, pretending, denying, surviving in the best way she knew. You must grasp that the rest of my story is about the wounded abused child trying to exist in the skin of an adult, and in a world that often just brought more pain, confusion and victimization. This is another paragraph that I wish you would read again. You need to fully understand what I am saying before we move on.

Now I want to speak to those of you for whom I tell my story. You are now beginning to understand that you are not alone. God loves you. You are precious. You are worthy. You are not crazy. There is hope for one like you. Please continue with me. There is still much to learn. I am right there with you.

But first, let us pause for a few moments of reflection. We have spent a great deal of valuable time preparing the canvas for this portion of my life story. All of this preparation was designed to help give you understanding about the inner turmoil I experienced as I struggled to keep the threads of my life from fraying into oblivion. It is here that the ugly, twisted effects of childhood abuse stormed into my life while simultaneously the all-consuming love and power of God imparted tender mercy to me, His precious wounded child.

We have washed across the canvas, sketched in the background, filled in the shadows, splashed about colors of despair and hope. But how do we draw into the centerpiece of this story the little girl who has become a woman, the abused adult/child whom I so desperately want

135

you to know before we put on the finishing touches of my painting? What colors do we choose; what size brushes do we use; what strokes will ultimately expose the confusion of a mind that must escape the reality of a life that must exist in a black hole so deep and so wide that only by the grace of God will the light of hope survive? How does one paint spiritual warfare, a battle fought over a desperate but not lost soul?

It will take unshakable faith to continue as I reveal God's redemptive work in me through my spiritual experiences. Once again, it will not be easy, but it will be victorious. Please bear with me as I may occasionally repeat for clarification some previously stated facts. This will be our final journey together before leaving the hospital. In many ways this part of my story is the most difficult to tell because this is where the wounds of my precious child festered.

Chapter 15

The Imperfect Church, God's Training Ground

B ecoming a Christian, or a Christ-follower, is a choice and not something into which you are born. In the Bible, Matthew 18:14 tells us that our Father in Heaven is not willing that anyone be lost. His desire is for all of mankind to believe in Him. Unfortunately, not everyone seeks to know Him; not everyone is listening to His voice.

I don't think anyone is really capable of explaining what happens when God calls us to step out in faith and believe in someone that we cannot actually see. Yet, supernaturally we who have sincerely done so know that Jesus is present within us the instant we make the decision to believe in Him—to believe He is who He says He is. We may not be fully aware in that moment that our eyes have been opened to the knowledge of God the Father, God the Son and God the Holy Spirit, but in time we will steadily gain understanding about the Triune (three in one) God. Water does not try to be water. Air does not try to be air. God does not try to be Holy and Jesus does not try to be God. It is as it is. Air is air. Water is water. God is God, and Jesus is the exact revelation of who God is. If you want to know God, then look at Jesus Christ.[1] I remember

---

[1] Ephesians 3:11-12, "according to His eternal purpose which He accomplished in Christ Jesus our Lord. In Him and through faith in Him we may approach God with freedom and confidence" (NIV).

my own experience so well. It was the moment when love came in and when seeds of faith were planted within my tender child-spirit. I heard God's call, accepted His invitation and believed in Him—not because I was waiting on Him to accept me, but because He was *waiting on me* to accept Him.

When I was a teenager, I began to walk away, not from God, but from the principles of my faith. Throughout those tumultuous years and into my early twenties, I never once let go of my belief that God was always with me. I sincerely believe, with every fiber of my being, that it was the faith He planted within my spirit and that I embraced as a young girl that enabled me to survive. After my divorce, I began to seek God, and I began to respond to His gentle tug within me. He was urging me to listen and to obey His voice, His precepts. He surrounded me with Christian friends who influenced me to return to church and be baptized. That is when I walked back into His always open arms, and that is when Jake walked into my life. When Jake and I met, my spiritual maturity was far from consummated. I brought into our marriage unreal expectations and the naive notion that all people who go to church are loving, kind and sinless. I thought that going to church and taking my family to church would somehow protect and heal all the ills of my life. Somehow I became stuck in the suspended spaces of those expectations. I had unwittingly put on a huge facade that never allowed me to put my guard down for fear of exposing my own deceptions. But just as sure as the powers of darkness roam this earth seeking whom they can devour,[2] the Spirit of the Living God roams this earth seeking those who have a heart for Him.[3] The holiness of God pushed through those deceptions, saw my faith and honored my heart for Him. I could never have imagined just how much I would need Him. I will be eternally thankful that He

---

[2] 1 Peter 5:8 says, "Be self-controlled and alert. Your enemy the devil prowls around like a roaring lion looking for someone to devour" (NIV).

[3] Hebrews 11:6 says, "Without faith it is impossible to please God, because anyone who comes to Him must believe that He exists and that he rewards those who earnestly seek Him"(NIV).

never let go of me and that I never abandoned my belief or my faith in Him. I am here to testify that there would be a very different story to tell had I not chosen to accept God's gift of love and forgiveness.

Shortly after we met, I began attending Jake's church with him. It took very little time to realize that this church/denomination was very different from the church of my childhood where the character of holiness was found in the lives of the people who worshiped there. I could not help but observe that the pious reverence I saw displayed on Sunday mornings was not always reflected in many of the lives of the people who served there. Although it has taken me a lifetime to learn the difference between judging and discerning, I rightly discerned from the very beginning that there were disturbing, hidden issues within those walls of worship. I felt there was something very out of sync. It grieves me deeply to reveal that Jake's church eventually became, for me, another dysfunctional family in which I had to learn to survive.

I made the decision to join Jake's church for several reasons. For one thing, he came from a family with deep roots in this particular denomination, but I had no church roots to offer him. For another, his parents went to church faithfully, and it appeared to me they had raised their children to do the same. This was extremely important to me because as a young girl, I was taken to church by a neighbor and I cherished my Sunday mornings there. I was frequently invited to a friend's house after church for Sunday dinner. I felt I was a part of something very special, and I recall desperately wanting what I saw in those homes for myself. Sometimes, I was even asked to say the blessing before we ate our meal together. I remember feeling so happy and proud because I was made to feel I belonged, and that I was loved. Since that time, and even throughout those lost years when I did not walk in God's will for my life, I longed to have a Christian family that worshiped together on Sunday morning, and then went home to a family dinner of roast, potatoes, carrots, gravy and, of course, a guest or two. I desired more than anything else in the world to have a family that worshiped, prayed and read the Bible together. I wanted my future children to have spiritual roots that I did not have. So in the beginning, going to church with Jake and his family was the icing on the cake for me. Aside from my preconceived expectations, Jake was on a mission to convert me.

My initial response to the church service itself left me feeling awestruck. The requiring of women to cover their heads before entering the church, the nearly absolute silence—hardly even a whisper, the soft lighting, the single lit candle hanging over the umbrae where the reserved sacrament was kept, signifying the real presence of Christ. The kneeling at the foot of the cross upon entering the church and throughout the service, making the sign of the cross on your forehead and across your chest, the beautiful words of the liturgy, the introduction to apostolic succession (meaning that at the time a priest is ordained he is touched by a bishop who is in direct apostolic lineage of the twelve apostles), the consecration of the wine and bread by the priest for communion bringing the *actual* real presence of Christ into the elements, the chanting, the incense—it all created an atmosphere of reverence and holiness that deeply touched me.

Jake and I became engaged only four months after we met. We promptly made an appointment to discuss wedding plans with his priest, whom I deemed as holy and the next best thing to God himself. Whenever I was around this man, I was practically shaking in my shoes for fear of doing something wrong because I mistakenly created for myself a holy illusion about priests.

We were not prepared for the ultimatum that Jake's priest presented to us during our brief visit with him. In order to get married in the church, I would first have to go before a panel of priests and have my first marriage annulled. I would also have to go through confirmation classes and be confirmed before I could take communion at our wedding. I wanted to rebel, I wanted to protest, but I could not. I agreed to the priest's demands. *Denial was always around to do whatever the abused adult/child needed for it to do.*

We had set a June date for our wedding, and therefore I had only four months to meet all the demands that were placed upon me and plan a wedding. I began to attend the weekly confirmation classes at the church. As required, I accompanied Jake's priest to the annulment hearing which he scheduled for me to attend. I can recall that my emotions began to shut down as we traveled down the busy expressway to the cathedral where the hearing was to be held. It was another one of those times when everything around me went black, and I disappeared somewhere into the background around me as the interview began. The all-too-familiar feeling of panic screamed at me to run out the door. I could not. It was not possible for me to run away. *Controlled panic attacks were not uncommon for the abused adult/child when she felt unsafe. They left her without boundaries. Depression followed closely behind the panic.*

In my mind's eye, I can still see about twenty men—all dressed in ominous black with their white collars radiating out into my darkness—staring at me and judging me as though I was on trial for some heinous crime. In reality, I think there may have been only six or eight men present. When they began to probe into my past and ask me degrading questions, I refused to sit there and tell a bunch of strange men what I could not even tell my future husband or worse, what I could not even face myself. I held my head high and, with justifiable dignity, avoided telling them what they wanted to hear. I was sure God would strike me dead. *The abused adult/child would do anything to avoid the truth and absolutely was incapable of facing honest confession to anyone.*

Confirmation classes should have been another warning to me. I am not sure what I expected, but the classes really had nothing to do with developing my relationship with God. In fact, they really weren't even about God. The classes were about how to *do* church. I was expected to know the seasons of the church year, what color corresponded with each season, what songs were to be sung, what scriptures were to be read, when you stand and when you sit, and so on and so on. I was never once asked about my relationship with Christ or even if I believed in Him. I began asking the priest and Jake questions that seemed rather important to my personal faith. I wanted to know why we were not studying the Bible, and although I loved the beautiful prayers found in the prayer book, I wanted to know how children were supposed to learn to talk to God if all their prayers were read from a book. I had been talking to God since I was a little girl and had never once needed to use a book to get His attention. I began to have a very difficult time understanding the significance of everything that was being tossed at me, and I expressed my unhappiness to my future husband. I am not sure exactly what happened, but all of a sudden, finishing confirmation classes did not seem so important to the priest. He changed his mind and allowed us to get married before I was confirmed, and I was also allowed to take communion at our wedding. I have wondered if they all got the feeling that I was about to bolt out the door and if Jake's father had put pressure on the priest to ease off the rules.

Jake's family connection to the church made it very easy for us to get involved. Therefore, we were quickly drawn into the core of the church. Jake was elected to serve on the vestry, which is like the deacon board in most protestant churches. I went to work in the church office as the priest's secretary. Eventually, we were invited to social parties held by members of the church. I was shocked to witness leaders in the church and church members drinking excessively and exhibiting what I considered inappropriate behavior, especially for Christians. Many of those same people would be serving Holy Communion and reading the Scriptures, all piously going through the motions of the liturgy on Sunday morning. Such behavior among Christians and in the church was unthinkable to me. To make matters worse, some of the young men on the vestry belonged to a nationally recognized philanthropic organization, which Jake was invited to join. While this group of young men and their wives did many good community services, it was also a group of people who loved to party. Alcohol flowed freely. *The mind of the abused adult/ child became a twisted mass of bitterness and resentment each time she was around groups of people drinking. She became consumed with a new anger that she did not understand. But no one would know this because she smiled and wore the mask of happiness.*

The effects of having been married to an alcoholic, my own addictive personality, and the history of alcohol abuse in my family haunted me. I wanted nothing more to do with people who drank, ever. Above all, I feared exposing my future children to the socially acceptable practice of drinking. Unfortunately, Jake was never able to perceive the terror that I held in regard to this indulgence. I had first ignored the practice in my husband's own family and then watched as it spilled over into our church and social life. *The abused adult/child put on the mask of disdain. A war began within her between good and evil as it related to behavior she did not understand. The rampant use of alcohol was confusing. She could not find where she belonged.*

And so it was that early on in our perfect marriage and our perfect life that alcohol's silent, cruel deception began to nibble away at the sweet love we had for each other. Unsuspecting spiritual battles, for which I was ill equipped, stepped into my pathway. From all outward appearances, I was an attractive, happy young woman; but secrets, deception and lies from the enemy of my soul fueled simultaneous, conflicting emotions and feelings. I desperately wanted to be good, but freedom from my past eluded me. My hope had been to find that freedom in Jake, in his family and in his church. Tolerance won, as I closed my eyes and sometimes joined them in the things I most detested and feared. *The abused adult/child's perpetual shift in and out of God's truth (right and wrong behavior) was unavoidable for her. It was impossible for her to control. She did not understand that no human could fix her.*

In addition to the confusing presence of alcohol, my expectations found it hard to believe that the church could be anything but a loving, safe haven for anyone. However, all too often I did not see the character of Jesus being expressed there. There were no Bible studies, no prayer groups and no Sunday school classes. The priest loved his pipe organ, and the people loved to party. Disunity was evident, and unkindness was found. With the exception of a few, I found little spiritual connection with the people in the church. *The abused/adult child felt a disturbing presence there and often did not feel safe, did not feel loved. Her secrets overshadowed her perceptions.*

Ultimately, it was within the ambience of this church that I truly came to understand that spiritual warfare is real. The work of Satan and his demons is to seek and to destroy the Church, the Body of Christ. It

143

was within this church that I saw those dark forces work in the lives of well-intentioned, but often uninformed, people. *The abused adult/child became victim to those dark powers while the wounded child listened to the lies and acted out in every way that she had learned she could—the depression, the ambivalence, the anger, the confusion, the denial. She constantly screamed out to be loved but often pushed people away if they got too close. The precious child guarded God's Spirit within her. The survivor emerged and wore all of their faces well.*

However, God loved me too much to allow my mind and spirit to stay trapped in the twisted betrayal of abuse. He used my church experience as a training ground for the spiritual battles the survivor in me would face. Slowly, He pruned the dead branches of my life away where the sins of others and my own sin and rebellion had rotted. In contrast to the behavior of my wounded child, He showed me that the strength and character of Jesus coursed through my veins and flowed into many areas of my life. He revealed to me that I had a goodness of heart for those who are hurting, and He gave me opportunities to exercise my faith in Him.

It was during this time of training that God led me to venues outside of our church that provided spiritual teaching I had not found otherwise. This was training that I desperately needed for the battles I would face. I honestly do not know what I would have done without Christian radio and television. *Insights for Living* with Chuck Swindoll taught me God's Word which has spoken to humanity throughout the ages to reveal who God is. Chuck taught me God's precepts—principles that work and do not work for us in this life. I listened intently to James Dobson's *Focus on the Family* radio program where his interview with Ted Bundy gave me insights into the mind of a sexual predator and the evil power of pornography. Dr. Dobson's programs on child abuse, marriage and raising children became invaluable to me. Evenings would find me in front of the television praying with Pat Robertson and my *700 Club* family. These godly men became my teachers, my counselors, my prayer partners, my lifelines to God. They fed my thirsty, immature spirit.

On the battlefield, God's gentle voice kept speaking—never giving up on me, until I finally learned to listen and obey. In the battle, I would also discover, with great dismay, how easy it is to fall short of listening to and obeying the still, small voice of God. I also realized that my choices, both good and bad, always had consequences. In the course of time, I would learn that my spiritual battles are God's to fight and not mine. I had to learn to surrender my battles to Him.

One of the most precious gifts of knowledge God has given me is to understand that He never closes His heart to me, and that He patiently *waits for me* to follow where He wants to lead me. God the Father, God the Son and God the Holy Spirit—the Triune God, has been the one sure thing in my life that has sustained me. As we continue on, you will experience God's incredible faithfulness to this wounded child.

Chapter 16

Yes, Life Can Get Worse, and It Did

From the beginning of our relationship, Jake and I had each expressed a strong desire to have a family. We were ecstatic when I became pregnant only eight months after we were married. Our precious baby girl was born two weeks after her due date in November of 1969. She weighed eight pounds, four ounces and was much too large for my small frame. The whole labor and delivery experience was so traumatic that it would be years before Jake would even talk to me about how really bad the whole experience had been for all of us. After many long hours, my labor stopped and it was determined that she was wedged in the birth canal. My doctor ordered an x-ray to determine what he needed to do and then gave me a medication to restart the contractions. These decisions would later come into question. We named our baby girl Katherine, which means pure. Katherine is also the middle name that was given to me when I was born. *Did the abused adult/child struggle against bringing an innocent baby into a world filled with so much darkness and pain? Had she desired to give her own name to her child in the hope of defining new pure life for herself?*

When Katherine was only a few months old, my brother-in-law appeared on our doorstep with his camera equipment in tow. He had come to take pictures of my baby girl. I still cannot believe that I even let him in the door. I remember feeling a rage inside me that wanted so badly to come out against this man. The entire time he was in our home, repressed raw emotions clawed the inner walls of my skin, begging for a way to be unleashed. Just as he was leaving, I found the courage to look him in the eyes and say, "If you ever touch her, I will kill you!" He never said a word to me; he just left. Shortly thereafter, he was diagnosed with colon cancer and suffered terribly, until he died several years later. *The abused adult/child had no power over her abuser—except when it came to her own child. She resolved never to let him near her.*

Delivery amnesia, which I am convinced is a gift from our Creator, must have kicked in, because six months later, I became pregnant again. Clearly, the blessing of having our little girl in our lives far outweighed the struggle of getting her here. We did not realize then that Katherine's difficult entry into this world was only the beginning of many battles for this beautiful, golden-haired baby girl who would touch so many lives.

When I took Katherine in for her nine-month checkup, our pediatrician sent us to a nearby lab for blood tests because he thought she looked a little pale. The results did not show anything particularly abnormal, and we laughed it off because fair skin was a trait that ran on both sides of our family. It was about this time that I began to have premonitions of dread concerning my baby. I cannot explain the uneasiness that began to consume me. I would have sudden unexpected moments when I would be engulfed with unbearable panic and fear. I would hold her close to me and weep, crying out to God to please protect her. I even began to resist getting in the car with her for fear that we would be in an accident, and she would be killed. The day finally came when stone-cold reality hit me between my eyes. I received some pictures I had recently taken of Katherine and another baby who was her same age. As I flipped through the pictures, I could no longer hide in stubborn denial. There was something seriously wrong with my precious little baby. I had previously noticed that she was bruising easily, and in these pictures I saw dark, bluish-green circles under her eyes and on her cheeks and arms. Instead of being pretty, baby-pink, like the other child in the pictures, her skin had a greenish tint to it. The pictures did not lie. Penetrating dread crept over me as I turned and looked purposely at my child. I knew that I had to do something. In desperation, I called and made an appointment to see her pediatrician. Wise mothers had clued me into the fact that a suspected ear infection would always get you in the door quickly. It worked, and within minutes, we were on our way into town.

The caliche country road left a cloud of white chalky dust behind us, reminding me of other cloud-covered roads that I had traveled, roads that were filled with so much fear and uncertainty. I did not want to travel down another of those roads. Physical pain clutched at my emotions and crushed my chest until I could hardly breathe. A familiar, foreboding presence sat beside me and mocked me. *Denial stuffed every persuasive thought and every dark emotion down, deep down into the center of my soul. My baby needed me. I had to think about her and not myself. I could not disappear.*

I checked in with the receptionist and settled into a chair in the waiting room of the doctor's office. Mothers chatted as they watched their toddlers scurry clumsily around the small room. Katherine, who obviously did not feel well, laid her head on my chest as she habitually caressed the satin binding on her soft blanket. Her tiny, plump thumb gave her much-needed comfort as she gently nursed on it. I nestled my chin over the top of her head and securely wrapped my arms around her as though trying to protect her from the ominous cloud that had been following us for weeks.

Her name was called, and I was directed into one of the small examination rooms. We were greeted by Dr. Stein, a young doctor who had the undisputable reputation of being the best pediatrician in the area. I would come to believe that divine providence had led us to this wise man. He gently examined Katherine and then cautiously suggested that we take another look at her blood count. In addition to her bruising, I observed that he was paying close attention to the lack of color under her fingernails and under her eyelids. I refused to let my thoughts linger, as once again I carried her to the laboratory for another blood test.

I firmly gripped my baby's hand and tried to console her as the technician stuck her tiny finger once again with the sharp metal object that caused a small amount of blood to rise to the surface of her skin. Tears rolled down Katherine's round, flushed cheeks as she looked at me in dismay. It was not enough blood, and the kind lady had to continually squeeze my baby's finger until she had produced enough to give her the information that she needed. The last time I had seen my daughter's blood, it was bright red. This time it looked like pale, pink Kool-Aid. Her white count was so high that the technician finally just stopped counting. *The familiar darkness that had often provided refuge when I was threatened lingered about me, trying once again to give me a place of protection. But I could not go there. Not this time.*

I chose not to comment on the color of the blood as I watched it being squeezed into the small vial. I chose instead to soothe this precious little person who had so trustingly offered her tiny finger to be pricked by a stranger. But I knew—and I denied the look of concern on the technician's face as she handed me the results and directed me back to the doctor's office. Our doctor, taking note of my condition while glancing at the report, asked me when my baby was due. I looked bigger than my four months along. He guardedly told me that Katherine was anemic, and that it was important for us to find out why. He suggested that I go on home, and he said that he would call me when he could make some arrangements for her to be examined by someone at Children's Hospital in Dallas, perhaps on Monday. He was gently preparing me.

The trip back to our country home seemed much longer than the trip into town. My body was aching from the stress of carrying my unborn child and baby Katherine, who was by now exhausted. Two of our cats, Spot and Mittens, greeted us as I pulled our blue sports car into the garage. I could hear the persistent ringing of the phone as I struggled to pull Katherine over my growing belly and out of the car. The steep steps leading into the house seemed like giant obstacles that were trying to hinder me from getting the news on the other end of the phone line. The significance of the call was mimicked by the gravity of our doctor's voice. He told me he had spoken with Dr. Lon at Children's Hospital in Dallas, and that he was willing to wait for us to get there—today. Dr. Stein did not wait for me to make a decision. His recommendation was that we leave immediately for the hospital. He gave me directions and instructed me to go to the emergency entrance. It was already close to 5:00 p.m. I called Jake, and he came home immediately to make the trip with us.

I never did like the city traffic, and it was especially annoying to me as we fought the heavy Friday afternoon rush. A light drizzle of rain dampened the windows of the car as darkness began to take over the light of day. Irritation nipped on my raw nerves. I did not like anything about this particular moment. Jake and I sat in silence; Katherine had fallen asleep in the car seat between us. Upon arrival, we found our way to the emergency room where the staff paged Dr. Lon. The head of pediatric oncology wasted no time meeting with us. I immediately liked this man who had an air of gentle wisdom about him. His thin, graying hair gave him a distinguished look, and he had the most caring eyes I had ever seen. When he quietly told us that he wanted to admit Katherine into the hospital, I protested, "She doesn't have any pajamas to wear, and she hasn't had her supper, and it's close to her bedtime!" A kind, gentle smile assured me that the hospital had plenty of pajamas, food and beds and that her needs would be taken care of. *I could not stop the inevitable.*

Jake was instructed to go to the admitting office while Katherine and I were escorted upstairs. That short walk from the emergency room to the third floor made me painfully aware, in no uncertain terms, that only the very ill resided in this place. We were greeted by dozens of little faces. Some were being pushed around in wheelchairs, while others were being pulled in little red wagons, enjoying yellow banana popsicles. Many were confined to their beds. All were accompanied by ominous steel poles that delivered fluids through tubes that were attached to frail, pale bodies. I tried to ignore the needles that disappeared into young flesh, and I tried to ignore the sadness in the eyes of the parents who hovered nearby these little ones.

Once we were settled into a room, Katherine was whisked away from me. The transition was handled so professionally that I hardly had time to think about what they might do to her. She did not protest. My child's sweet innocence did not know what was in store for her. She was so willing. She was so trusting. *I resolved that I would stand firm. I would not feel. I watched her go without emotion.*

When Jake found me alone in our room, he was greeted with deafening silence. We embraced. There was nothing to be said, no words to speak, each of us grasping for something to hold on to, trying to cope with our own fears while trying to comfort and reassure each other. We cringed at the news that Katherine would receive a pint of blood plasma; the IV was being inserted at that time.

When she returned to my arms, I dutifully wiped the tears from her crimson cheeks. Her golden hair, much longer than most eleven-month-old babies, was drenched with perspiration. Her long dark eyelashes were matted against closed eyes. She had fallen asleep from exhaustion and sighed every few minutes, her body trembling with each short breath. The nurse put her in the cold, uninviting bed where I covered her to make sure she would be warm. I fretted because she had missed her supper.

I examined the patch on her head where they had shaved off a part of her pretty blonde hair. I was amused by the fact that a Dixie cup, cut in half and taped to her skin, protected the needle that now penetrated her scalp. I familiarized myself with the machine that monitored the dark red liquid that flowed from the clear, plastic bag held high above my head by the icy, steel pole. I ignored the needle that dug into her tender flesh. I would be everything that my baby girl needed for me to be. I would give her my own life if I had to, but I would let no one see the massive agony that ripped at my soul as I stood and watched my child throughout the long and perilous night. Intuitively, I knew that death was knocking at our door.

The new life that was growing inside me occasionally reminded me of its presence as soft flutters momentarily drew me away from the unforgiving truth that blanketed my mind. Did my unborn child feel my sorrow? Did it sense what I sensed, the gravity of its big sister's condition? Was its little soul grieving with me or was it trying to offer me comfort and hope for life, not fear of death? I looked at my daughter and prayed for them both. *Numbness from the past and strength for the present merged into one as a part of me that I had not known before was born that night. Emotionally, I separated myself from my daughter. It would be the only way the abused adult/child would be able to survive. It would be the only way the abused adult/child could be strong enough for her baby, her unborn child and for her husband. I was a survivor and that is what survivors do. Whatever it takes!*

My parents came to the hospital early the next morning to be with their ninth grandchild. It was a Saturday, October 1969. Tired and weary from lack of sleep, I stood in the hall outside Katherine's room staring out the window that looked over the tops of fall-colored trees. The oranges, reds, golds and greens blended together as I tried to appreciate their beauty through thoughts of dread. Thick, heavy clouds hung low in the sky, and light rain tapped on the protective glass. A gust of wind rattled the window and shook the trees below, sending an icy chill down my spine, and pulling my attention back into the cold hallway. Without emotion, I returned to the colorless room, looked firmly at my husband and said, "It can't be leukemia!" Glassy, blue eyes reflected my own secret thoughts. Perhaps now it won't hurt so deeply when we finally hear the truth. We were given, in that moment, the first of many large doses of grace. I fell into the familiar warmth of my young husband's arms. *The abused adult/child's tears would flow no more. The survivor could not afford their luxury.*

We had been told that we would be given a diagnosis by noon that day, and with unappreciated punctuality, four doctors marched methodically into our small space and formed a semicircle around us. Mom and Dad quietly slipped out of the room. I could not begin to imagine how difficult it was for these men to hand over their verdict, "Your daughter has acute lymphocytic leukemia. There is no cure. For now, the blood transfusions have temporarily sustained her life."

Broken only by the small whimper of distress from our precious baby girl, disbelieving silence hung in the air. The jail-like bed with its metal bars kept me from quickly comforting her. I struggled to get the barrier free, lashing out in anger at the bed. *The abused adult/child displaced her anger, just like she had always done in the past, not wanting to look at the source of it, but always placing it somewhere else.*

Jake explained to the sympathetic doctors that he had turned in his resignation where he had been working just two weeks earlier. The insurance on Katherine had terminated at midnight Friday, the day before. With tears in his eyes, he first wanted to know what kind of expenses we would face. We were told that we would be out a minimum of fifteen thousand dollars (nearly Jake's annual salary) for every year that she lived. Hesitantly, his lips trembling and his voice shaking, Jake asked how long we could expect that to be. We were told that if she could tolerate the medication and stay in remission, she might live twelve to eighteen months. If not, it could be a matter of weeks or even days. They began gently to explain the treatment she would have to endure, kindly sparing us of all the gory details at once. Those we would experience soon enough. I can find no human words to adequately define the impact of what our ears heard, or what our hearts felt, or what our senses wanted to scream out. I only know that God's grace was sufficient for that terrible moment. *The survivor began preparing herself for unknown territory while the abused adult/child succumbed to numbness.*

The doctors left us alone as we faced giving my parents the dreadful diagnosis. I grieved for them. They had lost their third child, a little girl, who was just a few months older than Katherine when she died unexpectedly. Surely, this would be like reliving their loss all over again. Both of my parents remained stoic. In the 1930s, technology to determine the cause of death was not available to them like it is today. When our doctors began to ask us about family history, I began to wonder if the sister I had never known might have had this same dreadful disease. I knew that she had been given a blood transfusion but died shortly thereafter. We were also questioned about the x-ray that had been taken shortly before Katherine was born. In reality, there were no definitive answers to their questions or to our own. Mysteriously we never asked God, "Why Katherine?" Mom and Dad gladly stayed with their grandbaby when we left the hospital to tell Jake's parents the tragic news. We felt that a phone call was inappropriate.

As we walked in silent, intense sorrow down the long corridors of the hospital, the floors glistened beneath our feet. The walls, decorated with lions and tigers and bears, attempted to make us smile. Occasional quiet laughter would penetrate our thoughts, often broken by the cries of a child in distress. We left the enormous shelter for the suffering and dying behind us, dreading to spread our heartbreaking news.

Arm in arm we walked across the concrete parking lot. The steady mist of autumn rain dampened our shoulders while dreary, overcast skies persisted. Before getting into our car, I turned to my husband and looked with determination into his eyes. From some sacred place that I did not even know I possessed came these steadfast words, "Jake, God is going to take care of Katherine. I don't know how, but I know that He is going to heal her."

Seeds of faith, those sown in my simple child-heart so many years ago when a little lost bird flew down from a distant tree limb onto my shoulder, were now beginning to grow like an acorn that had lain dormant in the soil of my soul. Sprouts from within began to search for light as they reached toward Heaven for nourishment. From that moment on, I walked in complete faith and belief that Katherine would not die. In the days and months that followed, I shared with everyone I knew this unwavering faith I had in Jesus to heal our Katherine. I was not prepared for the lack of faith that surrounded me. Everyone thought I was in denial and that Katherine was doomed to die. *The survivor did not understand others' lack of faith. Her faith had overcome denial. The abused adult/ child secretly harbored anger toward those who scorned her faith.*

There were so many times when God would impart mercy to Katherine. There was an unexpected rise in her blood count that prevented the doctors from having to cut into her ankle in search of a vein sufficient enough for yet another transfusion. Consequently, we were able to take her home. She tolerated the horrible, toxic drug that was forced into her tiny, fragile veins and the weekly oral medication I was instructed to give her. I had to come to grips with the fact that I had been warned not to allow even a trace of the oral medication get into my own body because it could damage the baby I was carrying.

Everything within me wanted to rebel. I wanted to refuse to put my child through these horrible atrocities. However, it was Katherine's own God-given ability to endure that allowed her to be happy, in spite of the completely necessary, seemingly abusive *things* that were being done to her. Her strength and joy carried us through. *The survivor would not allow feelings to dictate the choices she had to make. Feelings would no longer be permissible where her child was concerned. She was an expert at not feeling.*

God met our financial needs in ways that we could not have even imagined. A neighbor wrote an article about Katherine for several surrounding newspapers, which was graciously published. Consequently, we were given gifts from people that we did not know. Envelopes filled with loving thoughts and cash arrived in our mailbox; they never had return addresses on them. We received a free turkey for Thanksgiving and free dry cleaning service. The list goes on and on. Another neighbor, who owned a fireplace business close to our country home, kept a picture of Kat beside a large red piggy bank on his countertop. Patrons tossed their coins and sometimes their bills into the slot of the smiling pig until it could hold no more. You can't imagine the surprise and awe-filled thankfulness we felt when one day this humble man knocked on our door and presented us with this money-stuffed, potbellied pig! One of the most amazing God-cidences came through a young woman whose husband I had once dated. She worked in the lab where we had to make weekly and sometimes semiweekly visits. When she realized our financial circumstances, that we had no insurance on Katherine, she went to the owner of the lab and petitioned him to drop all of our charges. We were faced with a minimum of forty dollars a month just in lab fees alone, which was extremely substantial for us. Thankfully, he agreed to this arrangement, and we were never charged for their services, no matter how many times we needed them. There are many people who touched our lives whom we will never be able to repay directly or tell how much we appreciate their kindness. But in time, we would return such kindness in the only way that we could—by helping others who are in need.

In March 1971, we were blessed with the quick and easy delivery of our son, Jay. Katherine was blessed with a desperately needed playmate and little brother whom she adored and could not give enough attention. The pain of Kat's illness only multiplied the blessing we felt in having our new son. But now, not only did I have a sick child to take care of, I had the added stress of a new baby. *There was no place for the abused adult/child's self-pity. She could not be self-absorbed. The survivor must stay in control.*

Several months after Jay's birth, we received a call from our pediatrician. He informed us that St. Jude Children's Research Hospital, located in Tennessee, had just released their experimental treatment for leukemia to hospitals around the country. He wanted us to consider taking Katherine back to Children's Hospital in Dallas to discuss entering her into this program. We did not hesitate. We felt we had no choice but to try anything that was offered to her. She was one of the first to receive this treatment in the Dallas area.

But once again, this mother's heart did not like what she was hearing. A complete bombardment of Katherine's cells was the proposed solution for a possible cure for our daughter. They were striving for a five-year remission with only a five percent chance that she would live beyond that time period. If she survived the initial treatment, she would be on maintenance drugs for two and half years. She would then be taken off all medication because her body would not be able to tolerate the drugs indefinitely. Although Katherine was accepted into the program, years later Doctor Lon told me they almost did not move forward with our daughter because she was showing signs of a relapse. "For some reason, we decided to take a chance with Katherine." Protocol typically denied such children from further treatment because they never did well. Such treatment would only prolong the suffering, the inevitable. This was yet another extension of God's immeasurable grace toward Katherine.

An extensive three months of chemotherapy began. The original intravenous drugs were repeated, and in addition, she received five injections of methotrexate into her spine. We had been told that this drug was related to the mustard gas once used in warfare. She also received a series of cobalt (radiation) treatments administered to her head. Bone marrow was painfully extracted from her delicate breast bone to chart her progress, and there were endless drops of blood squeezed from her tiny, tiny fingers and arms.

She had managed to hang on to her beautiful hair the first time around, but this time we sadly watched her shoulder-length hair come out in clumps. We sensed her humiliation, even at her tender age of almost two years old. During this period of time, her features changed so drastically that family members did not even recognize her. She was bloated and puffy and bald, but still the happy, sweet little person whose life became more precious to us with each passing day. *God gave Katherine the grace to endure and He gave the survivor the grace to sit by and helplessly watch. She lived on prayer by faith.*

I must share this one endearing story about little Katherine. I had taken her to the hospital for the final injection of the methotrexate into her spine. Throughout all the times that she had been taken away from me for those awful treatments, she had never once refused to go to the one who came for her. However on this last trip, she hit her limit and was no longer willing to accept any more pain. When the nurse reached out to take her from me, Katherine threw her little arms around my neck and dug her heels in around my waist and would not let go of me. I lovingly told her, "Katherine, you only have to do this one more time, just one more time! After today, your back will be all well, and we will never hurt your back again. Your back will be all well." She looked deeply into my eyes as with clear, trusting understanding and then turned loose of her mother and reached out to the waiting nurse. To this day, I can remember the aura of love that I felt around my child. It says so much about Katherine's own God-given, personal strength and character.

On the way home I felt a gentle tap on my shoulder. I turned and looked at my young daughter who was sitting next to me in her car seat. I asked her what she wanted. With big tears in her deep blue eyes, she leaned forward and pulled her little white dress with the tiny blue flowers away from her back and declared, "My back is all well. See, Mommy, my back is all well." I happily affirmed her declaration and marveled at this astounding little person. Overcome with emotion, it was difficult to respond. I whispered back to her, "Yes, Katherine! Your back is all well. Your back is all well!" She was only twenty-three months old.

We were faced with making some other difficult decisions. One of the hardest was the feasibility of living outside the city, in the country. Although we had absolutely great neighbors, they were all some distance from us, as were doctors and emergency equipment. Several incidents had frightened me and gave me reason to consider moving.

Early one afternoon, when Jake was at work and shortly after Katherine was born, I noticed a car creeping down the narrow, dirt road leading to our house. When the car stopped, several men jumped out of the car and tried to open our front door. When they failed to get into the house, they went to the back door and once again tried to gain entrance. Thankfully, they left without incident but stopped at another house farther down the road. I called the police, but the car was long gone by the time they finally arrived. I was a bit unnerved, and I never felt quite as safe after that.

Another disturbing incident occurred late one evening when a neighbor began to bang furiously on our front door. Much to our dismay, when we looked outside, we discovered that all of the land around our house was covered by fire. We had no fire department, and the only way to get water to the fire was by neighboring communities' fire trucks that could carry water. Jake drove Katherine and me down to a neighbor's house, where we watched from a distance as cars and fire trucks began to appear on the scene. The large propane tank behind our house was of utmost concern. A reflection from one of our windows picked up the flames, and it appeared that our house was burning. It turned out to be an illusion, and I was very thankful to learn that our house was never actually touched by the fire. Nevertheless, I had been horrified. Katherine had just been diagnosed, and I was pregnant with our son, Jay.

Another chilling event that impacted our decision actually happened a few months before Katherine was born. It acted as a warning bell that never stopped ringing in my ears after both of the children were born and when Katherine's health became a factor. Tiger, our gray tabby cat, had been sitting next to me on a chair watching me sew. I heard him cough, and when I looked up at him, there was a pink thread hanging from his mouth. When I pulled on the thread, Tiger went into a tailspin. He had swallowed the needle. For the first time since we had lived in the country, I was without a car. I finally found a neighbor at home who offered to take us to our vet's office in town. As I tried to maneuver Tiger into the car over my full belly, I managed to slam the poor cat's tail in the car door. He immediately lunged out of my arms and began throwing up all over my neighbor's new Chrysler New Yorker. It was a long ride into town, and when we finally got there, the vet wasn't sure who needed treatment more, me or the cat. X-ray revealed that the needle had actually broken in half, leaving both ends of the needle lodged in Tiger's throat. He was sedated, and the needle was safely retrieved. The cat was fine. I was a wreck. The importance of our being closer to doctors could not have been made clearer.

Even though we loved our first home very much and we loved our small country community where neighbors truly knew how to be neighborly, these and other issues had to be considered; we had a very sick child and a new baby. I was feeling the need to be closer to doctors and quick help if I needed it. Sadly, we sold our home and moved into town. I allowed myself to cry when Jake took the cats away.

With the dreadful series of treatments behind us and finally getting settled into our new home, we had another major decision to make. We were told that often kids with cancer die from secondary infections because their immune systems are wiped out by the chemotherapy. Chicken pox was a deadly enemy to be avoided because for some reason the virus would turn inward, and there was nothing that could stop it. With those threats hanging over our daughter's chance for survival, we decided to isolate our children from the rest of the world as long as Kat was on chemo. They would not be allowed to go out and play with other children or go to church or to preschool. I would not even take them to the grocery store.

We accepted our new way of life and settled into a routine that would last for two and a half more years. Our big adventure out of the house each week was when baby Jay and I took Katherine in for blood tests every Monday morning. Depending upon her blood counts, I would give her oral medications that would hopefully do their job in fighting the cancer, but it would also lower her resistance to zero. One of the medications, which is no longer in use, was so bitter and so difficult to get down her that Monday nights often brought me to the point of wanting to throw up because of the extreme anxiety I felt in trying to give it to her. Tuesday mornings became a nightmare for both of us. On one of those mornings she threw up what I had given her, and I foolishly gave her the whole dose again. Several days later she woke up literally foaming at the mouth. From then on, if it came up, it stayed up. Kat handled everything much better than I did. She continually offered her tiny finger to be pricked for blood tests, seldom ever shedding a tear or offering a protest. She was such an amazing little girl, and her sweet countenance carried me through those tough times. *The little child and the survivor were carried by grace. But the abused adult/child succumbed to the sorrow of what was being forced upon her little daughter.*

And so began a very long journey with my young family. It was a journey that would give me the greatest expressions of joy and happiness that I could possibly imagine, and at the same time plunge me into the depths of despair beyond description. It was the most rewarding time of my whole life and it was the most difficult. *It took every resource the survivor could draw from to keep from buckling under her conflicting emotions and feelings. She was weak. She was strong. She was happy. She was hopeful. She was depressed. She never stopped proclaiming that God would heal her child.*

My heart burst with love for my children and relished in everything they did. They were so teachable and so adorable. I had never been around children before I had children of my own. Each new thing they learned was a celebration and an adventure for me. We played together, read books, sang songs. I did all of the things for them and with them that were not done for or with me as a child. I think in many ways I was growing up with them. *The survivor was inadvertently nurturing the wounded child within.*

Initially, I tried desperately to stay somewhat involved in our church, but it became impossible, and I finally severed ties with the outside world. I made the decision to stay at home with my two babies. Our new city neighbors were unfriendly and distant. I longed for the country neighbors we had left behind. Jake coped with our situation by staying busy with work, church and the men's organization he had joined. Unfortunately, this left me at home alone in the evenings far too often. His being at home was my only outlet. *The survivor's loneliness fed the ever-present sting of depression that she tried so hard to deny.*

I had a spiritual connection with only a few in our church—Esther, Gaye, Kay, Sandra and Ruth—whose daily prayers, frequent phone calls and encouragement carried me through those tough years. They met together once a week to pray for my family. I honestly do not know what I would have done without these precious women of faith. Our church as a whole was distant and silent.

It was the day-to-day-to-day living without a break that finally began to wear me down. Mom and Dad were getting too old to drive across town in the heavy Dallas traffic, so they were unable to give me very much relief. My mother-in-law, who lived just three miles from us, did not offer to help. She was busy working on her master's degree. In addition, she was involved in her church and was active in her sorority and Junior League. She had little time for us and our problems. My erroneous perception told me that I could never rely on her, and pride told me that if I had to ask her for help, then I didn't want it. I called upon her only when we were in a crisis and I had no other choice. Those early years, unfortunately, set the tone for our future relationship. *The abused adult/child's preconceived expectations that Jake's family and his church would somehow be there for her began to unravel with devastating emotional results. She struggled to cope with her life.*

Isolation framed the lives of me and my children as the days slipped into weeks, weeks slipped into months, and months slipped into years. The exhaustion, loneliness and unrelenting depression forced me to cling to my faith in God. He was the binding that held the twisted threads of my life together as my guarded secrets fought within me. God used this time to teach me to abide in Him.

I needed the quiet, so He took me aside,
Into the shadows where we could confide,
Away from the bustle where all the day long,
I hurried and worried, when active and strong.

I needed the quiet though at first I rebelled,
But gently, so gently, by His patience upheld.
He whispered so clearly of spiritual things,
Though weakened in body, my spirit took wings
To heights never dreamed of, when active and gay,
He loved me so gently, He led me His way.

I needed the quiet, no prison my bed,
But a beautiful valley of blessing instead.
A place to grow richer and in Jesus abide—
I needed the quiet, so He drew me aside.
Author unknown

Several significant things happened during this period of isolation. Depression shrewdly skews every thought the brain tries to process. One night, when I crawled into bed, I cried out to God and told Him that if He didn't do something to help me, then He could just take me out of this life. I could not bear the pain I was in. *The abused adult/child wanted to cry, but she could not cry. She wanted to die, but she could not die. She had to live for her children. The survivor would not give in. She fought for her survival. Divine appointments awaited her.*

Aside from the fact that I never trusted anyone to stay with my children, we were so stressed for money we hardly ever hired a sitter to go anywhere. But occasionally we would scrape enough together so that we could attend a small sharing group that met on Sunday nights. About a week after my desperate plea to God, we attended one of those meetings. A doctor, who was a member of the group, overheard me telling someone about my awful headaches. I was considering seeing a neurologist because I had to keep the window shades pulled down during the day. I could not stand for the light to hit my eyes. Dr. John approached me about coming to his office for a medical checkup. He became the answer to my desperate cry for help. First of all, he did not charge me for all of my visits. Secondly, he put me on a hypoglycemia diet, which consisted of high protein and low carbohydrates. I was to eliminate refined products such as sugar and white flour and take nutritional supplements. Thirdly, he was an osteopath and had magic fingers that released the tensions I had stored in my back, neck and shoulders. Most of all, this kind, godly man gave me wise counsel and a listening ear. Life became more manageable for me after spending about a year under his care. He became a dear friend, and I will always be thankful that he heard God's call to help me. *The abused adult/child did not yet fully understand the faithfulness of God or that her hope and strength came from Him. Only He knew His plans for the survivor.*[1]

Television became an outlet not only for my children, but for me. They were allowed to watch *Sesame Street* and *The Electric Company* twice a day, but during naptimes the TV was my escape. One day a group of Asian children, who were singing a medley of Christian songs, came on the television screen. I was deeply touched by the beautiful harmony of their voices. They were representing an international children's ministry, and when a petition was made to help support orphan children overseas, I could not resist the nudge that I felt to respond. It was only ten dollars a month, but for me that might as well have been a hundred dollars. I did not have a clue where I would get the money, but it was always there for

---

[1]   Jeremiah 29: 11-13, "For I know my thoughts that I think toward you, said the Lord, thoughts of peace and not evil, to give you an expected end. Then you shall call upon me, and you will go and pray to me and I will hear you. Then you will seek me and find me, when you search me with all your heart" (NKJV).

me to make those monthly donations and eventually supporting World Vision International became a lifelong family commitment. Little did I know how God would reward that small step of faith. He has returned it to me a thousand times over again, and I don't mean just monetarily.

Except for the day when I felt God's call to invite Jesus into my life, this was the first time I recall hearing and following His quiet, gentle voice within me. In retrospect, I am always in awe to look back and realize that God has in some way spoken to me; however, the fact that He has spoken is not what I find so amazing. And the fact that sometimes I actually listen I find truly surprising; but when I obey—well, that is absolutely astonishing! I have come to believe that in different ways He purposely speaks to all His children. *The survivor did not know that God was testing her ears.*

Chapter 17

A Retreat and a Divine Appointment

About a year after Katherine was diagnosed, our small church was forced to merge with another church, whose priest was appointed to preside over the two blended churches. This young priest, who was outgoing, handsome and a gifted communicator, seemed to be idolized by those around him. With him and his congregation came a vibrant party spirit, which was embraced by many in our current congregation. Within a year of the merger, most of the families that I had made a spiritual and emotional connection with had left to attend another church of the same denomination. Jake was still on the vestry during the merger, and the new priest asked him to continue serving on the vestry as the junior warden. No matter how much I complained about being unhappy there, my husband defended his church and his denomination. He seemed blinded to the spiritual condition of the church and clearly had no plans to leave either of them.

The church grew by leaps and bounds. It was a very busy place with lots of energy, but with disturbing issues hiding behind the disguise of activity. Although Jake was extremely involved and constantly at the church, only a handful of people knew that he had a terminally ill daughter at home. Those who served with Jake on the new vestry made no effort to reach out to us. The new priest had not even been to our house to pray for Katherine. In fact, the church as a whole was not praying for our daughter. I believed that God was going to heal her, and somehow I knew He wanted people involved in praying for her. But the church was oblivious to that possibility. It was very apparent to me that our situation was of no great importance in the scheme of things. I tried to be obedient to Jake, like Sarai in the Old Testament had been obedient to Abram. Sarai followed her man and his mission, and like Sarai, I stayed with my man and his church. I like to think that in the long run God honored my obedience to my husband. *The roots of bitterness that had already taken hold just grew deeper and more deadly as untamed anger raged deep within. Frustration joined the abused adult/child's masks of bitterness and resentment. Her confusing, unmet needs multiplied.*

October of 1972 marked Katherine's second year in remission. The isolation had paid off as both of my children remained otherwise healthy. Katherine was no longer bloated and swollen, and the new growth of thick blonde hair complemented the simple beauty of a happy little girl who loved her little brother and loved life. We continued to isolate the children as much as possible, but Katherine constantly begged to go out and play with the neighborhood children. Rarely did I risk letting her be a normal kid, and I seldom left them, not even with Jake. However, when my friend Gaye called and invited me to attend a ladies' retreat being hosted by her church, Jake quickly encouraged me to go. He knew it would be good for me to get away. With mixed emotions, I left them for the entire weekend.

Before Jake and I married, I sternly told him there was one thing I would never do, and that was to go to confession. "I don't need a priest to tell my sins to!" As I piled into a car full of joyful, exuberant women who were headed north out of Dallas in search of spiritual refreshing and refuge from kids, husbands and housework, I discovered that the father confessor of the diocese was leading the retreat that weekend. He would naturally be talking about confession. I was a bit dismayed but kept my irritated thoughts to myself. The forty-five minute trip ended with a bit of a surprise for me as we pulled onto the premises of the retreat center. I had been there before!

It had been heaven on earth to have adult female conversation over dinner and to throw my bedding on one of the many bunk beds and just hang out. The sound of women's endless chatter ministered to my lonely spirit. Their laughter tickled me from head to toe, and their warmth and love comforted me. But during the Friday night session in the large meeting room, where I sat with Gaye and the ladies from her church, my pent-up emotions and poor, spent body sat rigid and lifeless. The priest, who was very tall and extraordinarily slender, spoke words that began to break through my walls of controlled resistance. When the session ended, we were asked to enter into a period of silence, which forced my reluctant mind to be still and to think about the words that had been offered to me that evening. The raging, relentless, all-loving pursuit of God's Holy Spirit began to tug at my consciousness, and in the quiet of the night, I began to listen. He began to lead.

By Saturday morning, I was feverishly taking notes during the first session of the day. By noon, I was making an appointment to meet with this wise and gentle man, who reminded me that Jesus taught we must forgive others as He has forgiven us,[2] and that we must confess our sins before God.[3] He told us the consequence of ignoring God's call to forgive would result in roots of bitterness that would continually haunt us and hinder our relationship with God and with others. We would not be able to love as Christ loved us. I had never before been faced with the convicting challenge of forgiving the people in my life who had hurt me. *The abused adult/child struggled. How could she possibly bring herself to forgive the ones whose secrets she could not even voice? Even the thought of it sent sharp pains throughout her body. She felt as though a knife was ripping out her heart.*

I searched my mind for those who had taken me by the hand, mentored me, guided me or taught me along the way during those lost

---

[2] Colossians 3:13 says, "Forgive whatever grievances you have with one another. Forgive as the Lord forgave you" (NIV).

[3] 1 John 1:9 says, "If we confess our sins he is faithful and just to forgive us our sins and cleanse us from all unrighteousness" (NIV).

years; I found no one. There had been no one there for me. I did not understand why God had left me to walk in this desert alone. After I moved away from my church family at the age of fourteen, I repeatedly chose paths of destruction and separation from God. I wondered why I had seemed so powerless to resist the pull toward darkness. I wondered why I sometimes wandered so far away from God, and why I had never heard these words before now. I had been like a ship without a sail that had been aimlessly tossing around in a vast troubled sea, alone and so very lost. The weight of my transgressions began to fall heavily upon my shoulders, and I knew I no longer wanted to bear their consequences. But, would I be able to openly confess them to this man of God? *The abused adult/child could feel her emotions shutting down. She was not capable of facing her own guilt and sins or those of her abusers. She just wanted to run and hide. She did not know that all along God had been trying to teach her to depend upon Him and only Him for her strength, her courage, her life.*

My appointment time wasn't until 3:00 p.m. This gave me some free time, and I could hardly wait to walk down to the chapel, the same chapel where Jo Ann and I had ridden our horses together, years before. The crisp, country air warmed by the autumn sun calmed my anxiety. And just for a moment, I forgot about the burdensome sorrows I carried. I relived happy and carefree moments that seemed a lifetime away.

Still unfinished, the large concrete pillars embedded in the vast, concrete floor held the flat roof in place. And just as before, it remained wall-less. I cringed at the youthful irreverence we had displayed and wondered about what strange fate had brought me back to this place, a place where I had known such joy on a horse and fun with a friend. It had brought healing to me then; perhaps it would bring healing to me again. I found a sunny spot, slid to the floor of the unfinished chapel and began to make notes in the small blue notebook I had brought with me. Not only did I have my own sins to bear, but I had the sins of others to bear as well. Time passed much too quickly.

The knot in my stomach seemed to grow larger with each anxious step I took as I walked slowly up the stairs to the small room where

Father Banning was hearing confessions. The all too familiar darkness hovered around me, inviting me to join the secrets that hid there. The secrets, the weight of them, reminded me once again of how weary I was from carrying their burden of never-ending pain. I wanted to endure them no longer, yet simultaneous conflicting emotions haunted me. There was a part of me that wanted to run up the stairs and confess every dastardly thing that had happened to me, and all of the secret hates that I harbored. Other parts of me wanted to run away and disappear into the shadowy comfort of the darkness.

When I reached the top of the stairs, I was warmly greeted by the man who wore a long, black robe with a white collar. Long, slender fingers graciously motioned for me to sit at the round table across from him. The first words out of his mouth were, "I lost my son to cancer." The darkness began to back away as this precious man of God began to share the heart-wrenching illness and death of his own young son to this unforgiving disease. The forever-fresh pain on this wounded father's face recounted the night his precious child left him. It had been snowing for most of the day. As the little boy watched the large flakes float softly toward earth from his hospital window, he said to his father, "It takes so long. It takes so long." With unrelenting grief, this godly man finished his son's thoughts, "I knew that he meant it takes so long to die." Quenched lamenting sorrow hung in the air as his salty tears quietly expressed what he could not put into words. We talked about my daughter. *God had provided one who could understand the survivor's pain. She felt his grief as her mask of compassion allowed her mentor to cry and feel his own pain.*

Father Banning's transparency assured me that it was safe to trust him. I looked at my notes and then began to whisper that which I dared not speak to others who knew me. With no hint of emotion, I simply told him that my brother-in-law had abused me as a child. I quickly moved on; it would not be safe for me to linger. In simple bits and pieces, I told him about my first marriage and divorce. I guardedly talked to him about my issues with the church and the resentments that I carried because my Christian community had not been there for me and my family. There was only so much that I would or could give to him, and the morsels that he tasted gave cause for him to have grave concern for me. He gave me counsel and then he administered the sacrament of absolution. "God, the Father of mercies, through the death and resurrection of his Son, has reconciled the world to himself and sent the Holy Spirit among us for the forgiveness of sins; through the ministry of the Church may God give you pardon and peace, and I absolve you from your sins in the name of the Father, and of the Son, and of the Holy Spirit. Amen."[4] Forgiveness to receive, forgiveness to give—I did not fully understand the importance of my divine appointment with Father Banning. *It was a new beginning for the abused adult/child, but it would be a very long time before understanding would come full circle, before forgiveness would be completed. The survivor felt the impact of the moment.*

I had wept bitter tears the night I was given my daughter's death sentence, and that was the last time I had allowed myself to really cry. Father Banning clasped his large hands around mine and looked sorrowfully into my eyes. I thanked him, and then I hastily opened the door, ran down the stairs and crossed the narrow road. I entered the monks' small chapel where candles in the dark circular room cast soft flickers of light. I flung myself across the simple wooden altar rail and sobbed deep, cleansing tears. Gaye had followed me. My friend, my sister in Christ, gave me what I desperately longed for—arms of reassurance, comfort and tender, unconditional love. Looking back, I believe that was the day my recovery process really began. It was the beginning of a new spiritual awakening for me. It set the stage for the months and years that followed. It was October of 1972.

---

[4]   Only God can forgive our sins. However, I believe God knows our hearts and hears our sincere prayers. I believe my feeble attempt at confessing and forgiving and the prayer said for me from a prayer book, on that day, did not go unnoticed by God.

Chapter 18

Such Faith Is Sure to Be Tested

In February of 1973, Katherine began to show signs of liver damage from the toxic medications she was taking. The alternatives were to leave her on the meds and risk permanent liver damage or take her off the meds and risk a relapse. Neither seemed good options to me; however, the doctors chose to give her liver two weeks of reprieve. One of the medicines I had to give her was extremely bitter. She received two very large tablets every Tuesday, providing her blood count was not too low. I would grind the tablets into a very fine powder and then mix them with something that I hoped would disguise the taste. It was nearly an impossible task because nothing I tried really worked. By the time she managed to finally get the last of it down, we were both in tears. Although I was not happy for the reason, I relished in the joy of having two glorious weeks of not forcing that medicine down my daughter's throat. Katherine received a much-deserved break and two glorious weeks of freedom from being made to feel ill again.

During the 1970s, there was a great revival sweeping our country, and the charismatic movement was widespread. There were many reports of miraculous healings, conversions and renewal experiences in the Christian community. My friend, Esther, told a friend of hers about Katherine and her grim prognosis. He was actually a priest who lived in Colorado and was in Dallas for a charismatic convention. During one of the conference breaks, he called me and asked if he could come to our house and pray for Katherine. I was ecstatic! Here was someone who lived hundreds of miles away wanting to come and see us, but most importantly, he wanted to pray for our daughter! I quickly agreed to his request and called Jake to tell him about the phone call. He left work immediately and came home so that he could be in on the visit. We loved Father Kemp from the moment we met him. He exuded the very presence of Christ.

After a short visit with us, this wise, enthusiastic man asked Jake and me to consider having Katherine take Holy Communion regularly as a purification of her blood through the blood of Christ. I told him that I had reservations about his request because I did not hold the same faith in communion that he held. Our church/denomination taught that when consecrated, the bread and wine was actually transformed into the real presence of Christ. However, I believed communion was to be taken as a remembrance of what Christ had done for us. I explained to him about the inexcusable behavior I had witnessed by some of the people in our church who took communion every Sunday. I had seen no evidence that taking communion ever changed anybody. Consequently, I had come to consider it as nothing more than a ritual, and I wasn't at all sure if I could believe that there was actual power in receiving the sacraments. I then told him about the anger and resentments toward our church that I had tried to deal with when I attended the ladies' retreat the previous October.

I continued with the disturbing news that our little girl was now facing a relapse of the cancer because of the toxicity that had built up in her liver. I exclaimed, "And our church is not even praying for her! I know that God wants to heal Katherine, but people need to be praying for her and they are not!" As Father Kemp listened to my heart-wrenching plea, this incredible man of faith bore witness to my own faith and was suddenly overcome with excitement and conviction. He encouraged us to go to our priest and ask him to get the people of the church involved in our lives. He believed, as I believed, that God was going to use Katherine's healing as a testimony to the healing power of

Christ to touch and change many lives, especially within our church. Before leaving our home, he gathered our daughter in his arms and prayed a simple, yet powerful, prayer. Jake and I agreed that we would talk to our priest.

The following Saturday morning we met our priest in his office. When I told him about my resentments, the retreat and Father Kemp's visit, he expressed shock that I had any problems. He had assumed we were being taken care of. Remember, this was not a mega-church, and it was very easy to know almost everyone who attended. We told him about the potential threat concerning Katherine's relapse, my frustration that few people in the church even knew about her having cancer and the dismay I felt because our congregation was not praying for her. As we continued talking to our priest, he too caught our vision and began to lay out a plan. He vowed to have a prayer card made up for Katherine and asked us to give him a picture of her. His plan was to send it to everyone in the church. The following day we took our children to the seven o'clock morning service where three year-old Katherine received her first communion. That same Sunday, all three services were dedicated to Katherine's healing. True to our priest's promise to us, the prayer card with Katherine's picture on it was mailed out with a letter explaining our circumstances and an urgent plea to place the card where it would be a daily reminder to pray for her. James 5:14-15 appeared at the bottom of the card. "Is anyone among you sick? Let him call for the elders of the church, and let them pray over him, anointing him with oil in the name of the Lord; and the prayer offered in faith will restore the one who is sick." *As God's ministering angels gathered tightly around the survivor and her family, she felt a mysterious relief. She was unaware of God's plan that was set into motion when the power of prayer was unleashed.*

At the end of two weeks, I took Katherine back to the hospital for a follow-up on her blood work. The test revealed that the toxicity level in her liver was within normal range, and she would be able to resume treatment. Years later when I asked Dr. Lon why he thought she had no more problems with her liver, he shrugged his shoulders and said, "You know I can't explain it. When these problems start, they always get worse, never better." I knew his answer before I even asked. I just wanted to hear the doctor confirm my belief that God had answered our prayers.

March 1973 came roaring into our lives as my young son, who was only a few days away from turning two, began to run a temperature. I made a late afternoon appointment with our pediatrician so that Jake could come home and stay with Katherine. I refused to take her into an office where there were a bunch of sick kids. Dr. Stein told me that chicken pox was going around and that Jay might be coming down with it. A sharp pain ripped through my entire body as I thought what this could mean for our daughter. I was instructed what I should look for and was a bit miffed that our doctor had not just given Jay an antibiotic to take care of whatever he might have.

Later that evening, after I had put the children to bed, I suddenly had a queasy, nagging feeling about my little boy. Jake had gone to a meeting, and I was home alone with the two children. I went into my son's bedroom and quietly reached over the rail of his crib. Immediately, I knew he was in trouble; he was blazing hot. I quickly grabbed the thermometer. His temperature spiked at 105 degrees as his body began to jerk; he was having convulsions. I went into total survival mode, and only in retrospect do I realize that God was giving me wisdom that I humanly did not possess. In fact, I had absolutely no experience in dealing with the events of the following twenty-four hours. I hastily undressed my baby boy and began to bath him alternately with cold water and alcohol. His fever came down to 102 degrees. Not knowing any better and waiting for signs of chicken pox, I put him back in his crib, praying and trusting in God's protection for my son. I shudder to think what would have happened if I had not looked in on my little son when I did, if I had just gone to bed, if I had not listened to God's voice within me. When I checked on Jay early the next morning, he was standing in his bed, talking. Although he was not yet two years old, Jay had already begun to say complete sentences. His hair was wet with perspiration, and I mistakenly thought that his fever had broken. When I gave him a sip of 7 Up, it came right back up. Instinctively, I knew that was not a good sign and took his temperature again. It was still 102 degrees. I called the doctor's office and was given another late afternoon appointment.

Throughout the day Jay would whimper and say, "Oh, my back hurts." I continued to offer him sips of 7 Up every fifteen minutes, which he managed to keep down, but I noticed that his diaper remained dry the entire day. A deep sense of dread, an uneasy knowing began to settle over me. Many times during the day, I shook my head disbelieving that anything could be seriously wrong with my son. But what I was feeling was all too familiar. Again, Jake came home early to stay with Katherine so that I could take Jay back to see his pediatrician. *Fear! Denial! Hope! Faith! They struggled within the abused adult/child who was physically and emotionally drained and just wanted all of this to go away. The survivor vowed to be strong. Her son needed her.*

When we arrived, the doctor's waiting room was full of mothers with small children. We were quickly ushered to an examination room where I was instructed to undress my young son. I held him close to me, not wanting to let him out of my arms. When Dr. Stein came into the room, he asked me to lay my hot child on the cold, paper-covered table. I stood close by as the doctor directed his attention to his sick patient. Jay was alarmingly lethargic, his chubby cheeks were bright red, and his clear, blue eyes appeared glassed over and dazed.

Our pediatrician placed a firm hand behind Jay's head and attempted to draw his chin downward to touch his chest. As fear and despair tore into my senses, I watched in numb disbelief. His neck was stiff. His head would not bend forward. I am sure our caring doctor held thoughts of my seriously ill child at home. He looked at me with gravity in his voice and said, "I think Jay has spinal meningitis."

I quickly demanded to know, "What is that?" I knew whatever it was, it could not be good. The concerned look in Dr. Stein's eyes said it all as he explained that it was a disease of the central nervous system. He did not hesitate to take control of the situation.

"Jay has deadly bacteria in his body, and you must get him to Children's Hospital immediately. Your son is critically ill, and you must not stop for anything. Call your husband and tell him to meet you at the hospital." Dr. Stein's nurse stayed with Jay as I rushed to use the office phone to call Jay's father.

When I returned to the exam room, my baby was dressed and waiting for me. He stretched out his longing, little arms toward me as he neatly tucked his bottom lip over his top lip. Quiet tears spilled down his flushed cheeks. I wanted to cry with him, but this grieving mother would not allow tears. It was so very obvious that my son felt dreadful and was frightfully sick.

I quickly gathered my precious little guy into my arms as he clung to his favorite blanket. I did not fully understand that I was about to drive down the Dallas North Tollway for the second time with a dying child . . . My mind has lost that space of time. I do not remember the long drive to the hospital.

The now-familiar sights and sounds of the hospital for sick and dying children swam around me as I tried to reason through the moment. I cradled Jay close to my chest—oh, so tightly—refusing to give in, refusing to hear and refusing to believe that my son could be taken from me. But I knew! Denial served no purpose! I knew that death was knocking on our door again and I pleaded, "No, God, please no!" I handed him over to the forever kind doctors and nurses. I was no longer ignorant to what they would do to him or what he would have to endure. Jake arrived. He had taken Katherine to his mother's house. The seconds dragged. The doctors returned. The news was not good. Once again, Dr. Stein's suspicions were confirmed. The deadly bacteria had gotten into Jay's bloodstream, and his spinal column was now completely clouded with the deadly killer. We were informed that a powerful, intravenous antibiotic was being administered to him. His condition was critical.

Dr. Stein, who had come to the hospital to check on Jay, was the one who gently, but honestly, gave us the total picture. "Jay may not live, but if he does live, he will be mentally and physically impaired. The bacteria will cause abscesses to form in the brain, which causes brain damage. We can hope the antibiotics will stop the progression of the bacteria and limit the damage it will cause." He went on to explain that if he had given Jay antibiotics the day before, they would have hidden his symptoms, and he would have died before we even knew what had happened.

For a moment I stopped breathing. I stopped hearing. I could not even pray. I would not, could not accept this doctor's proclamation. My mind raced with questions. How? Where? When? He never went anywhere! He had not been around anyone! How could this be? Again, there were no answers. I had locked up my emotions when I was told that my baby girl would not live. I would lock them up again for my little son. *Once again every skill the abused adult/child had learned for survival came to her aid in that dreadful hour, and she became very still. The survivor held on to her faith in God.*

When Jay was returned to us, his blonde hair was drenched with perspiration. His long, dark eyelashes were matted against closed eyes. He had fallen asleep from exhaustion. He sighed every few minutes, his body trembling with each short breath. I covered him to make sure he was warm, and I fretted because he had missed his supper. I examined the all-too-familiar patch on his head where they had shaved off a part of his light blonde hair. I was no longer amused by the Dixie cup that had been cut in half and taped to his skin to protect the needle that now penetrated his scalp. Once again, I familiarized myself with the machine that monitored, not the flow of rich red blood, but the flow of the powerful antibiotic that came from the plastic bag held high above my head by the icy, steel pole. Once again, pain from the past and strength for the present merged as one as I faced another long and perilous night of uncertainty. I stood over my son and prayed. Faith born in the heart of a child held fast. God's grace was sufficient.

The following morning I discovered that one of our little friends with leukemia was critically ill and also in the hospital. After making a quick visit with the young boy's parents, I made a phone call to a priest I had heard about. Father Neilson's church, of the same denomination as ours, held regular Friday night prayer and praise services. I had been told they had experienced many answers to prayer in these services, including miraculous healings. I told Father Neilson about our sick friend and asked if he would come to the hospital and pray for him. I then told him about Katherine and about the current crisis that we were in with Jay. Father Neilson did not waste any time getting to the hospital. He came straight to our room and said, "Let me pray for your son first." Our own priest had not visited us.

Jay's healing came softly as he slowly came back to us. His fever gradually declined, his color returned to normal, and he totally charmed his nurses with his ability to communicate at such a young age. Each time he was taken to the treatment room to make changes in his IV, and where yet another patch of blonde hair was shaved from his head, he would look at the attending nurse and, with big, blue tear-filled eyes, exclaim, "Oh no! Not more hair!" On the tenth day of his hospital stay, members of the hospital staff gathered around his bed to sing "Happy Birthday" and to present him with a birthday cake made especially for him on his second birthday. *The abused adult/child existed in a daze, refusing to feel and going through the motions of living. The survivor felt the peace that passes all understanding . . . somehow she knew her son was going to be okay. She remained strong in her faith.*

Dr. Stein, who knew of my faith in God, commented on my consistent calmness and told me that it was my excellent care of my son in those hours before taking him to the hospital that contributed to his recovery. I can take no glory, because I know it was God's strength and God's wisdom and not my own which had carried me and my precious son past death's dark door. Shortly thereafter, we returned home with a healthy, perfectly normal, rambunctious two year-old. There were no signs of physical or mental impairment, just a partially shaved head! It took me a while to realize the full impact of the illness that had almost taken my son's life, his intelligence and his physical capabilities. It also took me a while to realize the full impact of his miraculous recovery. When Jay was four years old, we had him tested. We were not surprised when the results revealed he was reading at the third-grade level because we were very much aware that our son was unusually gifted. *The survivor stood in awe with thanksgiving to God and His tender mercy toward her son and her family.*

We settled back into our routine, making the usual weekly trips to the lab for Katherine's blood work, followed by yucky medicine-day Tuesday. However, on one particular Tuesday morning, six weeks after bringing Jay home from the hospital, the still small voice within me spoke very clearly and firmly as I opened the cabinet door to retrieve the bottle of bitter pills, "Do not give her that medicine today." Because I was slowly becoming sensitive to God's voice, without hesitation, I took my hands away from the bottle I had started to pick up. I closed the door to the cabinet and walked away. I recall taking my emotions and disappearing into my place of refuge. I could not allow them to override my actions, even though I did not understand them. I had been tempted many times before to skip the medications that I literally hated giving to my daughter, but I had never reneged. On this particular day, even though I was haunted by the message, I would not question it.

The following day, Katherine began to run a low-grade temperature, and by late evening, she began to make a strange sound when she breathed. I slept with her that night, constantly waking to check on her. The familiar dread, the familiar numbness, the familiar denial began to run through my veins, again! As morning dawned, I quickly dressed, fed Jay, and made plans to get Katherine to the doctor. Without even knowing why, I grabbed a pillow on the way out the door and placed it between the seat and the car door. Once I had Katherine in the car, I propped her up against the pillow, tilted her head back, and belted her in. I was subconsciously trying to open her air passage in an attempt to help her breathe. *God's wisdom led the survivor. His mercy kept the abused adult/child from anticipating the unavoidable trial ahead of her.*

This time I did not even bother to call the doctor's office. We were on his doorstep when he arrived. His immediate reaction was in the form of a very stern reprimand, "Why didn't you call me last night?" I could not reply because I did not know why. My mind, my body, my emotions were void of any ability to reason. I could withstand no more, and for the first time, this doctor saw my tears. "It appears she has an infection of the epiglottis, and she will probably need a tracheotomy. This is a critical situation she is in. I want you to leave now. Don't stop for anything. I will call Children's Hospital and tell them you are on the way." *The abused adult/child did not want to hear these words again. She wanted to scream and take her child and run away to a place where pain did not exist. She did not want any part of this. She was so afraid. The wounded child felt anger brewing inside of her. The survivor was very quiet and subdued. It was much too much to take in.*

Dr. Stein quickly drew a picture for me explaining that the epiglottis is a flap that keeps food from entering the trachea. This flap had become inflamed and was swollen to the point of shutting off her air passage. This was very serious for a well child, but for Katherine it was deadly. Again, there are no human words to describe that moment in my life, but I would only allow that moment to last for just that, a moment. I called Jake and told him to meet me at the hospital. Again, I went into survivor mode. *The survivor had no choice but to shut down the emotions of her abused adult/child. There was no place in this moment for them. She was the survivor and she must take complete control or there would be no control. Her child needed her now more than ever before.*

In numb disbelief, I drove down the Dallas North Tollway, for the third time, with a child that would have died without immediate medical intervention. Every inch of my body was wrenched in pain. I was totally void of feelings. I would not allow myself to hear the dreadful lies that besieged me. I would not listen to them. I would not let go of my faith in God. I began to sing *Jesus loves me, this I know . . .* I was desperately trying to keep Katherine with me. I could not lose her! Not now!

I had been reading a book that my friend Lou Ann had given me to read. It was written by Merlin Carothers, called *Power in Praise*. Remembering his words, I simply said to God, "I don't know why this is happening. I don't know why my children keep suffering, but you have said to praise you in all things, so I praise you. I ask you to use this for our good and to your greater glory." I continued to sing to my precious, precious little girl as peace began to fill the space around us, keeping the ever-present darkness at bay.

In peace, I carried her into the emergency room. In peace, I handed her over to the doctors and nurses as glazed, pleading eyes looked after me. Once again, she was pulled away from her mother's protective arms. She had been through so much! She was so brave! She was so strong! She let go of me, and I had to let go of her. Her bewildered eyes forever imprinted in my mind, I could not bear to return her gaze. I turned away. Once again, God's grace was sufficient.

I was directed to go to the admitting office and then to the room that had been prepared for us. The doctors had confirmed Dr. Stein's diagnosis. Because of her weak immune system, and the cancer that threatened to eat away at her red blood cells, they were reluctant to perform surgery immediately.

The decision was made to give her a powerful intravenous antibiotic and to put her in an oxygen tent. It was the hope that the swelling would go down and the deadly bacteria would be defeated. I recalled the still, small voice that had spoken to me earlier in the week and confessed to Dr. Lon that I had not given Katherine her medications on Tuesday. He acknowledged that this had been a wise decision because had I given her the medicine, her immune system would have been totally wiped out. I don't even want to think about the consequences had I not listened to God's voice. I was in awe that He had spoken to me in such a direct and powerful way. The fact that I had listened and obeyed still astounds me. *How many other times had God spoken to the abused adult/child? How many times had the survivor failed to listen?*

The long vigil began as I watched the nurses get Katherine settled. This time I would not have to deal with the jail-like bars of a hospital crib. Katherine was put into a regular bed. It was not yet noon. This time I remained untouched by the hospital sounds coming from the halls—children crying, occasional giggles and sometimes eerie silence. I paid no attention to the needles and tubes. There was no Dixie cup this time. All of this had become our *normal*.

The part of me that was strong remained stoic. Faith remained intact, but that fragile, fragmented part of me plunged into unspeakable depths of despair as I watched over this little one. She looked so helpless and vulnerable in the large, plastic oxygen tent that encased her small body. She was no longer a baby. She was a little girl. She was three years old. I could not get close to her. I could not whisper in her ear to reassure her of my presence. I felt anger at the large tent that separated me from my child. She slept. I was thankful. *Typically, the abused adult/child displaced her anger, not looking at the real source that fueled it.*

I was surprised to see our young priest enter our room around noontime. He had never visited us before. I could not help but notice that there was more than genuine concern on his face. When he prayed for Katherine, he appeared overcome with emotion and quickly left the room. He had a little girl the same age as my daughter, and for the first time I realized that possibly he was putting himself in our shoes, and relating to the prospect of losing a child. I dismissed his quick exit as just being an emotional response, but I was later surprised to learn that he had actually called his secretary and told her to get on the phone and get as many people as possible to the church to pray for Katherine. He later explained, "I have seen the angel of death before, and I knew that Katherine was dying."

As a result of our priest's phone call, the unimaginable happened. A few hours later, close to fifty people gathered in the sanctuary of our church where they prayed for Katherine to be healed and for our family. Donations were collected to help us with our financial needs. It was about this same time, five o'clock in the afternoon, the doctors decided that she was not getting better. They feared having to do an emergency tracheotomy in the middle of the night. Surgery was scheduled for seven o'clock that evening.

It would seem impossible for this mother, whose life had been wracked with so much despairing anguish, to cope with yet another crisis. The human spirit can endure only so much before it finally snaps, and I had walked up to that precipice one time too many. But thankfully, God has given to all of us built-in mechanisms to help us cope with those unbelievable, outrageous, psychotic moments that life imposes upon us. For me, I had learned to hide in the unseen domain of depression, even sometimes tottering on the brink of suicide just to escape my circumstances. But always, miraculously, I was pulled along by an unseen, loving force that constantly beckoned me to hang on—to hang on with all my might—and not let go. For the past three years, I had not allowed my circumstances to be about me, and this moment could not be about me either. Mercy had placed a barrier between me and my child—my child who had fought so bravely and with so much dignity and will to survive. In this, my most insane moment of all, my faith was tested beyond my limits. I could only see my cherished treasure in the hands of my God, the arms of Jesus. Otherwise, I would have gone stark-raving mad. *The abused adult/child had survived a horrifying childhood and now she was watching as her own little girl struggled to survive her own nightmare. And though their circumstances were totally different—the illnesses, the treatments and the abandonment that her young child must have felt each time she was taken from her mother—all of it was perceived in the mind of the survivor as abusive. All of it was intrusive, and all of it was trespassing on her child's soul. She was forlorn. The survivor was stoic.*

I recall very little about the hours that followed except that my friend Esther called the hospital to tell me she had called the *700 Club*. She told them about our situation and asked them to pray for Katherine when the program began at seven o'clock that evening. I had never heard of the *700 Club*. She explained to me that it was a new Christian television program that had recently begun to air in the Dallas area. Esther enthusiastically continued, "They believe in the gifts of the Holy Spirit. The broadcast is live, so when people call in with their needs, they are prayed for immediately. Many people are experiencing miracles of physical healing and they pray in tongues." I knew we needed all the help we could get, and I was thankful for the prayers. I did not realize the true significance of my friend's phone call.

Shortly before seven o'clock, nurses arrived in our room once again to take my precious gift away from me. Too ill to speak, her hopelessly confused eyes filled with tears as they begged me not to let them take her away from me again. Katherine seldom cried. She seldom complained. The fear in my daughter's eyes glared back at me, pleading with me. I was powerless to keep her with me and powerless to stop them from taking her away. This had become her *normal*. I assured her that she would be okay and then I had to turn away—again—so that I would not have to watch her go. I clung to my husband as he wrapped his own grieving arms around me . . . When trials come, true love walks in. Life was calling on my young daughter to be like her mother, a survivor. *The adult abused/child, the precious child, the wounded child and the survivor quietly waited. Their facade removed, their masks exposed, they had nothing to hide. They lay prostrate before their God.*

As scheduled, the *700 Club* promptly began its nightly television program, and shortly thereafter, hundreds of people in our area and across the country joined the program's founder, Pat Robertson, as he prayed fervently for little Katherine. At the same time, the Lenten ritual of the Stations of the Cross began at our church. Intercession was offered for Katherine at each of the fourteen stations, which symbolize the steps of Jesus on the way to the cross. Others waited anxiously in Katherine's room with us.

The many blended prayers of faith opened Heaven's door as those of different denominations and different backgrounds came together as one in our dark, desperate hour of need. Almost exactly an hour later, the surgeon and the anesthesiologist appeared in our doorway, both men looking somewhat perplexed. My heart skipped a beat as I demanded to know what was wrong. One of them spoke, pausing between words, "Well . . . Katherine just suddenly got better . . . We have decided not to do the surgery . . . She is downstairs talking and playing with the nurses. We are going to watch her for a while and then we will bring her back to her room. We suggest that you hire a private duty nurse to spend the night in her room . . . just in case." One of the physicians later acknowledged that he had felt a divine presence in the operating room that night.

Although there was much rejoicing and praising God, I did not fully grasp what had just happened. At that point, I was too numb to feel or to think beyond the simple fact that my child was better and surgery had been canceled. Katherine was returned to us, understandably exhausted. She slept. An emergency tracheotomy kit was placed by her bed, and

I was introduced to a young doctor who appeared in our room every thirty minutes throughout the night. As early morning dawned, I told the doctor that she was better and that we all needed some rest. He looked at me and said, "Well, you are the mother, you should know." He said good night, and I did not see him again. Hours later, Katherine woke up talking. Her fever was gone, and the oxygen was removed. Still cautious, the doctors kept her for a few more days. She was okay! She had miraculously survived!

Throughout our five-day stay in the hospital, a woman, whom I assumed to be a doctor because of her white jacket and the stethoscope hanging from her neck, would periodically appear in our room. With her hands clasped behind her back, she would walk over to Kat's bed, look at her, turn and look at me, and then just walk out without saying a word. I thought it to be a very strange ritual. On the day that I was packing Katherine's things to take her home, this same woman waltzed into the room and proclaimed that I did not have a clue as to how sick my daughter was. I was so taken aback by her accusation that I just retorted, "Well, I guess that I do!" She glared at me and then turned and walked out of the room.

I thought I had missed a perfect opportunity to tell this woman about the grace and peace of God, but then I realized I really did not have to. She had witnessed it herself. Clearly she did not understand the calmness of this mother, but perhaps someday she would. Throughout that treacherous day when our Katherine's life had been hanging precariously on the edge of eternity, I had not been walking in depression or denial, but I had been walking by faith in that peace that surpasses all understanding, the peace of God. Already lives were being touched, as God had answered my simple prayer as I drove my daughter to the hospital five days earlier. It was a prayer of thanksgiving, petitioning God to use this deadly illness for our good and to His greater glory. His perfect plan for my daughter was set in motion. Her life and the life of her mother would touch many to the glory of God. *Life could never be—would never be—the same for the survivor, for her family.*

Chapter 19

It Is Not That You Have Been Waiting on Me—It Is That I Have Been Waiting on You

In the days that followed, I began to seek God in a new and different way. He had my attention, and I could not get enough of Him. Every spare moment found my nose stuck in my Bible as I sought to know my God. I could hardly stay off my knees. I was so thankful to Him for all that He had done. My husband was beginning to wonder about me.

One evening, shortly after our last crisis was over, Jake announced that he was going to visit his mother. I had not had an opportunity to watch the *700 Club* and quickly plotted to watch it while he was gone. I had bathed the children and was dressing them for bed in front of the television and had been only somewhat engaged in the program, until Pat Robertson began to pray. I stopped to listen. At that exact same moment, Jake walked back into the house. His mother had not been at home. He stopped, looked at Pat and then looked at me, and back at Pat again. God's perfect timing allowed both of us to hear Pat say, "There is a child who has had leukemia." He paused and then repeated, "There is a child who has had leukemia. Know that your child has been healed.—*pause*—Know that your child has been healed.—*pause*—The Lord has a message for you. God wants you to know, 'It is not that you have been waiting on Me; it is that I have been waiting on you.' I don't understand the message, but perhaps you will." *The survivor would spend a lifetime listening to God's message in her mind. The abused adult/child would spend a lifetime seeking to grasp fully its simple yet complex meaning.*

I knew, that I knew, that God was speaking to me through Pat—but this time, not just to me, but to Jake as well. It was not until that moment that I fully understood that Jesus, the One who heals, had truly given us the miracle that I had believed God for. That night in the operating room, not only had He miraculously stopped the pernicious infection that was threatening Katherine's life, but He had healed her from the deadly, insidious cancer as well. But the miracles for our daughter were not all that I came to grips with that evening. It finally sunk into my thick head that my precious little son had also been miraculously touched by the awesome, healing power of God through Jesus Christ. Jay's illness had come and gone so suddenly that I hardly had time to embrace fully what had happened. I gave God complete credit for my son's recovery, but I had failed to see it for the true miracle that it was. Bacterial spinal meningitis is an unrelenting killer of small children, a crippler of the mind and body. Once Jay was declared fully recovered, I had to move right back into life with Katherine, her illness and motherhood.

I received the message from Pat very calmly because, at the risk of sounding like a broken record, no human words can describe what I truly experienced that evening. I had been talking about a personal relationship with God through Jesus since I was just a young girl, but I don't think that I fully understood what that truly looked like. Throughout my life, God had gently revealed himself to me in many different ways, but His clear communication to me through Pat defies my ability to communicate the understanding of something that I myself can't even begin to comprehend. This Holy One, the Creator of all things, truly does care *personally* about His children. When we invite Him into our lives and seek His face, He honors our faith in Him. When we begin to listen to His voice and obey His precepts, He will work in ways that we cannot even think or imagine. And in those moments when we cannot pray, He listens to our hearts. His patience amazes me; if He can be patient with me, He will be patient with anyone.[1]

As a child, I had given God permission to work in my life when I believed in Jesus. He had been *waiting on me* for all of those years to listen and to obey. Honestly, I had been doing a lousy job on both accounts (and still, I often fall short). But when I attended the forgiveness retreat just months before, for the first time I heard the empowering message of forgiveness. I was given the opportunity to hear God's voice speaking to me through the Scriptures as He asked me to step out in faith and begin to walk in the power of forgiveness. That October day, I was only capable of taking a very small step in that direction. As it has turned out, that small step was truly just the beginning of understanding for me. But at that time, for my children, I believe it opened a pathway to God that set into motion the events that followed, the occurrences you have just read about. Had I turned away with a hard heart and refused to offer God a heart of forgiveness, I am not sure the outcome would have been the same. I believe that a hard heart toward God separates us from Him. He does not move away from us; we move away from Him.

Now, having said all of the above, I need to make it really clear that I don't believe we can put God in a box and expect to find a formula to fill our wish list. We are made uniquely different, and our lives are uniquely different. There is a unique purpose and plan for each of us. God had been *waiting on me* to follow the path He desired for me to

---

[1]   Ephesians 3: 16-21, "I pray that out of His glorious riches [to know God], He may strengthen you with power through His Spirit in your inner being, so that Christ may dwell in your hearts through faith. And I pray that you, being rooted and established in love, may have power, together with all the saints, to grasp how wide and long and high and deep is the love of Christ, and to know this love that surpasses knowledge, that you may be filled to the measure of all the fullness of God. Now to Him who is able to do immeasurably more than all we ask or imagine, according to His power that is at work within us, to Him be glory in the church and in Christ Jesus throughout all generations, forever and ever. Amen" (NIV).

follow. Your path will be different, but equally as rewarding when you fully understand that His love for you is personal. He desires to lead you into a deeper relationship with Him.

I also want to clarify that I honor and respect all of the sacraments and practices of God's Church, which I believe should not be limited by humans' interpretation of them. I believe that God honors faith, wherever faith in Christ is found, no matter how differently we may choose to celebrate that faith. Please do understand that I do not wish in any way to dishonor the many diverse observances of God's Church.

When Pat had finished praying, Jake silently left the room. I finished dressing my children, read them a story, tucked them into their beds and prayed with them. I paused to watch my beautiful miracles as they faded away into peaceful sleep. Pulling myself away from them, I walked to my bedroom where I slipped to my knees. My soul burst with thanksgiving and praise; I could not contain the joy, the gratitude, the humility I felt. *The survivor had chosen to trust her God, had chosen to walk in believing faith, had chosen to begin her walk down the path of forgiveness. The all-knowing, all-loving God had shown tender compassion and mercy toward His wounded, abused child. Out of His great love for His wounded child, He spared her the agony of losing her children. He knew that she could bear no more suffering. He knew her secrets.*

A few days after receiving the confirmation of my daughter's healings, I was on my knees praying. A vision of Katherine lying in her hospital bed suddenly appeared in my mind. I saw a circle of light around her bed, and I saw dark, black images trying to break through the light. At first I was startled, but then I began to realize that my eyes were being opened to see the spirit world around me. I was given understanding about the spiritual battle that had been fought over Katherine's life. Through this experience came the understanding that the dark, oppressive presence that had often threatened me was very real. At that time, I really did not understand about Satan and his demons. But I was beginning to realize, more than ever before, they are very real and not imaginary, make-believe beings. I had much to learn.

Daily, an insatiable hunger to know God dominated my every waking moment. My friend Dede gave me *Nine O'clock in the Morning*, a book written by Father Dennis Bennett. This book gave me understanding about words that I had recently been introduced to: charismatic, a second touch, baptism in the Holy Spirit, gifts of the Spirit and the fruits of the Spirit. Its sequel, *The Holy Spirit and You*, taught me about the preciousness of the work of God's Holy Spirit and the responsibility that comes with being committed to a relationship with God. Father Bennett wrote about the consequences of continuing to walk in sin and about the enemy of our soul. The book pointed out many things the Scriptures taught, that I had never heard before. I had so much to learn, and I sincerely sought to enter into a deeper walk with God. He definitely had my complete attention.

In the meantime, my friend Martha made arrangements for different ladies to sit with my children one morning a week so that I could get out of the house. Katherine still had seven months of treatment left. I had to fight the old resentments I had previously carried toward the church for not being there for me. We had been on this treadmill for almost three years. I would have deeply appreciated just a chance to go to the grocery store during the day, anything to give me an escape from the daily, never-ending routine of isolation and two small children. Additionally, it would have been so good for the children occasionally to see a face other than mine. I sincerely appreciated the offer, which I accepted, and I was truly thankful for my weekly daytime trips to buy groceries.

One day I received a call from one of the ladies who had signed up to sit with my children. She told me she was available all day the following Tuesday if there was something I needed to do. I thanked her for the offer and told her that I really didn't think I would need her all day, but would let her know. A few days later, Gaye called and told me that she and some friends were going to a prayer meeting in a small town several miles away. She wanted me to go with them. It just so happened the meeting was scheduled for the following Tuesday. God had already made arrangements for someone to keep my children.

The survivor did not know that another divine appointment had been planned for her.

The following Tuesday morning, a dozen eager and excited women piled into several different cars and headed south, across Dallas. None of us had a clue about what to expect, but we knew we were on a mission. An hour later, we walked into a large brick home where I met a group of women who possessed more joy in their little fingers than I had experienced in a lifetime. The family room was filled with energy and songs of praise. I wanted to possess such joy, and I wanted to experience the freedom that seemed to come with this joy. *For the abused adult/ child to express or even experience unadulterated joy was impossible. Her secrets held her joy captive.*

The woman in charge of the meeting appeared to be somewhat older and more mature than most of the ladies in the room. After getting everyone's attention, she spoke with confidence as she taught us from the Bible. My actual knowledge of the Scriptures at that time was extremely limited, and every word spoken was life-giving information to me. When she finished teaching, she turned to me and explained that she had heard about my daughter's illness and asked, "Have you received the baptism of the Holy Spirit?" I told her I had not, but that I wanted to. "Oh, honey, your baby needs for you to receive. The Holy Spirit prays in ways that we can't understand, and you need for the Holy Spirit to intercede for you. Will you let us pray for you?" When I nodded yes, this room full of women gathered around, laid their hands upon me, and began to pray in utterances that I had never before heard. I was in awe as these dedicated women prayed so fervently and with so much love. Even so, I stood before them like a stone statue, as though paralyzed. I knew that God had brought me there for a reason, and I sincerely wanted this special touch from Him. I wanted the evidence of speaking in the Heavenly language that I had been reading about. However, it quickly became clear to me, and to everyone else in the room, that something was hindering me from receiving this gift from God. I had read in the book *The Holy Spirit and You* that emotionally bound people often encounter this problem, and I certainly qualified as being emotionally bound. *No one in the room, not even her best friend, knew they were praying for an abused adult/child who guarded a pain-filled past, where shameful secrets kept her honor and purity shackled.*

Eventually the ladies stopped praying for me when they did not see the manifestation of speaking in an unknown tongue. They turned to my friend Gaye, who immediately received the gift of tongues, as did all of the other women who had come with me that day. As I stood by pensively watching, a young woman stepped up to me and said, "You came here today seeking, and God does not want you to go away empty-handed. Will you let me be God's vessel? Will you let me pray for you?" Without any kind of hype or exaggerated emotion, she softly touched the side of my face and quietly began to pray. And gently, ever so gently, I began to feel a release, a letting go of my will. Simultaneously, I lost all thought of myself as a sweet flow of energy swept through me. Just for an instant, I felt that I had moved away from the boundaries of this earth and was standing in the presence of Jesus, the One in whom I had put my faith and trust, the One who had carried me through the secret, inner hell in which I lived, the One who had healed my children.

It was then, for the first time, that I experienced worship for my God in a way that surpassed my own thoughts and my own understanding. It was as though I was suddenly looking through different eyes. Tears that never came easy begged for me to let go of the wounds of my soul. I was able to give God only a tiny crack into the window of my will, but that was all the Holy Spirit needed. My tears of restraint turned to tears of unspeakable joy, as words that I did not understand began to flow from deep within me. As certainly as this experience would prove to be invaluable to me, this moment would forever change the direction of my spiritual life. *Once again, the survivor thought about the forgiveness retreat she had recently attended, and she wondered . . . had God been waiting on her to give forgiveness to those in her family who had hurt her, so that she might receive forgiveness from God, so that she might in turn give back to Him all her worship of Him? Her road to recovery from the wounds of her soul had taken another step forward, but that road would prove to be very, very long.*

The book of Acts in the Bible talks about the experience of speaking in tongues. Jesus told His disciples that He must leave them so that the Holy Spirit could come to them. After His death and resurrection, the experience of speaking in tongues came to them along with a mighty outpouring of God's Spirit. The Holy Spirit came first to the disciples of Jesus and the Jewish nation and eventually to the Gentiles (all other people). There is much controversy about this "experience" being appropriate for modern times. Most Christian denominations teach that when people believe in and receive Jesus Christ into their lives, they also receive the Holy Spirit. That is what I believe, because you cannot separate one from the other. When you receive Jesus, you also receive the Holy Spirit; they are one. The controversy, it seems, is in saying that there is a separate experience where a person receives the Holy Spirit and it *must come* with the evidence of speaking in tongues. From my own experience of receiving this gift, I believe that when I came to a point of unrelenting seeking and total surrender, I was able to respond to the call of God and yield my complete will to Him. When this happened in that defining moment, I experienced a release of the Holy Spirit within me. At that time, He imparted an anointing of His power upon me. With it came the gift of speaking in a Heavenly language. Of course, that is just my interpretation of what I feel happened to me. Who am I to say how God works? He is obviously not limited by my simple understanding of Him.

I also believe that we are not limited to just one anointing, or second touch, or whatever you want to call it, by the Holy Spirit. I believe God empowers us for ministry, and also in our daily lives, many times and for different purposes. The New Testament in the Bible clearly reveals this to be true in the lives of the disciples, apostles and believers. As far as speaking in an unknown tongue is concerned, we are not puppets on strings, and God will not impose anything upon us that we do not ask of Him. I sought this precious and sacred gift that adds great value to my own personal prayer life. Sadly, this gift is misunderstood and sometimes abused by mortals. Consequently, many in the Body of Christ miss a blessing.

A few weeks after this experience, my sister's first husband, my brother-in-law, died from colon cancer. His illness had been long and filled with suffering. Before his death, he reached out to me for spiritual guidance, but I was incapable of reaching out to help him. *The abused adult/child struggled with simultaneous conflicting emotions. She had forgiven her abuser. However, she did not know that she continued to carry the painful emotions associated with the abuse: his shame, his guilt and the ever-present raging, suppressed anger that secretly taunted her. She was relieved that she would no longer have to worry about his being around her . . . or her children.*

Chapter 20

God Sees a Bigger Picture That I Cannot See

In the years that followed, we would say good-bye to almost all of the many young friends that had traveled down the atrocious road of cancer treatment with us. Many of their parents had the same faith in God that I had, but oh, the sting of death, how cruel it is. I often struggled with the impact of their deaths in relationship to the healings of my own children.

One such little friend was Cheryl, who was a few years older than Katherine. We went to the same lab on Mondays for blood work. Her mother and I were blessed to have each other to share our ups and downs over the disease that both of our daughters were trying so hard to survive. We became good friends, and I admired her so very much. She had miscarried several times before giving birth to Cheryl. During Cheryl's treatment, she had several additional miscarriages, finally carrying to term a little boy who was stillborn. The day Cheryl died her mother called me and pleaded with me to go see her daughter, our little friend. "She looks so peaceful!" We both knew the suffering that had preceded her death. Cheryl's mom had finally given birth to a healthy little boy just weeks before her daughter's death. Because we lived in the same community, we would occasionally run into each other. She never failed to ask me how Katherine was doing, always genuinely interested in her health. Through the tragic losses of her children, this amazing woman had greater faith in our God to let them go than I ever had to believe that mine would live. Her faith remained strong and eventually she was blessed with a whole houseful of healthy kids.

I will always be thankful to John, a teenager who also had the same type of cancer as Katherine. He became my daughter's mouthpiece. One day, he was listening to me tell his mother how frustrated I was because I could not get my toddler to eat. He quickly told me that when he came home from school, he would be starving, but just opening the refrigerator door and looking at food would make him throw up. It quickly dawned on me that food was probably doing the same thing to Katherine, but she did not know how to tell me. I stopped trying to force her to eat and instead, looked for things she would eat. Her main staples were Cheerios, milk, SpaghettiOs, scrambled eggs and diluted apple juice. John's mother bravely called me the day he died. I could not imagine the pain she felt, and I was grief-stricken for her. It was so very hard to say good-bye to John. He was such a really neat kid. His parents, who were also Christians, believed up to the end that he would beat this killer of children. My head knows that God sees a bigger picture that I cannot see, but my heart does not always understand. John did not finish high school before he went home to be with Jesus.

The little boy who was in the hospital when Jay had meningitis died that same year. He was very ill throughout his treatment, and his suffering seemed greater than any of the rest of the children I knew who had this awful disease. His parents had a very difficult time with Loren's death and, in fact, were very bitter. I think I felt greater sorrow for them than for anyone else who had lost a child.

The many faces from those difficult-to-explain years will always linger in my memory. At times the reality of so much suffering and so many young lives lost overshadowed the images of my faith. The sadness I felt for these parents would never leave me. However, the long drama of childhood cancer had been played out for us. The curtain was finally closing. The time had come for me and my family to move on. *The knowledge that her own daughter was going to survive when so many did not was a constant reminder of the survivor's need to give glory to God. The abused adult/child would never feel worthy.*

Christmas of 1973 was a turning point for our family. Initially, we had been told that our daughter would receive the latest chemotherapy treatment for no longer than two and a half years. In actuality, she had been on chemo for three years. Her delicate little body could only tolerate the powerful drugs for just so long because not only did they kill bad cells, they killed good cells as well. Therefore, the decision was made to take her off all medications in early December. I knew that she was going to be okay, and I was at perfect peace with the decision. Having our children alive and with us was the best gift of all. It was a very merry Christmas.

I was so thankful that we could finally all go to church together and be a normal family. My children could play outside with neighborhood children and have friends. I craved Christian fellowship, and I longed to be involved in a Bible study and a prayer group. The desire of my heart was to be used by God and to share my story. *But the abused adult/child did not realize that she was "not normal," and life would never be normal for her or for her family. There were too many things in her life that set her apart and made her different. Another journey was beginning . . . for the wounded child.*

*   *   *

Praying for the sick was understandably of utmost importance to me. God gave me the desire of my heart by giving me opportunities to minister to others through prayer. I often received phone calls from people who wanted me to pray for them or for someone they knew who was sick. Because of the miracles of my children, there were some who mistakenly thought I had the gift of healing, or some special connection to God. For a while I even believed it was true, but eventually, I had to learn that God loved me too much to leave me in a place of pride. I would be humbled to grasp that there is nothing any more special about me than anyone else. In time, I would understand that my greatest spiritual gifts are having empathy for those who are hurting and a faith/ trust in God to hear my prayers. However, in those early years after my children were healed, I reveled in being called upon to pray, especially when miracles were needed.

Late one evening I received a frantic phone call from a desperate wife. "Sandy told me to call you and to tell you to pray hard." I felt the burden of death heavily upon my shoulders. Her husband had terminal cancer. Sandy had been raised a "preacher's kid" but had chosen to leave the denomination of his youth to be confirmed in our church. He was considered to be a super intellect, was knowledgeable of the Scriptures and had been given the responsibility of conducting a class after church on Sunday. One Sunday morning, he declared that the Apostle Paul's *thorn in the flesh* was homosexuality, although there is nothing in the Scriptures to support this thinking. After the class ended, Sandy and two other men stood outside the classroom yelling at each other and shoving their doubled up fists into each other's faces. It was an awful sight and one that sent my already troubled-about-the-church spirit reeling. The two men who opposed him left our church that day and never returned.

Years later, when I visited Sandy in the hospital after he was diagnosed with cancer, he began to relate to me the pain he had carried all of those years over that ridiculous incident. I said to him, "Sandy, why are you telling me this? You should be telling those two men what you are feeling." The next day, he called the two men, and they both eagerly came to the hospital to see Sandy. Forgiveness was given, forgiveness was received and relationships were healed. Sandy was healed in Heaven the night his wife called in desperation for me to pray for him.

Several years later, I received a similar phone call from our most recent priest. His voice was serious, "Marcie has been taken to the hospital, and she asked me to call you. She wants to see you. It does not look good." I was getting ready for a retreat that I was leading, and I had only a few hours left to prepare. However, there was really no decision to be made. I would make the time to go see her. As I drove to the hospital,

I told God, "You keep sending me to people who are dying, and I go and pray in faith, and they die anyway. I just don't understand!"

When I entered her hospital room, Marcie was alone and appeared to be sleeping. It was in moments like this that I was truly thankful to God for giving me a prayer language. I did not know what God's will was for her, but the Holy Spirit did.[1] I quietly approached her cold, uninviting hospital bed. Marcie had lost a lot of weight since I had last seen her. Her head was wrapped in a brightly colored scarf, and I was sure she had lost all of her hair. I gently laid my hand upon her thin, frail arm. She stirred briefly. "Marcie, it is Nola, and I have come to pray for you." She whispered back to me, "Good, that is what I wanted you to do."

In the hush of yet another sterile hospital room, where death tapped on the door of one for whom I cared deeply, the same still voice that told me not to give Katherine her medicine on that fateful day, spoke to me again, "It's not about miraculous healings. It's about touching, loving and caring. It's about being there when called." I knew I did not have the gift of healing, but I did have the gift of faith to believe in my God who hears and answers prayers. Finally, I understood that it was not up to me to determine how He would respond to my prayers. My duty was to answer the Holy Spirit's call to go and to pray. Marcie's passing came much quicker and easier than the doctors had anticipated. *The survivor listened and was humbled to understand that the greatest miracle of all is finally to be in God's eternal presence.*

On another occasion, I was one of just a few women who were trusted to sit with a friend's teenage daughter who had cystic fibrosis. In her last days, the only way this sweet child could be comforted was by having someone sit behind her in her hospital bed with their arms wrapped about her body as she cradled a large pillow. As we held her,

---

[1] Romans 8:26-27, "In the same way, the Spirit helps us in our weakness. We do not know what we ought to pray for, but the Spirit himself intercedes for us with groans that words cannot express. And he who searches our hearts knows the mind of the Spirit, because the Spirit intercedes for the saints in accordance with God's will" (NIV).

we would gently rock back and forth with her for hours at a time. My prayers became one of freedom from suffering, for Christine. She was set free, healed for all eternity. *The survivor was beginning to understand that miracles come in many different packages.*

Only months before my youngest child was born, one of my very dearest friends, Jennifer, gave birth to a son who was quickly diagnosed with cystic fibrosis. Because of my own experience, I could understand her grief and her sorrow. And I could pray. Over the years I have watched Jennifer prevail with great dignity and grace. She extends an ever-present smile and a positive report to all who encounter her. She is a tower of strength and continually praises God in the midst of her family's struggles, grief and sorrow. For thirty-two years, Adam found reasons to smile and to embrace life to the fullest. He made those around him laugh, reached out in love to many people, and left this world a better place because he had been here. In spite of the long, difficult journey, in spite of her loss, she and her family never lost their faith in Jesus.

Why physical healing is given to some but not to everyone is a mystery to me. This dilemma has stretched my faith, and I think it probably stretches everyone's faith sooner or later. I had witnessed God's healing power through Christ, and there is no doubt about what I have seen Him do. However, after my children's miracles in 1973, I had to face my own health issues. I was attacked by horrible allergies. Recurring sinus infections resulted in the use of strong antibiotics and cortisone, which led to other complications. More than thirty years later, I am still plagued by allergy attacks, which now include a sensitivity to cleaning products, fragrances, certain foods and insect bites. I have consistently pleaded with God to heal me. His answer has consistently been no. *The survivor was learning humility, to be empathetic and to trust God in all things—perhaps to keep her balanced.*

However, I sincerely believe that I did have a personal experience with healing. In 1976, I was occasionally awakened during the night by an excruciating sharp pain in the top of my head. I would shoot straight up out of the bed and grab my head, as my heart almost raced out the front door. These episodes were very scary for me, and they continued for several months. I was concerned that I might have a brain tumor or an aneurysm. Jake was without a job, and we had no insurance, so I decided to go to a charity hospital in Dallas for tests. I am convinced that every person on the planet should, at least once, experience a charity hospital. It is a humbling experience that will teach you to be thankful for the problems you have and that patience can be a virtue.

It was during those long hours of patiently waiting to see a doctor that I met a wonderful old gentleman of color named Clayton. I will never forget this man of poor means who was rich in his faith and love for his Heavenly Father. We shared Jesus stories, and he promised to pray for me. Several nights after meeting Clayton, I think I must have had another episode within my head, but this time something happened that I can't fully explain. I awoke suddenly in the night and sat up in my bed thinking that I had been dreaming. I recalled that I had been ascending at a very rapid rate of speed. Suddenly I was stopped by a voice that said, "You can't come yet. You must go back." Then I felt myself descending, and that is when I woke up. There was no pain in my head, and my heart appeared to be very happy. I didn't know exactly what to think as I told Jake about it the next morning. I returned to the hospital for the scheduled brain scan and EEG. The test results proved that I did have a brain, but that was all. And I never had another one of those episodes.

I have often thought about Clayton and have wondered, "Did I have a dream or did I actually encounter the voice of God? Was my meeting this prayer warrior a divine appointment because in me, God had a life to redeem, a story to tell, a book to write?"

I have just one more story before moving on. Jake and I received a phone call from a friend who asked us to visit Pam, a young mother from East Texas who had leukemia. She was being treated in a Dallas hospital. Her husband's job prevented him from spending long hours in Dallas with his wife, and the grandparents were busy taking care of her very young children. They knew no one in the Dallas area. Pam, who was a very private person, had the sweetest countenance of anyone I had ever met. She was extremely ill and very scared, but solidly trusted her faith in God. She needed a friend who could understand what she was experiencing. I was honored that Pam allowed me to be there with her as she went through this dreadful journey. In retrospect, I believe God gave Pam to me, more so than He gave me to Pam. I was able to see firsthand some of the procedures that I had not been able to witness with Katherine.

One day doctors came into Pam's room to extract bone marrow from her hip. They asked me to leave the room, but I insisted on staying with her. She had been tearfully dreading the painful extraction, and I just could not bear to see her go through the procedure alone. The doctors relented, and I laid my head down on the bed beside Pam's head and gave her my hands to squeeze. I have never witnessed anyone endure so much pain. It was tough reality for me to realize that my own daughter had suffered this same unbearable anguish . . . without her mother's hands to hold. Pam eventually received a bone marrow transplant and has remained in remission. *By walking with Pam through her pain, the survivor finally allowed herself to grieve and to weep over her young daughter's own pain-filled journey, a journey which she was much too young to verbalize to her mother.*

There are so many names to recall, so many stories to tell. I am blessed to have had the privilege of carrying so many on the wings of prayer, with the understanding that God's mercy extends to everyone in different ways. Even though circumstances may be different from my own, when I am willing to let Him, He will use my sorrow, my pain, my empathy, my understanding and His love in me, all to reach out to others. The lessons I have learned from those who have shared their suffering with me have left their mark on my spirit and forever changed me. *The survivor was beginning to understand that God sees a bigger picture that she cannot see! He knows what she cannot know.*

Chapter 21

Meanwhile, Back at the Ranch . . .

"Meanwhile, back at the ranch . . ." means that I have just skipped through small segments of time from Christmas of 1973 forward. Now I want to go back and pick up my story there. I shared the stories in chapter 20, which actually occurred throughout the years I am about to take you through, because of the lessons I learned and because I wanted you to get to know the tender, caring side of me. It will be on this part of my life's canvas that you will further understand the dynamics of me—the wounded child, and me—the abused adult/ child, in relationship to the survivor who was *trying to do life* during the years just prior to my going into the hospital in 1990. As you will further discover, those years were filled with overpowering circumstances that almost destroyed me and my marriage.

Up until December 1973, my life had been anything but typical. No one can survive the things I survived, and subsequently be touched by miraculous supernatural acts of God, and not be profoundly affected. I had been changed in so many positive ways and truly did look through different eyes. There is, however, another side to every coin. It is only in retrospect that I realize how very vulnerable I was to the powers of darkness around me that joined the powers of the abuse that controlled me. My husband had no understanding about his responsibility to be the spiritual head of our family, and our church did not teach him otherwise.

We were totally clueless and powerless when it came to combating the powers of darkness of this world.[1]

In addition, there was still an abused child living inside me, and this wounded child was far from being healed from the wounds she was forced to bear. *Trying* to live a normal life in spite of the secrets of my troubled past that I tried so hard to deny—*trying* to rear children when I didn't have a clue how to rear children—*trying* to be a wife when I had no role model to follow—or even *trying* to have healthy relationships with people who walked in and out of my life—or even *trying* to be the Christian that I professed to be—were all monumental tasks for me. However, this was my life, and all that I knew to do was to continue on as before. I would wear my facade over my many masks, hold my head high, and trust in my God. I was a survivor, I was a wounded child, and I was an adult. My journey was far from over, and in many ways my battle to survive, to be restored, was just beginning when God gave us the miracles of our children in the early 1970s.

Once again, please understand that I truly struggle as I share the next seventeen years of my life with you. It is impossible for me to tell this part of my story on just a few pages. I hope you will hang in here with me because I cannot leave these word pictures off my life's canvas. If I did, it would be incomplete, and you would miss a valuable part of the abused adult/child's difficult journey that ultimately led her to

---

[1] Ephesians 6: 10-18, "Be strong in the Lord and in His mighty power. Put on the full armor of God so that you can stand against the devil's schemes. For our struggle is not against flesh and blood, but against the rulers, against the authorities, against the powers of this dark world and against the spiritual forces of evil in the heavenly realms. Therefore put on the full armor of God so that when the day of evil comes, you may be able to stand your ground and after you have done everything to stand, stand firm then with the belt of truth around your waist, the breastplate of righteousness in place, and with your feet fitted with the readiness that comes from the gospel of peace. Take up the shield of faith, to extinguish all the flaming arrows of the evil one. Take the helmet of salvation and the sword of the Spirit, which is the word of God. And pray in the Spirit on all occasions with all kinds of prayers and requests. With this in mind, be alert and always keep on praying for all the saints, God's children" (NIV).

freedom. So let's pick up our brushes once again and complete the work on our longest session of all.

* * *

By the end of 1973, I was understandably on such a spiritual high that I could not see the forest for the trees. I sincerely thought life would now be wonderful for me and my family. Everything would be perfect, we would have no more problems, and I would finally live the spiritual life for which I had always longed. Because I had seen how God was working in my life and was changing me, I expected that he was doing the same in Jake, his family, my family and the people in our church. All that I wanted to see or experience was the goodness of God and His love. I did not ever again want anything to come into my life that was going to burst this wonderful bubble in which I had found to live. But bubbles do burst, and you can't put your faith in a bubble. *Unrealistic expectations, foreboding, dark forces and secrets from the past would slowly begin to chip away at the survivor's newfound joy and peace. The abused adult/child was once again rendered powerless. The mask of the victim emerged.*

Ironically, just as I had unrealistic expectations of people in our church family, there were some in our church who had unrealistic expectations of me as well. I found myself placed on a strange pedestal. Occasionally, someone in our church would come up to me and say things like, "You have such great faith in God." "You are such a special person." "God must love you a lot." A young priest who had temporarily been helping out with our growing church approached me after one of the Sunday morning services and said, "I've been watching you, and there is something really special about you." And for a while, I even believed that I was special and chosen by God to do great things for him. I longed to be that spiritual person, but secretly I knew that I did not belong on anyone's pedestal. *The abused adult/child feared the pedestal because she knew sooner or later she would disappoint those who placed her there. The survivor would learn that pride does not fall gracefully.*

The wounded child was extremely fragile and wore her feelings on her shoulders.

People began to come into my life who wanted spiritual bits and pieces of me that honestly, I was not capable of giving to anyone. Subconsciously, I felt an obligation and a responsibility to live up to the reputation that had been molded for me. Consequently, the facade I wore had to become thicker.

Some in our church did not know what to do with my spirituality, and I sometimes felt consuming rejection. Our priest told me that I needed to sit on my enthusiasm, "It turns people off." I felt like a balloon that had been popped and deflated. I was devastated and crushed in my spirit by this judgment of me. After what God had done for my children, that anyone could even think that I should be less than enthusiastic about God was heartbreaking to me.

A lady in the church called me and accused the prayer group that I attended as just being an opportunity for gossip. I was shocked and hurt!

We began playing bridge with some other couples in our church. I considered these people to be friends, but once when I tried to explain to one of the ladies in the group that I suffered from depression, she quipped, "Well, we all think you are strange!" I played that mental tape every time that I was with that particular group of people, and I never felt safe around them again. *The abused adult/child was extremely sensitive and was incapable of handling unkindness. The least infraction would send her spiraling out of control. The survivor's greatest issue was trust. If someone hurt her, she would inwardly put up strong barriers to keep them out of her space, but the abused adult/child's lack of boundaries kept her going back for more unkindness. She rode in the roller coaster of ambivalence with rejection and acceptance, love and indifference, joy and sorrow, fear and faith, good and evil. The wounded child loathed being judged; criticism felt like poison in her veins.*

In very small ways I would occasionally try to explain to someone that I had childhood issues that had impacted me. My needs were always quickly dismissed, and I would often end up listening, sometimes for hours, to others' problems. One person even retorted, "You don't have any problems! Let me tell you what I've been through!" I recall retreating into my dark space as this person told me about the death of a sister. *The abused adult/child was always looking for someone to understand her. The survivor was a very good listener, but sometimes a resentful listener. The wounded child wore the mask of resentment. She took resentments and twisted them into self-pity.*

Although God enabled me to serve Him in many precious ways as I slowly grew in my relationship with Him, the unhealthy atmosphere in our church fed the depression that continued to suck the life out of me. Those unseen, midnight forces that wanted to hinder my testimony began slowly to steal my joy. Even though at times I would prove to be poorly equipped to handle the spiritual battles and adversities that whirled around me, my faith in God did not waver. He had proven Himself to me over and over, and I did not doubt Him. *The wounded child would falter as she collected additional wounds and held on to them. The abused adult/child would prevail upon her many masks to see her through. The survivor trusted her faithful God.*

Our new priest with his magnetic personality and his gift for public speaking brought a huge increase in the membership of our congregation. The miracles of our children had clearly impacted the spiritual tone of our church. There was more interest in Bible studies and prayer groups, and in 1975, our church became involved in an international renewal movement. The movement was designed for the purpose of bringing its people into a relationship with Christ through study and prayer. This resulted in the development of a community of brotherly love. Thus began an amazing spiritual awakening, which eventually developed into a three-day weekend event where lay people, with guidance from a priest, became the facilitators.

In 1975, the movement made its mark in the Dallas area. Jake and I were scheduled to attend the third renewal weekend held in our diocese. However, a ruptured artery in my nose and two trips to the emergency room prevented me from attending. Although I was very disappointed, it turned out to be a good thing for Jake to go without me because he needed his own space in which to grow. At the end of those three days, a changed man returned to me confessing, "I always knew about Jesus, but I did not know that I could have a personal relationship with him." For the first time in our married life, I began to understand why my husband, his family and many people in his church looked at me as though I had three eyes, green skin and a horn in the middle of my forehead when I started talking about having a personal relationship with Jesus Christ.

Every decision concerning Jake's spiritual life had been made for him from the time he was born. He did what was expected of him, but he was never taught to study the Scriptures or that God had come to earth in the person of Jesus for the forgiveness of his sins, the redemption of his soul and the gift of eternal life. He did not know that he had to personally make the decision to invite Jesus to be involved in his life. Jake had never been told that he had to be *born again*. The Scriptures tell us that understanding is the beginning of wisdom. Godly wisdom comes to us when we accept, by faith, the truths that God gives to us in His Word, the Bible. The renewal experience opened Jake's eyes to these truths, which he did not know, even though he had been going to church regularly since he was born, thirty-one years before.

I could hardly wait until I was able to attend one of the weekend events. Two months later I made the trek, along with a few other people from our church, to the familiar retreat center. The Friday night session began in the beautiful chapel where its walls had finally been erected. Its finished altar, now surrounded by glass, looked out at the clear, star-filled night. I wondered again at what strange fate kept drawing me back to this sacred place where I had found so much joy on a horse with a friend. The chapel was eerily silent as forty or so people gathered for the Friday night session. I sat among mostly strangers as the powerful thirty minute meditation began to fill the serene space around us. I could hardly breathe as the impact of its message reached out to a roomful of spiritually hungry souls, including my own. It was the most spiritually convicting thing I had heard in my adult life. Its closing words brought everyone in the chapel to the foot of the cross, to the crucified Jesus . . .

The meditation walked us through the life of the Messiah, Jesus. He had been unjustly accused, sentenced and finally handed over to be crucified. He had gone through the agony of the cross, and the agony of conquering death, a death that we cannot comprehend or understand. Some of his friends came to the tomb to prepare his body for burial. They wrapped him in a white shroud, laid him in the tomb and removed the wedge that held the heavy stone. The stone rolled forward and sealed the tomb. The meditation reflected these thoughts:[2]

> As cold and empty and silent as the tomb has been my heart . . . it has been locked up in my sin, and I have refused to open my heart to the quiet knocking of the love of Christ. I have chosen to be dead to His love and dead to life. Oh Christ, strike down the door of my unwillingness to know you. Dissolve my stubbornness. Call me forth from the tomb of my sin, and bring me to new life in you. While on earth you never mentioned your agony, your death, and your burial . . . without mentioning your resurrection into the glorious presence of your Father God. And you have promised that for me too, if only I would believe in you, if only I would take up the cross and follow you. This is your mystery, Lord Jesus—the mystery that you are now holding out to me. The mystery you want to share with me if I will follow in faith, hope and love. I accept by faith, Lord, that you are the Way, the Truth and the Life. I trust by faith in your love for me because you proved it on the cross, and I trust that you are God made flesh who offers me redemption from the sting of sin and death.
>
> I desire to begin to walk on this road of love to you, Lord, and I want to give to you the only thing that is truly mine to give you, and that is the total gift of myself . . . my will . . . given in love received from you. I understand that this road I choose may not be easy and I am not brave. I ask you humbly to be with

---

[2] Taken from *The Way of the Cross* by Virginia F. Randall, Ph.D

me on this road to you. I ask you to please carry me to my final
destination . . . to the dawn of resurrection . . .

As the meditation came to a close, many found they could not
control their tears, and quiet sobs echoed around the Spirit-filled chapel.
No one could speak. No one wanted to speak. Silence was welcomed.
We were asked not to talk to each other until we gathered for breakfast
the following morning. For many, it was a long night of wrestling with
God.

Big round tables had been set up in the spacious commons
room, with the huge rock fireplace. We were given permanent seating
assignments. This room became the heart and center of the weekend.
We gathered early Saturday morning to hear lay people give previously
assigned structured talks that allowed space for them to interject their
own personal experiences. By the end of the first day, we had entered into
a mystical realm that is difficult to describe. A spirit of commonality and
community immersed the room and tugged at our hearts. Unconditional
love began to fill us with a peace that can be akin only to a human
perception of what Heaven must be like. We were unaware of the
hundreds of people who had been praying for us long before and now
throughout our weekend. By Sunday, no one wanted to leave. *The abused
adult/child feared going back into a world where its challenges could
steal away the love that Jesus had once again poured into her wounded
spirit. The survivor did not want to leave this place of peace and safety.
The wounded child was begging to be noticed.*

Jake attended the final closing communion service on Sunday
afternoon. When we arrived back into the city, we went directly to a
welcome back party hosted by those who had previously attended one of
the renewal weekends. I was greeted with a bottle of wine, laughter and
a woman who pulled me aside to tell me all about her marital problems.
My expectation was to be embraced by the same love that I had felt over
the weekend with everyone eager to talk about and praise God, but that
did not happen. It was just another party where doors were held open for
the powers of darkness to steal the joy of the Lord. *The abused adult/*

child stuffed her disappointment. The survivor did not understand. The wounded child tasted their anger.

Along with many in our church, we became more and more involved in the renewal movement. To put on one of those weekend events required lots of preparation, time and effort. I learned to play the guitar so that I could play in the monthly Sunday morning folk masses and other renewal related gatherings. We both became licensed lay readers and chalice bearers, which meant that one or both of us were serving at the altar on Sunday morning. Jake regularly served at the altar at the monthly "renewal" closing service. We both went through training so that we could serve on staff and participate as leaders during the "renewal" weekends. Jake absolutely thrived in the leadership role he was asked to assume. I was given the opportunity to do what I most wanted to do, and that was to give talks that allowed me to share my faith and tell what miraculous things God had done for my children. We attended as often as they would allow us. *The abused adult/child was unknowingly seeking self-worth and approval. The survivor walked in spiritual pride. The wounded child tried to be happy but failed miserably.*

But not all was well. Initially, people were allowed to bring their own bottles of liquor to the "renewal" weekend. I had begrudgingly resigned myself to the acceptable practice of drinking within this church/denomination. However, the first time we served as part of the staff for the weekend, the designated lay leader walked around with a glass of scotch in his hand the entire three days. He would have ruined the weekend completely except for divine intervention. I could not be silent. Before the weekend was over, I went to the priest in charge and expressed my objections. God used my voice to promote change. After that, the use of alcohol was limited to wine which was served only at the Saturday night celebration. *The abused adult/child had learned at a very early age that she had no voice. The survivor was learning to speak out and wore the mask of courage. The wounded child was waving a huge red flag and wore the mask of unhappiness.*

My enchantment with priests completely waned over time. On one occasion, when Jake and I were serving as part of the staff during a "renewal" weekend, the priest assigned to the table I was to facilitate seemed determined to bring disorder into the whole experience. From the word go, his language was disruptive and his actions were inappropriate. I was totally disgusted by this man's demeanor, but by God's grace, I managed to interact with him in such a way that by the end of the weekend he came to me and said, "I think you are one of the few people I know whose baptism actually took!" I was so shocked that I could not even embrace the remark as a compliment. Instead, I shook my head in sadness because his declaration painted a thousand pictures about the heart condition of the church/denomination and the people in it.

Intertwined with the *many* good things that had resulted from the renewal experience within our church were rumblings of discontentment, divisiveness and eventually immorality. Worst of all, our children began to take second place in our lives. Any parent who was actively involved in the movement had neglected children at home. It seemed that we were always going somewhere and doing something, but instead of finding sustaining satisfaction, I began to find frustration. And although spiritual growth was happening in our church as a result of the renewal experience, the after-meetings and weekly gatherings continued to become another excuse to have a party. Wine flowed freely, hugs became too friendly and affairs happened. To make matters worse, the people in our church who did not participate in the renewal movement began to resent those who were involved. The secretiveness, the meetings, the close relationships—all became sources of contention and division. I was often approached with complaints. What I saw happening within our church was beyond my understanding. Unknown to those around me, the depression that consumed me pushed me deeper and deeper into its black pit. I felt that I did not fit in. I did not want to be there. I would often go home from these meetings filled with anger and crying. I did not like what being involved was doing to me and my family. Eventually, I chose to back away. No one understood my unhappiness, especially my husband.

Something that had been created to bring glory to God became a tool of the dark forces in this world, because humans allowed the darkness to enter into their personal space. In time, those powers of darkness won, and the renewal movement in our church died. *The survivor grieved and was confused and struggled as she juggled her many masks behind the facade she wore. The abused adult/child's constant conflict with ambivalence was maddening. She hated what she witnessed within the church . . . she loved the Church. The wounded child connected the actions of a few to the whole—condemning them all.*

Chapter 22

Connecting All the Dots—the Church,
the Abuse, the Enemy of My Soul, and Jesus

It was during our involvement with the renewal movement in our church that Jake felt a call to become a priest. I supported his decision completely. Our priest was ecstatic. Along with about eight other men and their wives, we were asked to attend a long weekend meeting where Jake's *call* would be analyzed. We would both be evaluated. These evaluations were done by other priests within the diocese, who would then report their observations back to the bishop. The bishop would then decide if there was a true call to the priesthood or not. From the very beginning, I had reservations about this process. I did not feel that any human had the right to judge a person's call to ministry. *The abused adult/child unrealistically perceived that if her husband was a priest they could change things.*

February in Texas is often the coldest month of the winter season. As we pulled our car into the retreat center parking lot, the brisk wind whistled its chilling song around us. And once again, I wondered about the strange irony that kept calling me back to this beautiful, peaceful place. I had not been feeling well, and once inside the building, I was delighted to see the huge, rock fireplace in the commons room offering the comfort of warmth to my chilled, aching body. I quickly claimed the chair closest to the roaring fire and nestled in for the first session. My husband, being warmer by nature, could be found at the opposite end of the room. I claimed the same spot for most subsequent sessions.

On Saturday morning, we were assigned to small groups in which we would participate throughout the weekend. Husbands and wives were separated. Almost immediately, I began to get bad vibes from the priests who were interviewing my small group. When we broke for lunch, I mentioned my feelings to Jake. He was having the same uncomfortable feelings. By nature he is not inclined to be as sensitive to intuition as I am.

One priest in particular caught my attention when we first arrived. He was tall, solidly slender with styled dark hair, dark skin and very macho in demeanor. He smoked constantly. For some reason, I had been apprehensive about being in a meeting with him. When it came time for him to interview my group, he had everyone sit on the floor in a circle. He began asking each of us a series of questions, expecting each of us to give him an answer. One of those questions was, "What do you expect out of a priest?" When it came my time to respond, I simply said, "I expect a priest to be led by the Holy Spirit." This man, whose black attire and white collar should have defined him as godly, banged his fist on the floor, swore at me and made a negative remark about the Holy Spirit (which I won't repeat). The men and women who sat on the floor around me wrenched at his actions. I am sure that my mouth dropped open as my personal space around me turned black. *The abused adult/child, once again, refused to stay where she felt unsafe. Her hiding place waited for her. This time, the survivor went with her, right along with the wounded child.*

During each break, Jake and I would compare notes and express our bewilderment to each other. We kept asking each other, "What is going on here?"

Our very last interviews on Sunday evening were one-on-one. The priest who interviewed me was extremely nice and seemed gentle in spirit. "I see that you grew up in the Pentecostal Church." I am sure that my mouth fell open, again. When I explained to him that I did not grow up in any church, he showed me the form that our priest had filled out. Suddenly, it was all very clear to me and I knew why this group of men had been so rude to me and my husband. They thought that I was one of those "holy rollers" who was ecstatic in worship, babbled senselessly and also handled snakes! They had judged me and, consequently, my husband as well. These priests had sentenced us as unsuitable before we had even started the process. I was bewildered and just could not understand why some people were so judgmental when it came to any mention of the Holy Spirit.

Not only was the misinformation a factor, but this group of men also decided that because we did not sit together, we really didn't like each other. In addition, they had issues concerning the healings of our children and *my* open enthusiasm for God. It was totally and completely a bad experience for both of us, but for Jake it was especially disappointing. Neither of us could wait for Sunday night to arrive so that we could get away from this peaceful place which was turned uncharacteristically hostile by some of the men who did not appear to have brought love with them.

Jake had developed a personal relationship with the bishop of our diocese. He felt no hesitation in calling the bishop's office early Monday morning to request a meeting. We immediately received an invitation to meet with this powerful leader, who listened intently as we presented our case to him. It was during this meeting that we learned that the priests who interviewed us were randomly picked. Those selected to interview were primarily whoever was available for the weekend. In other words, the men who were judging our suitability for service were not necessarily men who were qualified to make lifelong decisions for anyone. We were most grateful when the bishop recommended that we attend another evaluation weekend in a different diocese. We later learned that our voices helped to make needed positive changes in the interviewing process.

Within several months, we attended another weekend. The tone and the atmosphere were totally different from our first encounter. We respected those who interviewed us and were able to accept their recommendation. They were concerned that Jake felt a need to repay

God for healing his children. Additionally, they either wisely understood or foolishly assumed that all engineers are not always personable. Engineers are, however, great administrators and organizers. They gently suggested Jake needed a little more time before making a final decision. Jake told me they also had a problem with my enthusiasm. I just didn't get it! I didn't understand why everyone wasn't enthusiastic about God.

When we told our priest that Jake had again been denied entrance into the seminary, we were reprimanded, "Well you've just ruined my record [for yearly sending someone to seminary from my congregation]!" There was no consoling, no love, no sympathy, no concern expressed for what Jake was feeling. Neither of us really understood the call that Jake sincerely felt. Perhaps God was testing Jake's obedience to follow His voice. Or perhaps God was calling Jake into a deeper relationship with Him or perhaps teaching Jake to trust. Nevertheless, Jake did not pursue the priesthood again. In hindsight, it appears to have been the best decision in the long run. God understood what we did not understand. *Neither the abused adult/child nor the marriage could have survived if Jake had become a priest, at that time, in that particular denomination. The survivor had to pretend that all was well. She had to keep their secrets locked away; no one could ever know about them . . . because she was not worthy to be the wife of a minister.*

I struggled deeply and continued to be troubled as I witnessed the move of God's Holy Spirit being quenched. Like the renewal movement, the charismatic movement was a topic of controversy, and I know, I was as well. I was labeled as one of *those people* who was too fundamental, too far reaching in my beliefs and *too extreme* about God. Since miracle healings were often directly associated with the Pentecostal/Charismatic persuasion, there were even times when I actually thought that the people around me could have come to terms with my children's deaths easier than their miracles. I was cruelly asked how I could justify my children being healed while others were not. I was once asked what I had done to bring all of *this* upon my children. I often felt a general unkindness toward me, and I felt so misunderstood. People talked and gossiped—people judged. People still do. *The abused adult/child rebelled in inappropriate ways and often expressed her frustration in anger to those around her. The survivor was having a difficult time keeping her facade a secret. Sometimes she didn't know which mask to wear.*

The fact is I was never outspoken about my charismatic experience. I did not broach the subject unless someone asked me about it first. I didn't raise my hands in church and I certainly did not use my prayer language in public or flaunt it in any way. Nevertheless, I kept getting approached by people on both sides of the fence about the charismatic experience. All of the negative comments that were made to me about the "spiritual gift" nibbled away at my peace. I just did not understand what the problem was and I continued to be baffled by so much controversy. I began to feel a need to defend the Holy Spirit. *The abused adult/child did not understand that the Holy Spirit did not need her to defend Him. She took everything personally.*

I longed to be in a charismatic church, but God never opened those doors for me. In retrospect, I believe that is because He wanted me to find and walk in spiritual balance. Eventually, when I became serious about studying the Bible, I realized that this same controversy existed in the early Church. Even then, the Christians were encouraged to seek balance and unity. To stay in balance, we must keep our eyes upon the *Giver* of the gifts of the Spirit and not on the gifts themselves. When the gifts become more important than the Holy Spirit, we get out of balance.

There was, however, a remnant of people within the walls of our church who sincerely desired a deeper walk with God and began to embrace the charismatic movement. Occasionally, some of us would caravan over to Father Neilson's church on Friday night to attend the non-denominational prayer and praise service he led. Remember, he is the priest who came to the hospital to pray for my son when he was so ill. Jake and I were approached by some of these folks about having a weekly evening prayer meeting. By this time, I was close to being thirty-six years old and had been pleasantly surprised by the arrival of a third child into our family. Katherine was nine, Jay was seven, and Kim was one year old. Since no one else in the group had small children, we decided to meet at our house on Monday nights. Before Sandy's death from cancer (see chapter 20), he introduced me to his friend and co-worker Drew, who spent a lot of time ministering to Sandy through the Scriptures and prayer. It occurred to me that he would be a great facilitator for our group, so I contacted him about leading our meetings. Drew accepted our request and spent the next several years devoted to teaching us God's precepts.

We all agreed that it would be wise to tell our priest about our plans, so I made an appointment to see him in his office. In spite of the issues I previously had concerning this young man, it was difficult not to like him. He possessed a charisma of his own that caused you to want to overlook his shortcomings. I honestly believe he was sincere about his faith in Jesus Christ and his desire to serve God.

When I told the priest about our plans to host a weekly prayer group in our home, it was apparent to me that he was not exactly happy about the news. The issue of speaking in tongues came up, and he shared with me some of his own negative experiences surrounding the issue. Ultimately, I think he was afraid that bringing the charismatic movement into the church would bring further division and controversy to his congregation.

As our conversation unfolded, the priest remarked that speaking in tongues was the least of the gifts. I responded with, "But what is so small about any gift that comes from God?" He just stared at me and did not respond because he knew what I said was true. After all, what is so small about any gift that comes from the hand of God? It finally dawned on me that it was the speaking in tongues with which people had a problem and not the Holy Spirit. The gift of tongues is another gift from God like faith, healing, spiritual wisdom and knowledge are gifts. The twelfth chapter of 1 Corinthians in the Bible tells us this is so. Unfortunately, well intentioned people, probably on both sides of this controversy, were often turning God's heavenly language into something other than what He intended for it to be. Many centuries later, we mere mortals are still making an issue out of praying in the language of the Holy Spirit, which was given to us as a way to intercede with God's understanding and not our own. Do I understand it? No, but it is not my job to understand the mind of God or His plans for us. He has clearly shown me that He works in many different ways and has many different gifts for different people at different times. His blessings and His love for His creation are forever diverse and boundlessly unlimited. God never changes, and clearly He is still pouring out His Spirit upon those who desire to know Him. For me personally, it is a humble blessing and a very personal encounter that connects me with the all powerful love of God.

I was constantly tormented by lack of understanding as to why people could not comprehend that God is not limited by our limitations or why people want to turn Him into who they want Him to be instead of letting Him be who He is. Having given humans freedom of choice, He will not impose His will upon anyone, but promised that if we seek Him, we will find Him.[1]

I left the meeting with our priest feeling bewildered. Nothing else was ever said to my face about our group, but unkind remarks occasionally traveled back to my ears. A local newspaper magazine wrote a story about the healing of our children. The article mentioned the *700 Club* and our church. One day, the church secretary briskly quipped, "That article made us sound like a bunch of holy rollers." I never ceased to be shocked by the unkindness of the people with whom I worshiped. That statement was so far from the truth. The magazine simply told of our journey and the power of faith and prayer. *The abused adult/child's hurts continued to multiply and burrowed deeper as she tried to hide the anger and the inner turmoil of her wounded child, who could not accept others' opinions. Her mind magnified criticism. The survivor held her head high.*

It was also during this time that several significant things happened to me. One day, I had gone to the church to work on a project. I was standing at a long table with several other ladies when out of nowhere I

---

[1]   Acts 17:27-28, "For God did this so that men would seek him and perhaps reach out to Him and find Him, though He is not far from each one of us. For in Him we live and move and have our being. As some have said, 'We are His offspring'" (NIV).

felt someone literally pat me on the bottom. The horror of the moment is indescribable with words. When I turned around, I saw a priest passing behind me. When our eyes met, he just laughed and said, "I couldn't resist myself." He disappeared around the corner as I stammered for something to say to hide my humiliation.

I was enraged and confused because I did not understand why men felt they had a right to own me, to use me for their personal amusement. I was not a raving beauty! I was attractive in my own way, but I did not exude sexuality. In fact, I ran from it. So, why did these kinds of things keep happening to me? This was not a new reality for me. *The abused adult/child had learned to deny her disgust for men's unwanted attention. She could not face the reality of truth. Denial never let go of its grip on her. She continually heaped one more insult upon another, causing the wounds of her wounded child to fester. They were raw to the touch by the world around her. Being the constant victim of others was literally making the survivor physically ill . . . she cried out to God, continually . . .*

When Jake got home that evening, I told him what had happened. Sobbing my heart out, I pleaded, "Why do men keep coming on to me, Jake? I did nothing. What is wrong with me?" In spite of my walk with God, I had always felt that there was some controlling force, a veiled darkness that tormented me. I was convinced that *something* out of my control had drawn this man, whom I really believed to be sincere about his faith and not a bad person, to make this shameful, abusive act toward me. Drew had just been teaching our prayer group about Jesus' ministry concerning demonic influences that roam the earth. He had mentioned that he knew a man named Steven who had a ministry that dealt with this subject. Jake agreed that perhaps we should seek Steven's counsel. The call was made, and an appointment was set for us to meet at our house.

I had no idea what to expect from our visit with Steven and his wife. I recall feeling very subdued as we discussed what this priest had done and the humiliation and guilt I felt. I also admitted to them that I had often felt a dark presence around me. They asked permission to pray for me. Jake, Drew, Steven and his wife laid their hands upon my shoulders. Almost immediately, we all sensed a resisting presence. I physically felt this dark presence closing in on me. The more intense the prayer became, the stronger the force became. My mind could not reason what was happening. I felt oppression and fear and even sick at my stomach. I told everyone what I was experiencing, and they all confirmed to me that they too felt the oppression. I was confident that Steven knew what he was doing when he discerned that a *whoring* spirit was tormenting me. He explained that the evil spirit was not defining me as such, but that it had attached itself to me through some means and was causing men to be physically attracted to me. I immediately thought of all of the sexual predators who had put their despicable evil upon me. Then I thought about the perverse pornography that I had been exposed to as a child and that I had been involved in as an adult. I was certain that he was probably correct, even though I did not understand it. Neither Steven nor Drew knew anything about my secret past.

Intense prayer continued until, for some reason, Drew stepped back and said, "It's getting late, and nothing is happening. I think we should stop." The unwelcome presence received a reprieve and seemed to have backed away. Somehow I knew that it was not gone. I was completely drained and overwhelmed. Fear does not come close to defining what I felt. Drew and the others left our house, and as the front door closed behind them, my concerned husband took me in his arms and tried to comfort me. "Jake, what am I going to do? You felt it too. This is real. This evil thing is in some way hanging on to me or hanging around me." He had no answers for me, but as always, I had his unconditional love. *Panic such as she had never experienced before gripped the abused adult/child. Terror consumed the survivor as the wounded child disappeared faster than ever before.*

After a long, sleepless night, I put on my facade and went on with life—breakfast and lunches prepared, kids to school, Jake out the door, Kim and I off to work. I was the Director of our church's Mothers' Day Out and preschool program and I had to be there. *The survivor of child abuse was very responsible and very capable of rising to meet most any demand placed upon her—no matter what the cost to her, personally, might be. But the abused adult/child felt no peace.*

I put on my sweet and friendly demeanor and proceeded to gather my teachers for prayer, greeted parents and kids, conducted the chapel service, collected tuition and smiled as though I did not have a care in the world. This was the story of my life—the mask of deception I wore. I could never let anyone know that I was dying on the inside while living life on the outside. At the end of the school day, I could not wait to pick up Kim from the nursery and get home. I quickly put her down for a nap. I had serious business to confront.

I went into our living room and fell on my knees before God and prayed as I had never prayed before in my life. I had read many accounts in the Bible where Jesus took authority over demons, and before His death He gave this same power and authority to His disciples who cast out demons in His name.[2] I reasoned that because I had the Holy Spirit of God living within me, surely I possessed this same power to overcome this tormenting spirit. I stepped out in faith and commanded the *whoring* spirit to leave me in the name of Jesus. Immediately, I felt the power of God rising within me as I commanded the evil spirit to be bound and to return to the pit of hell and never to return to me again. Instantly, I physically felt the ominous presence flee from me. I can explain it no better than that. Exhausted, I fell asleep. When I woke up, I knew that I had been set free from the bondage of this evil, tormenting spirit . . . whatever it was. Time confirmed that men were absolutely no longer being inappropriately attracted to me, except for one time many, many years later when I was inappropriately approached by a man that was in our square dance club. The incident terrified me and I could not even

---

[2]   Luke 9:1, "When Jesus called the 12 disciples together he gave them power and authority to drive out all demons." Acts 5:12, [After Jesus' resurrection and after they received the Holy Spirit] "The apostles performed many miraculous signs and wonders." Acts 5:16, "Crowds gathered also from the towns around Jerusalem bringing their sick and those tormented by evil spirits and all of them were healed" (NIV).

tell Jake about it for days afterward. However, the Holy Spirit quickly gave me peace and revealed to me that I was not the problem. Very soon thereafter, the man in question was no longer a part of our lives and I have never been threatened by anyone again.

This part of my story is shocking, even to me as I tell it. No doubt it will bring about lively discussions. It certainly did within my own family when my now grown children helped with the editing of this book. To think that something so evil can somehow be lurking around me is a terrifying thought. I sometimes think that if we could see the spirit world around us, we would all be terrified. I don't understand why it is so, but the Scriptures clearly teach that Satan and his demons have been given permission to roam over this earth. They can torment, tempt and oppress believers in Christ. However, they cannot possess the soul of a true Christ-follower. We are warned to put on the whole armor of God so that we can stand against the evil darts of the enemy.[3]

In retrospect, as I think about my own experience, I can't help but believe this spirit clearly manifested itself when there were men around me who were susceptible to its wicked temptation. Perhaps at other times, it was there to torment me and tempt me. Perhaps, it drew me into and kept me in bondage to pornography. I don't really know. But Dear Reader, think about it. How many times in this book have I written that ever since I was a little girl I had felt a dark presence around me? As an innocent child, I had been captured, held against my will and innocently drawn into others' evil. I sincerely believe that was the avenue by which this spirit entered into my life. Because of circumstances beyond my control, I had unknowingly continued to invite that evil to have a foothold in my life by allowing the effects of the sexual abuse and the pornography to control me.

---

[3] Ephesians 6:10-12, "Put on the whole armor of God so that you can take your stand against the devil's schemes. For our struggle is not against flesh and blood, but against the rulers, against the authorities, against the powers of this dark world and against the spiritual forces of evil in the heavenly realm" (NIV).

As a Christian, I had not been taught; therefore I did not understand the seriousness of my choices. Not only does pornography invite those dark forces into our lives, there are many other avenues by which we invite evil into our lives. It can happen when we have surrendered our control to addictions such as alcohol, drugs or sex. It was not until I finally understood the truth about these things that I was set free. Hear me when I ask you to understand completely that I am not one to look for a demon under every rock or behind every bush, but please know who the enemy of your soul is. Above all else, know that the name of Jesus has all power over this enemy. Conviction by the Holy Spirit moved me to repentance and turned me away from the sins of my flesh.

It is very important for you to understand that this dark presence is not to be confused with the all consuming darkness of depression that compounded my issues and in many ways was just as deadly to the abused adult/child. They were not the same.

Shortly thereafter, I attended a prayer and praise service at Father Neilson's church where he spoke about demonic influences and the need to renounce any and all involvement dealing with the occult. When he gave an invitation to come forward to be prayed for, I felt compelled to respond. As I knelt at the altar, Father Neilson placed his hands upon my head, prayed, and then prompted me to verbally renounce any previous involvement I had, from a long list that he reported to me. That list included horoscopes, fortune tellers, Ouija boards *and* pornography. As soon as I made the proper repudiations, I knew that I was totally set free from the powerful addiction pornography had over me.

Our quiet, unassuming group continued to meet for several years. I have often wondered how anyone could have found fault with us just because we embraced Jesus through the work of the Holy Spirit. The needs within this small body of believers were many as God's Holy Spirit ministered through us, to each other. We all needed and invited His sweet, gentle, loving presence to be with us. We were all strengthened in our faith. While some came in and out of our meetings to praise, worship, and to hear Drew teach, there was a core to the group that remained consistently faithful in attendance. Among those was Jonathan, a wonderful man of color who had been shot during a robbery. He was wheelchair bound. His love for God was reflected in his enormously contagious smile. Every Sunday morning he would sneak a piece of chewing gum to our young Kim and then just laugh like a little kid. He spent his nights at home alone connected to the *700 Club,* taking phone calls from desperate people who needed someone to pray for them or just to listen. He died during my six-week stay in the hospital. He was truly a great prayer warrior, a man of faith and my true friend. I still miss Jonathan.

One of the women in our group suffered with terminal cancer while another grieved over a troubled son who would eventually take his own life. The son's grieving widow followed in her young husband's footsteps by taking her life as well. One of our dearest friends would die unexpectedly in his early forties with a brain aneurysm. It was not common knowledge that there were actually three abused adult/children in our group who were searching for inner healing. There was also one couple in our prayer group whose marriage ended in divorce because of an affair. Eventually, I came to understand that life is about the choices we make, and also that Christians are not exempt from sin or the trials of this world. My own story bears witness to this truth, just as my story bears witness to the redemption Jesus offers to us and the strength He gives us to walk through the uncertainties of life. Miracles do come in many different packages. *The survivor was beginning to learn the difference between judging, discerning and unconditional love. The abused adult/child had a long way to go before she would finally put it all together.*

As surely as summer follows spring and fall follows summer, winter will follow them all. Our young priest had enjoyed great seasons of success. He had increased the number of baptized members to around 1,500, or approximately 700 families. Additionally, he had built a large new sanctuary, a new office building with classrooms and social space. He was successful in sending a number of men from his flock to seminary (minus one). But those seasons that had been very good to him fell hard into the dark days of his winter, when he was caught having an affair with a woman in our church. His youth, his inexperience and his vulnerability to the unseen dark forces around him ultimately became his downfall. Strong winds of despair and disbelief carried the dead leaves of his actions to many who had put this man up on a very high pedestal. For others who, like me, had discerned the darkness within our walls of worship, enough was enough. The unhealthy atmosphere in our church led yet another group of my brothers and sisters in Christ to leave, and once again, I felt so alone. I pleaded for my husband to do likewise, but he would not leave. Jake's roots were too deep.

Turmoil and division roamed the forlorn premises of our church as the search for a new priest began. In the meantime, I continued to build the Mothers' Day Out program. When I became the Director, it was mostly a child care program and struggled financially. Prayer, commitment, love for moms and kids, a desire to serve God, plus organizational and bookkeeping skills culminated in turning the program into much more. I raised money to buy preschool furniture, went before the city to change zoning requirements and worked very hard to meet all the state guidelines, which resulted in acquiring a license to operate a preschool. I hired degreed teachers, even at the nursery age level, attended training workshops with my teachers, extended the number of days we were open and published a monthly newsletter. It was a place where I could share Jesus with children.

I met with my teachers before class each morning for prayer and added a weekly chapel service for the older children. One of my favorite memories connected with the chapel service happened one year during Lent, just before Easter. I took an apple into the service and began by telling the children that God is like an apple. Showing them the apple, I explained that the apple has three parts, and each part has a different purpose. I cut the apple in half to reveal the flesh and the core. I pointed out to them that the apple has the pretty, red outside peeling, which protects the apple, the yummy, sweet inside part which gives nourishment, and the core which holds the apple together and produces more seeds to make more apples. I sliced the apple into several parts and asked them how many apples I had in my hand. Curious, wide eyes watched as I folded the apple back into place. "One apple!" they exclaimed. They were correct. No matter how you cut up an apple, it is still just one apple.

It was the perfect example to teach those young children how the Father, the Son and the Holy Spirit is always One, but with different purposes. The Holy Spirit is like the beautiful outer peeling—He is our teacher, comforter and protector. Jesus resembles the sweet stuff—He is our nourishment, our Savior, and our Redeemer. The Father represents the core—He holds everything together; He is our God and Creator. Little Adam, who was only four years old and suffered with cystic fibrosis (I told you about him earlier), went home that day and told his mom that he understood all about God. I loved my job!

The Mothers' Day Out/preschool program ministered not only to children in our own congregation but to the community as well. New families joined our church as a direct result of the program that I ran, with God's immeasurable help. It also ministered to me. It was a wonderful healing experience, and I loved every aspect of it. *The survivor found great joy in sharing her faith, especially with children. She was a good teacher/communicator and very capable of being a leader. The abused adult/child and the wounded child tried to behave themselves.*

There always seemed to be a silent *however* to all my happy, positive experiences when it came to my involvement in our church. Things began to change when I needed to put a chain-link fence around the playground. A man in our church recommended someone to do the work for me. Since he was a building contractor himself, I had no reason to question his recommendation. The young man that I hired foolishly poured the concrete all around the perimeter, and tried to set all of the steel fence poles up at one time. It was a mess to say the least, and I refused to pay him. He, in turn, threatened to sue the church. I paid the man to avoid a lawsuit, and he attempted to mend his mistakes. The fence was functional, just not very pretty. From that point on, everything I did was challenged, and the joy of the position began to ebb away. *The abused adult/child could not get away from falling into the victim role where she often found herself. She wanted to run away. The survivor began to stumble.*

At the end of the school year, I was approached by one of the school board members about getting an early childhood development degree. The church was even willing to pay my tuition. I was actually excited and grateful for the offer, but I expressed my concern about taking on any additional responsibility until my youngest child was in school. I told the board member that I would prefer to wait until Kim was in kindergarten before taking any classes. Just before the fall session began, I received a call summoning me to the church. The school board had held a meeting without my knowledge. Although I received a great pat on the back and a raise in salary, I was told that if I did not acquire a certain number of hours toward my continuing education by the end of May, I just might not have a job. I was offended that I had not been included in the discussion. I was also offended that my request for a delay until Kim was in school had not been considered. I really don't know why this particular incident sent me so far over the edge. Perhaps it was just the straw that broke the camel's back. Suddenly, the suicidal depression that I had fought since my childhood began to overpower me completely. *The abused adult/child did not know that the depression was a very large symptom of many underlying problems. It was so easy just to give into its power, and she did.*

Several weeks after this meeting took place, the school session began. One day during the school hours, a recently ordained priest, who had been working at our church as a trainee, stopped me in a hallway and said, "I want to tell you something. When I graduated from seminary, someone gave me a sweatshirt with an inscription in Latin on the front. It said, 'Don't let the b******* get you down." He then put his hands squarely on both of my shoulders, looked me straight in the eyes, and sternly evoked, "Don't let the b******* around here get you down. You are doing a great job!" We talked for a while, and I thanked him for his encouragement and support. But it was already too late. My emotional downward spiral had already begun. Ultimately, the powers of darkness at work within my church did get me down. *God always managed to encourage the survivor in unexpected ways, just when she wanted to give up. The abused adult/child was drowning and wanted to give up. Once again, the wounded child wanted to die.*

I continued the school year as usual, but I refused to enroll in the continuing education classes. Being a good mother was the most important thing in the world to me. To put my family through the stress of my working and going to school was not an option for me, even if it meant that I would lose my job.

The demon of suicidal depression that had methodically built a haunted house within my mind, where monsters lived solely to destroy this child of God, once again began to tell me that I did not want to live. I was going to die. And I needed to get my affairs in order. I told Jake to put his guns where I could not get to them. He traveled extensively and was often away from home. I feared what I might do in a moment of complete despair, because I could not find a way out of the indescribable abyss I had slipped into. *Suicidal depression cannot be trusted under any circumstances, especially for an abused adult/child who is indefensible and subject to attack. She cannot control her thoughts like a normal person. The wounded child was slowly dying. She could see only the negatives in her life. They canceled all of the positives in her life. The survivor held on for all of them.*

Fortunately, I had gotten my husband's attention. One morning, Jake pulled me to the side of our bed, and for the first time in our marriage, he knelt with me and desperately called out to God for help. Apparently, Jake told his mother about my state of mind because several days later she called and told me that I needed to come to her house and get an article she had just read. Dr. Truss, a doctor who lived in Alabama, had written a book called *The Yeast Connection* that discussed the harmful effects of taking antibiotics, which can result in an overgrowth of yeast in the intestinal tract.[4] One of the side effects is depression. I called the phone number mentioned in the article and discovered that there was a doctor who could treat me only three blocks from where I lived. I called immediately and took the next available appointment.

---

[4]   For additional information go to www.knowthecause.com and listen to Doug Kaufman. He has done amazing research on fungus/yeast and the human body. He has a daily program that you can view online as well as valuable resources.

I was eager to hear what this doctor had to say, and I clung to his every word. He shared parts of his professional journey with me. He, like Dr. Truss, had become frustrated with the medical profession's use of medicine and the inability to help people get well. He explained to me the vicious cycle that can result when antibiotics promote an overgrowth of yeast in the intestinal tract, consequently destroying all the good bacteria needed to keep us healthy. Unaware of the deadly condition developing within us, we add sugar and other simple carbohydrates for yeast to feast on. He told me to imagine what warm water and yeast does when added to white flour and sugar—it rapidly multiplies and grows. If left unchecked, the same thing happens in the intestinal tract. Over time, the yeast will crowd out the good bacteria that are there to fight harmful bacterial infections and viruses that invade our bodies. In addition, he explained that where there is an overgrowth, the yeast gives off toxins that will cycle throughout the body, causing a breakdown in the immune system. Fatigue, moodiness, depression, mental confusion, poor concentration, poor digestion, bloating, gas, poor nutritional absorption and overall poor health can result. The doctor was describing many physical symptoms I had struggled with for most of my adult life.

Since there was not a specific test that could tell us if the condition existed, I would be treated based upon my history. I reported to the doctor that during my twelfth year, both my tonsils and my appendix were removed, and I had also been in the hospital with the flu. It was the norm to give anyone who went into the hospital penicillin shots every three to four hours around the clock. Later on, I also had a history of taking birth control pills, which only exacerbated my problem. Candida, a female related yeast infection, had been a constant problem for me. Since yeast needs warm, moist places in which to grow, it made perfect sense that yeast could also become out of control in the intestines.

The doctor asked me about my diet. As I began to tell him about it, I watched a deep furrow form between this man's eyes. He actually looked perplexed as I told him I had been raised on southern fried chicken, fried steak, fried potatoes, fried okra, biscuits, gravy, peach cobbler and vegetables that were doused with bacon grease and cooked until limp.

As an adult, I added to my wonderful diet a daily sugar-filled Dr Pepper. Of course, I fed my growing family accordingly. The doctor politely, but sternly, told me those foods would have to go. I don't think he had been raised in Texas! When I told my husband about my change in diet, he humorously asked, "Why live, if you can't eat all those things?" I had turned my northern-raised husband, who had never eaten a fried steak before we married, into a true Southerner!

I was given a prescription for an antifungal drug called nystatin and was instructed that I would begin by taking a few tablets each day and gradually increase the dosage. The process of killing off the yeast can make you feel bad, and it is best to approach it slowly. I was instructed to eliminate all processed white foods and to eat a high-protein diet with mostly fresh, green vegetables and nut meats. That meant no sugar, white flour, potatoes, no fruit, no juice, no dairy products and absolutely no fried foods! He gave me a list of supplements to purchase, including acidophilus to restore the good bacteria. And then, he sent me to a lab for blood work to determine the nutritional levels in my body.

Two weeks after I began the doctor's regimen, the deep suicidal urges miraculously disappeared. I felt like a different person, and for the first time in my life, I did not feel that I had cobwebs in my brain. Getting the overgrowth of yeast in my body under control and changing my diet literally saved my life. We have long been a society that lives on antibiotics and cortisone. It is now believed by some that many illnesses are yeast related, including chronic sinusitis, bronchial conditions and even some cancers. Antibiotics are given to children and adults as if they were candy, and no one can deny that juvenile and adult suicides are epidemic in this country. I cannot help but wonder if many illnesses and these senseless deaths are often fueled by this condition. While many doctors are beginning to take precautions and advise their patients when prescribing antibiotics, there are still many who do not believe in this diagnosis. The Internet now has a lot of information about the effects of yeast in the body. *When the depths of suicidal depression were lifted, new life emerged for the survivor. It was another step toward recovery for the abused adult/child.*

Once again God had shown mercy to me, His wounded child. I will always be thankful for my husband's desperate prayer, his unconditional love and the important awareness that was given to me. Those deep suicidal tendencies have never returned since I was treated for this overgrowth of yeast. However, this was not the end of my depression, and in some ways, it was a Band-Aid that temporarily covered up the oppressive emotional and mental pain that seemed would never, ever go away.

In the meantime, our church hired a new priest, the school season progressed into the autumn months, and the opening of hunting season began. Jake had become obsessed with hunting. The children and I had learned to live with his frequent absence while he and other men from our church indulged their new pastime. Occasionally, he would take one of our kids with him. On one such occasion, when he came home from a hunting trip, I sensed that something was wrong and was puzzled by his advances toward me. In all of the years that Jake and I had been married, he had never been sexually aggressive toward me. His understanding and patience have always been his gift of love to me.

Several weekends later, we were at a social gathering when one of the hunters' wives asked if I knew that the senior warden of our vestry had driven his motor home to the hunting camp and had shown X-rated movies on his VCR. Unaware of the bomb that she was setting off inside of me, she jokingly began to describe the sex orgies that our husbands had watched. Jake, who was a member of the vestry, was in earshot of the conversation. He turned and looked at me. When our eyes met, I saw red and literally shouted, "Where was my son?" My husband came to my side and assured me that he was in bed asleep. "And where was Joe?" Again, I was assured that Jay's friend was in bed asleep. I shook my head fearing the answer to my next question. "And where was Phil?" By now the blood had drained from Jake's face. He said nothing. "Don't tell me that you allowed a sixteen year old . . ." My voice trailed off, and I disappeared into one of my dark hiding places. I was beyond angry, and I honestly do not know what I did or what I said after that moment. These were men who were supposed to be leaders and some who regularly read the Scriptures and helped serve communion on Sunday. I had already been made aware of men in our church who had boasted about watching pornography with their wives and sometimes with each other. I had no right to judge them because of my own previous history and lack of understanding, but this was where I had to draw the line. This was inexcusable and intolerable. I would not be silent. *The survivor's rage could not be contained. The abused child grieved for innocent children who depended on adults to protect them. The wounded child lost all control.*

The following Monday morning, I received a phone call from one of the church secretaries who was a trustworthy friend. She told me that the priest was going around telling everyone that I was emotionally and mentally disturbed. I could only imagine what the senior warden had told him about me. If being mentally disturbed meant speaking out against so-called leaders in the church who were exposing children to pornography, then so be it!

I already had a reputation to live up to; I was the complainer, the troublemaker, the one who could not keep silent when I saw the ever-present darkness working in the church, wounding God's children, when injustices were done. There was always a price to pay for my inconsistent personality, but I was powerless to control who I was. There was a raging war inside of me that I did not understand, and unfortunately, those around me did not understand it either.

The abused adult/child wanted to fight, and she did. The survivor did whatever she had to do to survive. The wounded child, as usual, acted out her hurts.

I could not be silent when a priest came to speak to the congregation about stewardship and spewed swear words all over the congregation during his presentation. I voiced my objection of this man's inappropriate language to our priest and to the office of the bishop. I also wrote a letter to the guilty priest. No one even bothered to respond to me. When a young woman hired by the church to oversee adult education came to my house and fell into my arms sobbing because the senior warden, in the presence of our priest, verbally chopped her into little pieces over a small incident, I was not silent. I felt she had been targeted because she was "charismatic." When the men's group gathered monthly, year after year after year, to drink beer and play poker at the church, I constantly protested. At every church related event, alcohol flowed much too freely. I could not control my anger and made no excuses for it. When a girl in the youth group was molested by a boy in the youth group, I confronted the parent. I was ignored. When my children came home from Sunday school telling me they were told it didn't matter *who* they believed in, Jesus or Buddha, I raged. When a shaman was brought into the church and told the adult congregation the same thing, I really lost it. Worst of all, often when I heard people in the church talk about my children's miracles or any answer to prayer, I seldom heard God, and certainly not Jesus, get the glory. Instead I most often heard, "Look at how great *we* are! Look at what happens when *we* pray!" It was a place that appeared to glorify itself. *The survivor wanted God to get all of the glory. The wounded child seethed as she found fault and judged.*

When friends of mine in our church became involved in a suspicious "religious" movement, I attended a weekend event so that I could try to understand what they were involved in. I was shocked at the mind control, manipulation and spiritual deception that I witnessed. The leader was a priest who was mixing New Age thinking that embraced Eastern religious teachings with his own brand of Christianity. I felt an ominous presence throughout the weekend. Once these extremely long sessions began, no one was allowed to leave the room or to speak to anyone without permission. No one was allowed to eat or drink anything or even go to the bathroom without getting permission. People were drilled unmercifully and humiliated into submission until they agreed with what the leader wanted them to believe or accept. If someone openly disagreed with the leader, degrading responses followed. Participants were openly questioned about their sex lives. I witnessed this large room full of people submitting to this man as though he had cast a spell upon them. By the end of the weekend, they would do anything he told them to do. It was all very strange and very unnerving for me. I could hardly wait to leave and had the very clear impression that I should have nothing further to do with this organization. At the end of the last session, I approached the leader and began to ask him questions because I really wanted to understand why and how a priest could justify making life all about *us* instead of making life about developing a relationship with God. Life is not about what we can do for ourselves, but how God's redemptive love restores us. I will never forget the look in this man's eyes. He had no answers for the questions I asked of him and quickly ended the encounter by inviting me to come to Houston for an interview—if I really wanted to talk to him.

I am sure he thought he had put an end to me, and I am sure he was rather shocked when I actually appeared on his doorstep a week later. God-cidently, while I was meeting with this leader/priest, he received a phone call from a man whose wife had just committed suicide. This couple, in their mid thirties, had been to the same weekend event that I had attended, and I knew them through a mutual friend. I am sure the caller was seeking direction, comfort and even sympathy from this man who had, just one week earlier, appeared to be someone who cared about him and his wife. However, there was no love or compassion extended to this grief-stricken husband. All that this leader could say to him was that it was a *life-changing event*, and he just had to deal with it. I was stunned by this priest's cold and hard-hearted response. The more time I spent talking to him, the more confusion and pain I discerned within him. I could see it in his eyes and the expression on his face. Very suddenly, I felt the need just to get out of his office as quickly as possible. I excused myself and left, not being sure of what was accomplished by my visit. I felt great sadness for this man, this priest, who appeared ill-equipped to help another human being face the tragic death of a spouse or the ensuing, unbearable grief. I did not understand how this could be. The deceptions taught to others, in turn, failed the one who taught the deceptions.

I felt compelled to express my concerns to my friends who were involved in the movement. I talked to our priest about the weekend event and my concern about people in his congregation who were being drawn into its grip. My words fell on deaf ears. If the leaders in our

Christian churches do not teach and warn their congregations about the snares and traps of the enemy of our souls, if they do not warn them to be watchful and to pray for discernment, if they do not teach them how to be grounded in God's Word, then those under their leadership will be easily swayed and deceived. The Old Testament in the Bible clearly reveals that God warned the Israelites not to have anything to do with *other* religions. They did not listen; and the consequences of their disobedience resulted in a continual, vicious cycle of destruction to the nation, separation from God, repentance and restoration.[5]

I discovered that many of those involved in this movement were Christians, and many also belonged to the same denomination as Jake and I. And by the way, the man whose wife took her life shortly thereafter also took his own life. But it didn't really matter because it was just another *life-changing event.* Or so we were led to believe. I do not feel the weekend training seminar caused the woman to take her life, but I feel it added fuel to her existing problems. She was one of the women with whom the leader had openly interacted several times, and I recall being embarrassed for her at the time.

Yes, I suppose I did allow all of these things to drive me somewhat crazy. Considering the childhood issues that no one knew about and that I did not even understand myself, I guess I didn't have far to go! My preconceived ideas about Christians being perfect had turned into

---

[5]   Jesus warns us in Matthew 7:15-16, "Watch out for false prophets. They come to you in sheep's clothing, but inwardly they are ferocious wolves." 1 John 4:1-3, "Do not believe every spirit, but test the spirits to see whether they are from God, because many false prophets have gone out into the world. This is how you can recognize the Spirit of God: Every spirit that acknowledges that Jesus Christ has come in the flesh is from God, but every spirit that does not acknowledge Jesus is not from God." 2 Peter 2:1-3, "But there were also false prophets among the people, just as there will be false teachers among you. They will secretly introduce destructive heresies, even denying the sovereign Lord. Many will follow their shameful ways and will bring the way of truth into dispute. In their greed these teachers will exploit you with stories they have made up. Their condemnation has long been hanging over them and their destruction has not been sleeping" (NIV).

disappointment and despair. I had desperately needed for something in my world to be surefooted, and when I found the church not to be so, *I* assumed the job of trying to make it perfect. I had not understood that it was not *my* job to change lives, but God's. Even so, I could never accept the carnal behavior exhibited within the church my family attended. What I had witnessed over the years was sacrilegious—irreverent to that which should be held as sacred, and I could not keep silent. And now this, while on a hunting trip a child was exposed to pornography by leaders of the church. What was I supposed to do now? *The survivor could not be silent when it came to defending others or her faith. But the wounded child found it impossible to speak out for herself.*

The church secretary's phone call concerning our priest's opinion about my mental state received a very different response from past experiences. The darkness of suicidal depression was not controlling me; I was emotionally and spiritually in a good place. I was seeing things very clearly, and I really did not care what anyone thought about me. I had seen what pornography does to children at the hands of a pedophile who will use porn to entice children to accept their advances as normal. I knew firsthand just how vulnerable a child's mind is and that those first sexual triggers will be the very thing that he/she keeps going back to for sexual pleasure. I knew that young souls become entrapped in the grip of the images they see and that innocence cannot discern or process the right or wrong of it all. I knew that pornography is like a drug or alcohol. You cannot "un-see" what you have seen. Once it gets into your mind, you can't get it out, and it takes more and more to satisfy the need for it. I knew the evil that lies therein, the demonic power that dances with pornography. The natural beauty of sex is vulnerably courted and swayed and twirled around and around to the music of pornography's deception. All the while, it entices possible rapists, murderers and abusers of children and women into the dance of death—death of mind, body and soul. Pornography invites unsuspecting, innocent men, women and children to be its partners. Worst of all, it distorts human perception of God and hides His face from view. My reaction, no matter how crazy it may have appeared, was completely justified.

The course of time had moved us into the early 1980s when I finally found the courage to remove myself and my children from a situation that was obviously spiritually and emotionally unhealthy for them and for me. When I told one of the school board members that I was resigning from the Mothers' Day Out/preschool program, her response was an ugly expletive. I simply turned and walked away. Eventually, this very successful program dissolved because those who had personal agendas wanted to control it instead of letting God guide their decisions. The powers of darkness prevailed. The priest, like his predecessor, was later dismissed because he, too, had an affair with a woman in the church. The senior warden's wife divorced him (he was the one who had exposed the teenager to porn at the deer camp), and he left the church as well.

Even before I became a parent, the desire of my heart was to have my children in a church where the precepts of God were solidly taught. I wanted them to have a strong spiritual foundation on which they could firmly stand throughout their lives. Alcoholism ran in their veins from both sides of their family, and I never wanted them casually to slip into its grip. They would soon be teenagers. I would no longer allow them to stay in this church where alcohol and pornography had a hold on many of its members and where so much darkness prevailed. We would attend a different church, even if it meant no longer following my husband. *The abused adult/child was hyper-vigilant. She was constantly on the lookout for danger, especially concerning her children. The wounded child could not feel big feelings for herself; she shut those down.*

From the very beginning of parenthood, I had felt so totally unprepared to guide my children spiritually. Surprisingly, Jake, who had spent his entire life going to church, was even more ill-equipped than I. Consequently, in an effort to counteract our shortcomings, the negative influences of our church and our extended families, I made the decision to put our children in a Christian school while they were still at the elementary school level. I was desperate to give them what I had not been given as a child. The only time that Jake and I ever really fought was over things that happened in our church. As far as I was concerned, I was through fighting and through being judged and through being defeated. I told my husband that the children and I would no longer attend his church. We began to attend the church associated with the school our children attended. We left. He stayed. No one really seemed to care.

By now I am sure you are asking, "What took you so long?" That is a good question and one that eventually I had to answer for myself. In reality, an emotionally healthy person would never stay in a place where the environment was so unhealthy. A healthy person would not have a need to fix the world around them. But this is what child abuse does; it creates emotionally unhealthy adults who will continue to act-out inappropriately until they take back their power, find their precious child, love their wounded child and change their behavior. Because I was not emotionally healthy, I stayed in a place that for me was not safe. Consequently, I lost the precious gift of joy which I had found in knowing Christ.

It would be many more years before my husband and I became unified spiritually, but I will save that story for my next book . . . the next twenty years! *The abused adult/child stayed in situations that were familiar, because in her twisted thinking, she thought she had no choice. In her mind, familiar was safe because she wore the mask of denial. She had no understanding about her need to fix whatever she perceived to be broken. She could not see her own brokenness . . . the wounded child within her.*

*   *   *

I welcomed Sharon's punctual knock on the door. Her inviting smile peeked through the gap in the door where she pointed to her watch, reminding me it was time for our small group session. I waved at my friend and told her I would be there shortly. I had spent a very long time alone in my room trying to climb over the top of an insurmountable mountain. I felt as though I had been swimming upstream with a weight tied to my feet. Child abuse had held onto my ankles, and life's circumstances stood on my shoulders . . . only Jesus kept me from sinking. There was so much more I could relive, but the struggle had been enormous, and I was so very tired of digging through the twisted threads of my life. I wanted to be done with it all, but I knew I was not finished just yet.

I had allowed myself to get in touch with memories, feelings and emotions that touched the very core of everything that had culminated in bringing me to this climactic moment. There had been so much to face and to process—so many obstacles, so much unbearable pain—and I had worked so hard. But in the face of my tragic circumstances, there were also many, many victories and blessings. I was humbled to look back over my life and realize the great extent to which the Creator of this Universe had gone to reveal Himself to me. Yes, this Holy Being, who is not the Universe as some proclaim but the One who created it, is much greater than time and space and matter. And I don't know how, but I know that He knows *me*. I felt so unworthy, but I knew that my feelings of unworthiness had nothing to do with His great redemptive love for me. He had given me free will, the choice to make both wise and unwise decisions. I had made plenty of unwise choices, but even when I got off His divine course, He had patiently *waited on me* to respond to this incredible, unconditional, unspeakable love that He could not withhold from me.

As I continued to think about my faith journey, with all of its struggles and trials, it boggled my mind even to try to comprehend this great love, which, like the wind, moves all around us. We can feel it, but we cannot see it. Its strength is so powerful that it can turn the worst of human nature into the sweet submission of compassion and forgiveness. We all know it is there, and even though we may try to ignore it, it will not go away—it cannot. Love is the very nature and character of God—to create, not destroy. Who of us can really even begin to perceive this Holy God who designed this one-of-a-kind, singularly-made planet among billions where He breathed His own breath of life and love into existence in the form of the nature we enjoy? Who can grasp, except by faith, this Creator of all things who birthed His own Spirit into humanity, becoming the man—Jesus, the sacrificed Lamb, the object of our faith? How can we comprehend His birth, His death and His resurrection? He was *born* to give us new life, right standing and a personal relationship with our Creator/Heavenly Father; *died* to give us freedom from the darkness of this world, the power to overcome temptation and forgiveness from our sins; and *resurrected* to give us eternal life. Honestly, I cannot wrap my mind around these things, but I know that the power of my story lies within these holy mysteries.

On the other hand, how can we begin to understand the opposing forces of evil? We also cannot deny these forces or their power as they whirl all around us, unseen but deadly to the human spirit, taking their own wickedness and turning it into cancerous malevolence. I cannot deny the presence of both good and evil in this world. The evil that I have seen and experienced in my life is real. Evil things happened to me. Evil is not an illusion. The ungodly acts that I write about within the Christian community exposes the power of these evil forces. They seek to thwart God's plan of salvation and His great love for mankind. Religion was created by man, and it is sadly polluted by man. If I had put my faith in the religion of Christianity, I would have walked out a long time ago. I repeat: if I had put my faith in the *religion* of Christianity, I would have walked out a long time ago. But my faith is not in this religion, it is in the object of this religion, Jesus Christ. I had been carried, by God through faith in Christ and by the power of the Holy Spirit, to this moment, with my faith in Him stronger than ever before.

I had read in the Scriptures many times that I am to take the log out of my own eye before I take the speck out of others' eyes. I knew in my head these words spoke of a great truth that I needed to heed, but in my brokenness, I did not understand it in relationship to my walk with my God or with others. In *no way* do I condone the inexcusable behavior of those who hurt me, but it is not my place to be their judge. Hurting people hurt other people. Our churches are full of hurting and needy people. The world is full of hurting and needy people. Therefore, my wounded abused child was often in conflict with the wounded abused adult/child of those around me. I had been looking for self worth by trying to make my personal, imperfect world perfect. I desperately wanted *people* to love me and to heal my hurts, rather than looking totally to God to fill and to heal those voids in my soul. I expected Jake, his family, and the people in the church to make me happy. In reality, no human being can make another human being happy. Happiness grows from within a relationship with God. I had been searching for significance and acceptance, but now I had to face the reality that I had been doing so in all the wrong ways. That is what abused adult/children do, and will continue to do, until their wounded child is healed—until they find their precious child.

If I was to stop and evaluate my walk with God honestly, I had to first admit to my own shortcomings. The Church, the Body of Christ in which I sought to serve God, was not there for me, but there were also times when I was not there for the Body of Christ, either. As Christians, we have been called to be a conduit of love. But when we fail to do so, we hurt each other, and we hurt the cause of Christ. This, in no way, means that we turn our heads and ignore the sins of fellow Christians. In fact, to ignore sin is to ignore God's call to truly love one another. There is balance, which I believe the Scriptures clearly teach, and the time had come for me to begin walking within that balance.

I looked down at the sheet of paper clutched in my hand. I had been making a list of all the people who had hurt me, those toward whom I held resentments, bitterness and anger. The list had become unbearably long, beginning with my own family and then Jake and his family, and finally those within my church family. I knew very well that there was a great price to pay for withholding forgiveness. If unconditional love walks in forgiveness, then the principles of my faith hung between the two, and I had to make a choice. *The abused adult/child had known the answer all along, but she had failed to connect all the dots. She had been so tangled in the twisted threads of her wounded child that it had been impossible to move into a place of peace and live within the boundaries of unconditional forgiveness. She had been set free spiritually, but she had not been set free emotionally. Her threads no longer twisted, she could now move on.*

Without hesitation, I slipped off the bed that had become my holy space. Once again, I gathered my furry friends into my arms and hugged them tightly. I fell to my knees. My hospital room was suddenly tranquil, serene. Only faint sounds filtered down the hallway and through the door. Soft shadows danced in the sunlight through my single window. The chill from the air-conditioning suddenly felt warm. Tears welled up inside of me as I buried my face into my hands. Agonizing groans came from deep within my spirit as I lay my life at the foot of the Cross—once again. It had been almost twenty years since Pat Robertson had spoken a word of knowledge to me, after Katherine and Jay were miraculously healed. He told me he had a message from the Lord that he did not understand, but perhaps I would. I can still hear his words to me, "It is not that you have been waiting on Me, it is that I have been waiting on you." When Jesus was dying on the Cross of Calvary, He prayed to His Heavenly Father, "Forgive them (those who rejected him, beat him and crucified him), for they know not what they are doing." In that moment, while on my knees, I believe that Jesus was asking my Heavenly Father, "Please forgive her, because she did not know what she was doing." Throughout my journey, God had continually *waited on me* to hear His voice, to follow His call and learn His precepts as taught in the Bible. Ultimately, He had been *waiting on me* to understand that Jesus holds the key of forgiveness that unlocks the door to unconditional love. The great mystery is that He died for the forgiveness of my sins so that I might have eternal life, and although I had understood the eternal value of forgiveness, I had missed the earthly importance of forgiveness. Without unconditional forgiveness, I could not fully love, unconditionally.

For you see, what I had failed to grasp, to understand, is just how sin separates us from God and from each other on this earth. God gave us a history book, the Bible, which repeatedly reveals to mankind what works and what does not work when it comes to loving others. What works in relationships is kindness, compassion, honesty, gentleness, temperance, self-control, purity, respect, generosity and forgiveness, to mention a few. These attributes walk toward love. What does not work in relationships is hate, rudeness, self-centeredness, immorality, drunkenness, bitterness, lying, cheating, anger, gossip, deceit and so on. These attributes walk toward depression, suicide, guilt, self-loathing, unhappiness, hate, broken relationships, divorce, murder, addictions, abuse, poor health, etc. God calls these actions/choices sin, and sin separates us from God and separates us from each other. They hinder our relationships both earthly and eternally. The root of my sin was bitterness. My sin became inappropriate anger and its tentacles reached deep into every area of my life. I had come to this place to find answers because I wanted to live . . . not just survive. It was time to step into that place of healing and to move forward.

"Oh Lord . . . my God . . . please . . . forgive me for the bitterness and the anger that I have held on to for so long against so many . . . those who have felt anything but love from me; they did not understand me. And for those who have hurt me so deeply . . . give me the grace to forgive them; I did not understand them. In Jesus name, forgive me." And He did . . .

Chapter 23

The Canvas of My Life Completed—
Well, Not Just Yet

It seemed that I was almost always the last one to enter the meeting room, and this day was no exception. I quickly found the nearest available chair and slid into the waiting seat. I examined the questioning eyes that gazed back at me. Many faces had come and gone within our small group during the past month and a half. Some faces had changed; they reflected a hint of peace. Some had stayed the same; depression manifested sorrow. New faces mirrored fear and anxiety. I understood them all. I really liked Michael, the coordinator of the unit and also facilitator of my small group. He had been a solid rock for me. He was a good listener and was stern, yet fair in his responses to everyone. He knew that my stay on 3E was drawing to an end. "Nola Katherine, tell us what is going on with you today."

Time would not permit me to take them down the long road that I had just traveled. Most of them had heard bits and pieces of my story during the past few weeks, but none of them, except for Sharon, were fully aware of the agonizing mental, emotional and spiritual work that I had done. Like me, they were just trying to find their own way. I struggled to find my voice. My emotions were all over the place as I sought to give these wounded souls some final thoughts about my own recovery process. It was my hope they, too, would find the courage to heal, the courage to get their power back, and the courage to move forward. I chose my words carefully . . .

During the past six weeks I have learned many things about the wounded abused child that lives inside me. All of my adult life I have unknowingly been trying to protect her, but instead I have caused her more pain by denying her. I smothered her. I tried to shut her out of my life because it was just too painful to look at her. I just wanted her to go away. I did not know that all this time she was just begging to be loved, and I did not know how to love her. I have spent the past six weeks learning about her and trying to understand why she has affected my life in so many complex and confusing ways. Now I finally understand how horribly she was abused, and I understand the raging anger that she harbored. I have also discovered that she is really a very special part of who I am, and I have come to embrace her tenderly.

Since being here, I have dissected and examined a lifetime of experiences that have molded me into the person that I am. I have had to be very strong willed, and I have had to have very strong survival skills in order to overcome the circumstances life has imposed upon me. Those strengths have worked both for me and against me. I have been at war with myself trying to be strong when I was weak and being weak when I should have been strong. I think that finding balance has been one of my reasons for being here—letting my strengths overcome my weaknesses and letting my weaknesses become my strength. It has not been easy to sort through the maze of confusion to determine that for me, this means that in my weakness God's unconditional love in me will be strong, and in my strength I will choose not to be weak by withholding forgiveness. I will choose to love unconditionally, but with healthy boundaries. This also means that I must take off my masks—all of them—and be who I truly am.

Today my wounded, abused child and I accepted our responsibility for the bitterness, resentments and anger that have controlled me, the survivor. No matter how justified those emotions might be, and I fully understand that I have every right to have them; if they are harbored, protected and nurtured, they will undermine and destroy everything that my God has designed for me in this life. I can no longer afford the luxury of wallowing in them. I must completely forgive those who have been the object of those destructive emotions and their resulting behaviors. If I firmly believe, and I do believe, in the redemption of my own sins, paid for me when Christ shed His blood for me on the cross, then how can I ever withhold forgiveness of another? This does not mean that what was done to me is okay. Abuse of any kind is never okay. It just means that I set the captive free, and the one in captivity turned out to be me.

About six months before entering the hospital, I attended a workshop for survivors of abuse, and simultaneously, I had a very disturbing dream. The dream and the workshop were instrumental in leading me to seek help. I dreamed that I was standing on the shores of a large lake watching a little brown dog drown. I kept going out into the water and rescuing the little dog, but it just kept going back into the water. Finally, I just let it go and let it drown. In my dream, I became the little dog and I felt the sweet release of leaving my pain-filled life—letting it go. When I awoke, I realized that I was both the one drowning, as well as the one rescuing. I knew that if I did not get help soon, I would drown and the survivor in me was not willing to let that happen.

Today, I think I finally understood that the little, brown dog in my dream was my precious child . . . the little one that I have been trying so hard to find. She has been with me all the time . . . we have been clinging to each other and rescuing each other all of my life. She is the core of who I am—my soul, my spirit. And she is truly precious.

Michael picked up on my words and continued, "I rarely use the words intestinal fortitude, but when I was writing about Nola Katherine that is the term I used. That is what I have observed about her. She is very unique. She lost her core, the very essence of who she is, when she was a child. It is very unusual to get that core back and then work on the issues of child abuse. But, somehow she did get her core back and then worked out her issues. Nola Katherine, I am really concerned about you. I have seen you go to such depths of despair that I was not sure you would be able to come back. It's like an archeologist who can dig and dig through centuries of treasures, but then after a while, he has to stop digging because the treasures he finds begin to crumble. I think it is time for you to stop digging."

I knew that Michael was right. It was time to stop. It was time to go on with my life. I told my small group that I would be leaving soon. When the session ended, I was showered with lots of hugs and well wishes. When Michael put his arms around me, he said, "You have made a tremendous impact on my life." I had seen tears in his eyes more than once when he talked to me. We both knew that I had one more mountain to climb.

*   *   *

Since entering the hospital, no one on my side of the family had visited or called me. I am not really sure why. It is possible that my mother had not told anyone where I was. Perhaps fear and denial kept my family away. However, I could not delay the inevitable. I knew that before I left the security of the hospital and my therapist, I needed to confront my sister. The knot in my stomach tightened as I picked up the phone to call her. She willingly agreed to come to the hospital, but I really don't think she was prepared for what was coming. I was sensitive to the fact that she had just lost her second husband to cancer, and I really did not want to hurt her. But she came from the same family I came from, and I knew that her childhood, her life, could not have been easy for her either. Perhaps subconsciously, I hoped that through my journey she would see the need to seek her own path of healing. I sincerely wanted for us have a healthy relationship. I knew that would never happen if I did not talk to her about what her first husband had done to me and her part in protecting him . . . and not protecting me.

The hallway just outside of the locked doors leading into 3E was lined with small rooms that were designated for therapy sessions. Long narrow windows on the doors allowed visual entrance into the rooms. The elevator on the opposite wall guarded these small rooms where there was just enough room for four chairs and a table. My therapist and I waited in agonizing silence for my sister's arrival. When I entered the hospital, I had been told that I had no boundaries. Anyone could get into my space, and I would not object. Almost six weeks later, I was uncomfortable with the close proximity between my therapist and myself. I was not afraid of him; I respected him. I was just suddenly aware of the fact that I didn't want him so close to me, even though he was sitting in the chair opposite me. *The survivor was feeling healthy boundaries.*

The gentle tap on the door broke our silence. Sis was motioned to come in. She smiled, like she always smiled, as I introduced her to my therapist. There was something clearly different about her. She seemed much older to me. I noticed her shoulders slumped slightly forward. There was nothing about our appearances that would connect us as sisters. She was five inches taller and carried a larger bone structure. I was short and petite. She had just turned sixty, and I had just celebrated my forty-seventh birthday while in the hospital. Even though her auburn hair had turned white, her complexion remained flawless. She had inherited the darker skin, which I envied, from our native American roots and tanned beautifully, while I had inherited dark hair and the fairer Irish skin that burned, blistered and peeled when exposed to too much sun. She sat down in the chair next to me.

My therapist explained to my sister that I had been working through child abuse issues, and I had some things I needed to talk about with her. With her smile still in place, Sis replied, "Okay." When I asked her whether she knew that her first husband had abused me, as expected, she denied any knowledge of the abuse. As I disclosed snippets of information, her smile turned harsh and she even tried to put the blame on me, "You always wanted to go with him! You were always sitting in his lap! You always have had an overly active imagination! It was just photography (when he was taking pictures of you)!"

Her accusations caused me to catch my breath, and when I gave my therapist a sharp, panicked look, he quickly intervened, "If a child is not getting the attention it needs, even negative attention is better than nothing. A young child will almost always go to its abuser." The air in the room churned thick and heavy with sorrow, sadness, grief and denial.

When I asked her whether she had been abused as a child, I saw a flicker in her eyes that said yes. Her answer was emphatically, "No!" It was not a good encounter and nothing was resolved. She left angry and hurt. I don't really know what I felt. We hugged when she left. My therapist wanted to know what the hug was about. I told him that we always hug. I loved my family—in spite of everything. *If only I had known then that my sister was very ill. I had not told her that I forgave her, and I had not asked her to forgive me. I knew I had hurt her, too.*

Dr. Kamen took me off all my medications. We both felt that I no longer needed them and could make it on my own. He made the necessary arrangements for my discharge. Healthy, ambivalent feelings raced around me as I began to pile my belongings onto the metal cart that would transport them to my car. I could not help but wonder what the days and weeks and years beyond would mean for me. I had been warned that the world I had left behind had not changed, just because I had changed. People will have me in a box, and they will not want to let me out. One of the nurses on staff appeared at the door of my room to escort Jake and me off the unit. "For someone who did not feel very loved when you came into this place, you sure do have a lot of cards and flowers. In fact, you had more visitors than anyone I have witnessed on this unit." *The wounded, abused adult/child had been able to focus only on those who rejected and hurt her. She could not see that there were those who loved her. The survivor now looked through different eyes. She saw hope for new beginnings.*

The sound of the large metal doors clanging behind me as I left Unit 3E of the adult psychiatric hospital for the last time was music to my ears. The familiar rattle of keys remained on the inside of the door as it closed behind me. My little girl had been lost, but now she was found. She had been a prisoner, but now she was set free. My husband, my soul-mate, the love of my life, took my hand, and we disappeared into the elevator. *The passion of my precious child had caught my vision for a life that is still worthwhile. We joined our hands and reached out far beyond what we had done. Like dreamers, we had awakened to the new life that was yet to come. For new beginnings are not just for the young . . . and so we did . . . begin again!*

*   *   *

Well, our journey together has come to an end. I thank you for taking the time to bring wonderful life to my painting. We have worked hard together sketching in the outline, washing in the background and painting in the shadows. Moist tears shed along the way reflect the brilliant colors of joy, and rays of victory now shine through those beginning efforts. As I stand back and examine this beautiful masterpiece, I thank God for the privilege of being the Artist's brush. I would never have chosen this life canvas for myself, but I would not trade it for any other life canvas on this planet because I am truly blessed.

But the canvas of my life is far from being covered, and the painting is not yet entirely complete. Wisdom has not fully revealed all of its magnificent hues, and truth etched in the drawing is waiting to be more fully disclosed. Gleeful hope lies at the tip of every shape, every pink, purple and lavender, every yellow, blue and green. There is so much more of life to come my way, so much more to sketch and paint. The good news is that whenever I do make a mistake, I can pick up my brush, and I can begin once again to strive to make it right, until someday, when this life is over and the canvas is finally completed, the Master Artist will say, "Come home, my good and faithful servant. Come home."

Post Script

Just so that you are not left wondering, I am going to answer a few questions you might be asking just now. I will begin with the health of my children. As of the conclusion of my writing, Katherine is forty and is married to Patrick. She graduated from Southwest Texas State University, has never had a relapse of the cancer and remains in good health. Jay is thirty-nine, has no mental or physical signs of having had meningitis, graduated in the top ten of his high school class, summa cum laude from Texas A&M, with honors from the Naval Officer Candidate School and is currently Director of Data Applications for a company based in California. He is married to Zoe, and they have two sons, Andrew and Samuel. After graduating from the University of Tulsa, Kim married Anthony and worked as a deputy sheriff until Luke was born. Eighteen months later she gave birth to twins, Hunter and Heather. I am thankful they all live close by.

Jake and I began attending a Bible church over fifteen years ago. God made it perfectly clear to my husband that we could no longer stay in the church of his youth and family. Once we left, we never looked back. We have grown spiritually and relationally, both individually and as a couple, and we have enjoyed developing trusting and loving relationships with the people in our new church.

As for me, I truly turned a corner and moved on with my life. I am no longer haunted by the memories of abuse. The memories only remain for me to look at when I need to. They no longer have power over me. My fickle handwriting remains a mystery to me. When it changes,

I consider it to be an indication that there is something going on within me that is trying to get my attention. However, I no longer feel controlled by the fragmented compartments of my mind. I rejoice and thank God that I have a sense of who I truly am. Only occasionally do I find myself slipping into those strange places in my mind. However, I can come right back out, just as quickly as I went into them. Awareness is everything.

Depression no longer gives me a dark place in which to hide, nor is there inappropriate anger to fuel the depression. I can get angry, but I don't let anger turn into bitterness because I understand that God gave me the capacity for anger. I believe there is a redemptive side to this strong emotion and that God's intent is for us to use it for good, not turn it into something bad. He has shown me how to use anger in constructive ways rather than letting it cause me to be destructive. If I acknowledge my anger and do something about it, then I can be relatively healthy in mind, body and spirit. I have learned that I must never sleep with anger because if I do, I will get into trouble. I must openly talk about the things that bother me because being immediate and genuine prevents the accumulation of anger's poison. Sometimes I forget and sometimes I fail, but recovery is usually quick.

One of the most difficult things for me to overcome was playing the victim role. I had to train myself to be aware of circumstances that put me in that mind set. It is amazing to me that I am sometimes targeted by others' dysfunction. One of the most important tools for correcting victimization is healthy boundaries. I have worked very hard to identify and maintain healthy boundaries. But sometimes, I forget those, too.

What I want you to understand is that I am far from being perfect; my life is not perfect, but I have come so far. I can allow myself to have feelings and not shut them down. I no longer see myself as the same wounded, fragmented person that I write about in this book. By the grace of God, I have been changed. Most importantly, I am okay with who I am.

After this book went into publication, but before printing began, I received an e-mail from a man who knew me between the fourth and eighth grades. That was during the time when a lot of the abuse I write about happened. Because I had blocked out so much of my childhood memories, I did not remember the very close relationship that I had with this man as a young boy, even though I had often thought about him. He shared with me that while serving in Vietnam he awoke one night thinking about me. It was an extremely difficult time for him, and on that fretful night, I brought him peace. Following is a portion of a poem he wrote about me that night. His words brought further confirmation that all I have shared in my book is real and not imagined. I am thankful that Bill opened his heart to me at this time. He is an amazing man who has served his country well, and I have the greatest respect for him.

> But something about her was missing
> From the times that we shared.
> An emptiness, a darkness, a cover
> I could not pare.
>
> She held a part of her away from me,
> But I knew it was not because of me.
> Something else within her hides,
> An ebb and flow of deeper tides
> That I could not reach,
> That I could not breach.
>
> I sensed within her a frailness, a sadness,
> That she tried to hide,
> And to bring it out of her,
> I truly tried.
> I gave of myself all that I had
> In hopes that with me
> She would not longer be sad.
>
> Though my eyes may never again behold her,
> Within my heart I will always hold her.
> Even today after so many years,
> She still is with me, so far . . . yet so near.

June 18, Republic of Vietnam

This poem was written eleven days before I married Jake.

It is my plan to write a sequel to this book, and I hope you will be there to help me put on the finishing touches to my painting. *Waiting on You*, the next twenty years, will let you in on how life has been since leaving the hospital. Life is never dull for an abused adult/child—we tend to keep God very busy.

Suggested Guidelines
to Help You Begin Again

If you are an AAC—an abused adult/child, it is my hope that you will pick up your own brush, find your own canvas and seek others whom you can trust to help paint your own unique picture. You are precious. I cannot emphasize enough how heavy my heart is for you. I understand you. I understand your pain and confusion. I pray, ever so fervently, that you will find freedom from the devastating grip of your abuser(s). I will always be an abused adult/child; you will always be an abused adult/child. That will never change. But your knowledge and your perception about the abuse and your power over it can and must change. You do not have to live in defeat. You do not have to remain stuck in your pain. Medications are often needed to help with the recovery process. If you are suffering from depression, I encourage you to seek professional help to determine if you need to be on an antidepressant for a while.

Finally, I want to suggest some guidelines to help you get started toward your own healing. I realize that not everyone will be able to go into a treatment center or be able to afford therapy. Each of us travels down a different path, at our own rate of speed. I believe that God will meet you exactly where you are, to help you let go, to grow and to change. I am not a licensed professional; therefore, please understand that I give you these guidelines out of my own experience and from my heart's desire to use my experience for good. I want to help you to do more than just survive. I want to see you live life fully. If recovery is to

257

come, you must be in a place where you are completely willing to do the work, let go of your pain and be set free. I do pray that the following suggestions will be of some help to you and those who love you.

Prayer

When I first began to take seriously the reality that every horrible thing that happened to me as a child was affecting and controlling every area of my life as an adult, it was overwhelming. I did not know where or how I was going to get help, but I knew that I could not go down that road without God. I memorized the following prayer, and I said it over and over, every day. For how long, I cannot tell you because I just don't remember. I do know that in time, God did answer this prayer.

> *Come Holy Spirit, and heal my understanding.*
> *Heal the deep, innermost realms of self.*
> *Heal that which only you can heal.*
> *Heal the dark unconscious cellars of my mind.*
> *Heal my hurtful memories.*
> *Heal my hidden griefs and sorrows.*
> *Heal my wrong desires and ambitions.*
> *Heal my disappointments and vain strivings*
> *for those things that I should not have.*
> *Heal the pangs of frustration.*
> *Gently release the chains that bind me.*
> *Lead me into the light and freedom of your*
> *sufficiency so that I shall be filled with joy*
> *all the days of my life. Amen*
> —Author unknown

I urge you to memorize this prayer. Prayer is the key to Heaven, but faith unlocks the door. Put your faith and trust in God, and He will lead you. God loves you in a way that no one on this earth can love you. Believe in Him to answer your prayers. His mercy has no boundaries, no limits.

Explore your history of origin

If you have family abuse issues, find out as much as you can about your parents, grandparents and siblings and how they were raised and what happened to them as children. This can bring great understanding about the way you, in turn, were treated/raised. As of this writing, out of my family of seven, there are only two of us still living. Please don't put off too long getting answers that will help you understand who you are. Ultimately, it will bring great healing to your wounded child.

Write

Write about your abuse. Spare no details. Express how you felt at the time of the abuse, and how you feel about it now. Express how you feel about the abuser. Don't try to imagine something that is not there. Be absolutely honest. However, physical memories are very important. Do not discount them. You may not be able to recall who has hurt you, or the details, but you may recall physical symptoms and pain that is very real. Ask the Holy Spirit of God to reveal truth to you. If they are real memories, you will eventually have peace about it, one way or the other. Writing is safe and brings a wonderful gift of healing to the AAC.

I must caution you to share this information *only* with those you can completely trust. When you have turned that corner and started walking in freedom, then you will be able to share, as I am now sharing, with others.

Talk

Find a safe and trustworthy person who will listen to you and not judge you. Such a person will be able to help you talk and talk and talk. If your safe person is a friend or family member and not a professional, be careful not to wear out your safe person. Abused adult/children have a habit of doing this to those who are willing to listen. Once everything has been said, you *do not need* to keep rehashing your abuse. In fact, it is not healthy to keep rehashing it over and over, again and again. Be done with it. You will know when it is time to stop.

With all due respect to therapists, I must say that I have known women who have been in therapy for years, who are stuck in their pain and never move on. If you are seeing a therapist who does not move you beyond talking, especially if you have been talking for several years, then it is time to find another therapist. Don't be afraid to ask your therapist for a treatment plan. Find out what methods the therapist uses to help people move into recovery. Realize that everyone is different and that everyone moves at a different pace, so please don't look for a set formula or place a time limit on your progress. Just ask for some guidelines so that you will know there is at least a plan.

About talking in general, guard what you casually say to people you don't really know or even people that you think you know. People in general will not understand what abuse really means, and consequently they will most likely judge you. The AAC has a very strange way of communicating at times. Don't put yourself in situations that will cause you further rejection and pain.

If you really are trying to get someone you care about to understand you, this book might be a great help. Use discernment when trying to talk to anyone about your abuse issues. This is a difficult issue for anyone to try to understand. Keep this in mind as you want *normal* people to understand where you are coming from; be sure to try to understand where *normal* people are coming from also. Remember, they do not process life in the same way that the AAC processes life. And by-the-way, *Normal is just a setting on your dryer*, as Patsy Clairmont so wisely declares in her book of the same title.

Role-play (with your safe person)

This can be invaluable to the abused adult/child (or to an abused child). When I work with a woman who was abused as a child, at the appropriate time, I put a firm pillow in her lap because usually she is going to feel that she needs an outlet, something to beat on. I will ask her to allow me to take on the role of her abuser. This allows her to verbalize safely what she needs to say to the one(s) who have hurt her. In most instances, it may not be wise or safe to confront an abuser directly, or the abuser may even be deceased. Role-playing is safe and nonthreatening to an abused adult/child.

This exercise will allow you to get in touch with the anger, guilt and shame that has been locked up inside. It will also allow you to identify the deep emotional repercussions they have fueled such as poor behavior, depression, self-loathing, resentments, bitterness, unhealthy decisions, etc. Remember that a poor past is a poor excuse for poor behavior, and what needs to be changed is poor behavior.

As an AAC, you should passionately verbalize what you are angry at the abuser for. Speak to the one who has stolen the very essence of who you are, the one who has stolen your innocence, your joy, your life, your ability to be intimately healthy. Be specific! Place that anger back on the abuser . . . say, "I give your anger back to you! It is not mine!"

This next step is so important. Give the shame back to your abuser. It is not *your* shame that you have been carrying for all of those years. You don't own it, so give it back to the person to whom it belongs. You have nothing to be ashamed of, and any shameful thing that you have done as a result of being abused is covered by the love and grace and mercy of God. Please understand this and let it go. Again, verbalize it! "I give your shame back to you."

Now, let go of the guilt. Take back the power that has been stolen from you. **Children are vulnerable and innocent**! Adults have great power over children, and children lose their power when abused. Anyone can get into the space of an AAC at any time because the AAC is powerless to say no. The AAC does not have healthy boundaries. But that must stop! You have permission to have good and healthy boundaries. It is time to stop constantly playing the victim role. It is your life, and you deserve to be empowered as an individual. Make the choice to take your power back. Again, verbalize it! "I give your guilt back to you and I take back my power."

Role-playing can lead to a very powerful turning point. The pillow, not the person, will get the well-deserved punches that you have secretly harbored.

Suggestions for the *safe person*

If you are not a professional and someone has asked you to step into this role, pray fervently before proceeding. Be prepared to stick with your friend/loved one until the end. Please, do not judge. Please, give unconditional love. Just listen, and don't be too quick to give advice. Let them get their pain out. When role-playing, it is your job to ask leading questions such as, "Who hurt you? What did she/he do? How did you feel when it happened? How do you feel now? What do you need to say to that person?" Help them to get in touch with their anger. Let them yell and scream and cry and then help them to release their anger and their shame back to the abuser. Respond with positive affirmations back to them, saying, "I am sorry you were hurt," etc. Encourage them to verbalize; they need to say to their abuser, "I give your shame, your guilt and your anger back to you." And finally, help them to choose to turn the corner and move on. You are a valuable gift to the abused adult/child. Thank you!

Forgive

Forgiveness is always a choice. If you choose not to forgive those who have hurt you, then you will stay stuck in your pain, and you will not move forward. If you are a Christian, then you understand the unconditional forgiveness that Jesus personally bought for you, at great price. It is part of the great mystery of our faith. We have done nothing to deserve it. We have not earned it. It is a gift. Understanding that, how can you possibly withhold forgiveness toward another human being, regardless of who they are or what they have done? You must choose to forgive.

If you have not yet come to understand this great mystery, I ask you to step out in faith and choose to forgive your abuser(s). Ask God to give you the courage, the power and the grace to do so. It is of utmost importance to understand that forgiving is not saying that what was done to you is okay. Abuse of any kind is never okay. Forgiveness is about getting your power back, the power that was stolen from you.

I love my parents, my siblings and my aunt. I don't believe they ever meant to bring harm to me—especially my mother—anymore so than I ever intended to bring hurt to my own children. There is absolutely no comparison, but I know that sometimes I did wound my children. But as you have read in my story, my family of origin suffered with their own childhood wounds, and those wounds transferred over onto me. It does not excuse their behavior, but forgiving sets me free to love them. Understanding my family was huge for me. It is hard to hate those you understand, and you will never be free until you are set free both spiritually and emotionally.

And finally, don't forget to forgive yourself. No doubt, you have done many things in your life that you wish you had not done. Let those pain-filled memories go, and forgive your wounded child. She didn't know what she was doing. Memories never leave us, but they do not have to have power over us. They don't have to plunge us into a dark pit every time we think about them.

Turn the corner

A little bit of caution here. It is very difficult to break the pattern of being everyone else's beating post/victim. I have learned that I must have healthy boundaries. First of all, I do not have to be with whom I do not feel safe—those who do not honor me, respect me or give me lots of kudos. Secondly, it is okay to say what I need to say in order to take care of myself. This did not come easy for me and sometimes I relapse, but everyone has a right to be heard and to feel safe.

Finally, walk up to the wall that has held you captive, turn the corner and walk to the other side. Make the decision to go on with the rest of your life. Take responsibility for yourself and your happiness. And above all, trust God to walk with you. Healing takes time. Give yourself time to heal. But please, don't stay stuck in your pain. Choose to move on with your life.

Confrontation

Once you have turned this corner, you may then consider confronting your abuser. However, you may no longer feel that it is necessary. If you do feel you must confront your abuser, never go alone. Take someone with you. Go empowered and leave empowered. Be prepared that confrontation may bring repercussions such as denial, anger, and possibly, further abuse. Be discerning, be wise and be cautious. You might consider writing a letter to your abuser. Don't mail it right away . . . you may eventually feel that it is not necessary.

If you are feeling that you have hurt others because of your own confusing behavior, again, be discerning, wise and cautious about going to them. Some will respond favorably, but some will not have a clue what you are talking about. Do what is best for you. Letters are good ways to communicate, but always remember that apologizing is about what *you* have done, not what the others have done. I have found the following statement to be effective: "Please forgive me if you have ever felt anything but love from me." Leave it at that. You don't have to explain yourself. If they respond, then you will know they care and want to have a healthy relationship with you. If they choose not to respond, that is their problem. You will have done what you needed to do for yourself. Move on; you don't need them in your life.

Thoughts for the spouse, friends and family members

If you are one who lives with an AAC, I applaud you for hanging in there. It is not always easy, but remember that you have in your presence one that is cherished by God. Your loved one holds many admirable qualities, and I am sure you acknowledge them. However, often these qualities are unseen, because they were tragically stolen and hidden by the effects of the abuse. In other words, there is a precious child living inside your loved one and the precious child is worth finding. It takes unconditional love, and that is what your loved one needs from you more than anything else.

I hope that my story has given you new understanding of past experiences you may have had with the AAC you live with or know. We are, not by choice, complex individuals. The abused child will always live in us, and we will always look through very different eyes. Remember that healing takes time. It is a process.

If you are a parent, a teacher or a friend and you suspect child abuse, please get help immediately. Please don't be in denial. It is your place to protect powerless children. Children depend on adults. Act now! Pray hard for guidance and for discernment. You can make a difference. In fact, you may be the only hope they have.

Sexual/gender confusion

I really feel that I have to touch on this subject because I sincerely know the confusing sexual messages that go on in the mind of an AAC. We are totally "not normal" when it comes to our sexuality. We experience so much shame, guilt and confusion because we don't know who we are. I have often wondered how many abused adult/children have become gay or lived in the fear that they might be gay when, in actuality, they are wounded and confused because of childhood sexual abuse. We have every right and reason to be confused.

When I have asked women, "Do you think you would be gay if you had not been abused as a child?" the response has always been, "I don't know. I need to think about that." Clearly, it is something to consider for several different reasons. For one thing, because perpetrators are often members of the opposite sex, if we become gay, we can avoid ever having sexual encounters with that particular gender again. (Recall that was Sharon's sole reason for being gay.) On the other hand, if a child is abused by someone of the same sex, there is a strong probability that same sex relationships will be perpetuated. Secondly, there are spiritual ramifications to consider. Having said that, I truly believe in God's tender mercy toward wounded abused children, but as adults we are accountable for our decisions.

And then, there are genetic occurences that happen, like with my aunt. She did not choose to be born the way that she was. Yet, she had to live for over eighty years hiding her secret and living a life in limbo, never knowing who she was.

If you are one who struggles with sexual/gender confusion, I pray that you will seek God's perfect truth for your life. He has promised that if you seek Him, you will find Him. The Scriptures tell us that Satan is a liar and a deceiver, and I believe that the lust of the flesh is one of the greatest weapons he uses against mankind. I say to you, know that the enemy of our soul is Satan. Jesus commanded us to know the truth, and He promises that the truth will set us free. For those without gender issues, please do not be too quick to judge. We must all reach out in love and leave the judging to God, who is the *only* One who truly knows the human heart, the only One who knows our true stories. God's children deserve our mercy, just as He is merciful to *all* His children.

If you struggle with your sexuality or if you know someone who does, I recommend that you read *Love Won Out* by John and Anne Paulk.

Pornography

I must have one last word about this subject because I am passionate for you to understand the dangers of pornography. Once again, let me be absolutely clear, I don't believe in looking for a demon behind every bush. I do not go around screaming and casting out or rebuking demons every time something strange happens. I do, however, understand from experience the battles that we mortals face. You must be wiser than the enemy when it comes to overcoming this or any evil addiction. I know that this addiction would come back to me in a flash if I invited it in, and my fear is that I would never be able to get free again. You cannot play with it . . . ever! That is how powerful I know pornography is. Its grip on the human mind is beyond extraordinarily strong, and it will, like abuse, affect every area of your life. And I believe it has the potential for being passed on to your children if left unchecked. Please, hear me when I say that your involvement in pornography will adversely affect your family as you invite these powers of darkness into your life, into your home.

I would like for you to consider that behind each pornographic picture or video you view, there is possibly a story like mine. You do not know who is behind the camera—an abuser, or a manipulator. You do not know why this young girl, woman, boy, man or even child is being exploited. When you engage in pornography, I believe you are actually participating in the abuse of the one who is giving you lustful, self-seeking pleasure. I have to ask you—is the momentary pleasure worth the consequences you will bear for choosing to participate in the wounding of those whose bodies you lust?

I recently heard about a survey that was done in a Christian college that revealed a shocking percentage of men and women who viewed pornography at least once a week. These are young adults who were most likely raised in good homes and have Christian backgrounds. You may think that your children, especially your daughters, would never go down that road, but don't be too sure. In November 2009, a popular talk show host reported that one in three women are viewing pornography, or erotica as it is now being deceitfully disguised. *Familysafemedia.com* reports the following statistics which were gathered through a number of resources listed on their website:

- 53% of men who attended a Promise Keepers weekend, a Christian event held for men, had watched pornography the previous week.
- 47% of Christians interviewed admitted to having a problem with pornography at home.
- 72% men and 28% women visit pornographic websites.
- The average age children are first exposed to internet pornography is 11.
- There are 4.2 million pornographic websites,
- 68 million daily search engine requests for pornography,
- 1.5 billion monthly porn-related downloads, and
- 116,000 daily child porn requests.

Enough.org reported that child pornography is the fastest growing business online and the content is becoming worse. In their 2008 annual report, *Internal Watch Foundation* found 1,536 individual child abuse domains.

You may say of yourself that you would never have an affair, have same-sex relations or engage in some unthinkable act such as child abuse, rape or even murder. I know that sounds extreme, but porn is extreme. It will rob you of your self-respect, and it will anesthetize your sense of right and wrong. It is insatiable and has the potential of pulling anyone into a self-centered, destructive, bottomless pit. If you are into porn, you have opened a door that I beg you to close immediately. You are inviting the powers of darkness—Satan and his demons—to enter into your world, your home, your mind, your soul. It will touch those around you that you love the most . . . your husband, your wife, your children. Our prisons are full of people who are there because of pornography, and I am sure they never intended for it to lead them there.

Christians are extremely vulnerable to the lure of sexual immorality. To prove my point I want to share the following story. I was working as the bookkeeper for my church when one day a young woman came into my office, closed my door, and began to sob uncontrollably. Her expressions of guilt and shame were almost unbearable to watch. She was a committed Christian and a single mom with extremely high morals. Yet, she had been unwittingly pulled into a relationship that involved alcohol and telephone sex. She was devastated by the choices she had made and didn't know how to get out of evil's gripping power. Her need and desire for human, physical intimacy became skewed; it overcame her desire for spiritual intimacy with God. She knew that she had broken her relationship with Him, and the agony of that lost relationship left her empty and defeated. The devastation she felt far outweighed the momentary pleasure she found in insatiable, unfulfilling sexual pleasure. Thankfully, she did get free from her addiction, and today is a beautiful, joyful and fulfilled woman.

God desires intimacy with His children. When we are not spiritually connected to our Creator, when our relationship with Him is broken, our search for intimacy will become skewed. We search for alternative ways to fill the deep void that we feel. Every human being craves intimacy, and for us, sex is the most physical, completely intimate act we experience. However, when sex becomes an idol, as it has become in our nation and throughout the world, it will ultimately bring loneliness and emotional bankruptcy—not lasting pleasure and not lasting happiness or fulfillment. More than ever before people are searching for true significance in the idol of sex. If people who are heavily involved in porn were honest, they would tell you that what I am saying is true. They are not happy and fulfilled. Fulfilling sex outside of God's plan is an illusion. Sadly, innocent children whose bodies and spirits have been violated are carrying this idol on their shoulders. I repeat . . . **innocent children are carrying the idol of sex on their tiny shoulders.**

Trust me, only a relationship with God will give you the inner peace you desire. I know I have said it many times already; however, I don't want you to forget that Satan is a roaring lion seeking whomever he can devour. Know your enemy, but also know that we have a God who roams this earth seeking the lost and those who have a heart toward Him. For this, He gave us Jesus and the healing power that is in His name.

Before I move on, I want to tell you about the rubber band trick. It has great potential for working. Wear a strong rubber band around your wrist. Every time a thought comes to your mind that entices you to go to your addiction, pop, with gusto, your wrist with the rubber band. Continue until the moment is lost. Sooner or later, your brain will associate the thought with pain and not pleasure, and let's face it, we humans don't like pain. Something goes crazy in our brains when arousal of any kind takes place. We can't fight it, we can't stop it, until that urge is somehow satisfied . . . except, perhaps with a simple rubber band and the grace of God. Having said that, you have to want it to work and you have to be consistent in order to get the success you deserve.

Alcoholic beverages

I wrote a lot about drinking in my story, but I really didn't say much about it. I want to put my thoughts toward the subject here for you to consider. Jesus told his followers in Ephesians 5:15-18 (NIV), "Be very careful, then, how you live, not as unwise but as wise, making the most of every opportunity, because the days are evil. Therefore do not be foolish, but understand what the Lord's will is. Do not be drunk on wine, which leads to debauchery. Instead be filled with the Holy Spirit." The Bible appears to make allowances for drinking wine, but it clearly warns about drunkenness. The problem is, anytime you find people drinking alcohol, you will find a measure of drunkenness. It is an accepted drug that alters the state of mind.

I have been in both camps—one camp that drinks excessively and one that sits and watches others get drunk. For me, neither is a place where I am comfortable or where I want to be. Personally, I don't want to separate my mind, my body or my spirit from God. I believe that when we are in an altered state of mind, it's very difficult to be connected to God or to be sincerely connected with others. Alcohol gives a false sense of connection. Countless times I have watched people who, when first entering a gathering, hardly speak to each other, and in fact, act like they don't even like each other. After a couple of drinks, all are "best friends." I have witnessed the worst of human behaviors, all of which started with just one drink . . . after another . . . and another. Whatever your basic personality trait is, it will manifest when under the influence of alcohol. Your conscience guard is lowered, and your true self will emerge in an exaggerated way. In other words, there is no one mentally minding the store. If your personality is bent toward anger and violence, you will be a mean drunk. If you are kindhearted and loving, you will be overly vulnerable to anyone who comes near you, and you may be rendered powerless.

I have seen people use alcohol to dull their physical and emotional pain, their boredom, their stress, their loneliness and their insecurities. The problem with this is that people never get to the source of their problems because they just keep drowning them in alcohol and never get real, lasting help. The real danger in drinking is the potential for alcoholism, a devastating disease. Lifetimes are wasted, lives destroyed, families disintegrated, abuse perpetuated . . . there is no end to its destruction.

My greatest concern is the children. Monkey see, monkey do. They watch parents drink and grow up with the idea that this is a cool thing to do. However, the potential for these children to end up as alcoholics or even worse, drug addicts, is off the charts. Car accidents, promiscuity, unwanted pregnancy, rape, suicide, overdose . . . the deadly list is endless. I beg you to be an example for your children and educate them about the dangers of alcohol. It is a tough world we live in, and they are so vulnerable.

During my journey, I discovered the closer I get to God, the less I need other things to fill my life. Alcohol and drugs produce a temporary high that will eventually make you crash and burn. Instead, be filled with the Holy Spirit. It is a wonderful, joyful and powerful high that will fill your emptiness. And the supply is free and limitless. Please be wise; be discerning.

The Christian community

If you are one who has been hurt as I have been within the Christian community and have walked away, I am so very, very sorry. I encourage you to go back to your roots in Christ and renew your walk with Him. He knows you, and He is *waiting on you*. His arms are always open. There are many healthy churches with genuine, accountable leaders. I believe the Holy Spirit will show you whether or not you are in a church that is filled with genuine Christ-followers. Please, always remember that where there are human beings, there will never be perfection. Christians are not perfect, and sometimes we make awful mistakes, but we are forgiven. It is for us (sinners) that Jesus came to this earth. As for me, I know I am perfectly imperfect.

Pastor, priest, evangelist—you are called to lead, to be shepherds. But if you are not accountable, and do not strive to live by the precepts of the Christian faith, then the darkness you invite into your own life will trickle down into your congregation, into your ministry. As never before in the history of our nation have we needed the Church, the Body of Christ, to be strong and solid. Teach your congregation how to be true disciples of Christ, true Christ-followers.

And finally, before moving on, I want to challenge the Christian community to wake up. Church is not about *doing* church, it is about *being* the Church. It is about meeting the spiritual needs of the people who walk through the doors. When you go to church on Sunday mornings, I challenge you to look around you. Find that one who is alone, that one who looks sad, or that one who, perhaps, was abused and needs someone to tell them, "It's going to be okay. I care about you." You may be the first *face of grace* they experience.

If you do not believe in God

If you have never come to know your Creator, God, I pray that something in my story will compel you to seek Him. He knows you; He knows everything about you. He is also *waiting on you* to receive His provision of love. Just because you deny His existence does not mean that He does not exist, and just because I believe that He does exist does not mean that He does exist. Truth is truth; it is objective, unchanging and not something we can make up. As I wrote earlier, water does not try to be water. Air does not try to be air. God does not try to be Holy and Jesus does not try to be God. It is as it is. Air is air. Water is water. God is Holy God, and Jesus is the exact revelation of who God is. God is who He has revealed Himself to be, or He is not. It is that simple.

On your journey to find Him, if you come across something that you do not understand, I encourage you to put your questions and doubts on a shelf in your mind and ask God's Holy Spirit to reveal truth to you. This has worked for me. In time, God's love will override any confusion you might have.

I ask you to consider the following precepts:

God's love is personal. The Scriptures say, "God so loved the world that He gave His only Son, that whoever believes in Him shall not perish, but have eternal life."[1] God loves you!

The problem for mankind is that all of us have done, said, or thought things that are wrong. This is called sin, and our sins have separated us from God.

The Scriptures reveal that "All have sinned and fall short of the glory of God."[2] God is perfect and holy, and our sins separate us from God. The Bible continues to say, "The wages of sin is death."[3]

The good news is that over two thousand years ago, God sent His only Son, Jesus Christ, to die for our sins. Jesus is the Son of God. He lived a sinless life and then died on the cross to pay the penalty for our sins. "God demonstrates His own love for us in this: while we are still sinners, Christ died for us."[4]

Jesus rose from the dead, and now He lives in Heaven with God, His Father. He offers us the gift of eternal life . . . of living forever with Him in Heaven if we accept Him as our Lord and Savior. Jesus said, "I am the way and the truth and the life. No one comes to the Father except through me."[5]

God is *waiting on you* to receive His love. He desires for you to know Him. "Yet to all who received Him, to them He gave the right to become children of God, even to those who believe in His name."[6] You can choose to ask Jesus Christ to forgive your sins and come into your life as your Lord and Savior.

---

[1]   John 3:16
[2]   Romans 3:23
[3]   Romans 6:23
[4]   Romans 5:8
[5]   John 14:6
[6]   John 1:12

If you want to accept Christ as Savior and turn from your sins, you can ask Him to be your Savior and Lord by praying this simple prayer:

"Jesus, I accept by faith that you are the Son of God. Thank you for dying on the cross for my sins. Please forgive my sins and give me the gift of eternal life. I ask you into my life and heart to be my Lord and Savior."

Invite the Holy Spirit to actively work in your life and praise God for what He is doing in your life:

"Holy Spirit, fill me to overflowing with your love. Anoint me with your power to overcome temptation and wisdom to know your truth. Teach me God's precepts, protect me from the enemy of my soul and use my life to glorify God."

And finally, begin by reading the New Testament in the Bible. Ask the Holy Spirit to guide you and teach you. Praise God and thank Him for what He is doing in your life. I sincerely hope that today you make the decision to become a disciple of Christ, a Christ-follower. Perhaps someday you will become the first *face of grace* for another AAC to see.

*   *   *

In closing, please know that I am praying for those of you who have just read my book. If the telling of my life experiences in any way helps just one of you to make the decision to step out in faith and begin to reweave the threads of your life, then meaning has been given to my existence on this earth. If my story ultimately leads you into wholeness and freedom from the afflictions of any kind of abuse, then value has been given to my own pain and suffering. If my vulnerability leads just one of you to find God, my life has been worth it all. No matter where you have been or where you are today, I pray this abused adult/child has helped you begin your life again.

Blessings,
Nola Katherine

My family, c 1945

About 3 years old

School picture, 9 years old

Age 14, in front of the
screened-in porch

My Childhood

Senior year

Me with Lady

Billye after moving
to California

Mother and her family

Sis, Alice Ann, and Jack

A
n
c
e
s
t
o
r
s

My dad's mother

My siblings, Uncle Ben,
and my dad's father

Billye, Ruby Ellen, Eva,
my dad, and his father

Nola Katherine and Jake
June 29, 1968

True love walks in

Sweethearts

Marriage & Family

Katherine's first
Christmas after
diagnosis

Katherine
welcomes Jay

Katherine loses
her beautiful hair

A Miracle for Katherine

Prayer Card under A Miracle for Katherine

A prayer of faith will heal the sick, and
the Lord will raise him up.
St. James 5:15

Jesus, Son of Mary, You have ordained and
constituted the services of Angels and men
in a wonderful order: Mercifully grant
that as Your Holy Angels always serve You
in heaven, so may they guard and defend
Your child Katherine on earth. Through
Jesus Christ our Lord.
Amen

O Lord, Jesus Christ, who with joy did receive and bless the children brought unto
You: Bless Your child Katherine and grant
that she may be restored to that perfect
health which is Yours alone to give so that
she may live to serve and glorify You all
her days: Through Jesus Christ our Lord.

Amen

God's Grace
is
sufficient

Katherine's hair is
growing back

Tickle time with Dad

Cuddle time with Mom

Just before life gets really tough

Jay's 2nd birthday spent
in the hospital

Finally healthy –
our two miracles

Katherine and Jay
welcome baby Kim

A special moment between
Kim and her Granddaddy
while Grandmother watches

Dickie Bird by NK, c 1955

Chewy and her 12 puppies

M
e
m
o
r
i
e
s

Jo Ann and I ride
the Old Chisholm Trail

Falling Off the Horse
by NK, c 1967

My family – Easter 1990 – Just before…

Edwards Brothers, Inc.
Thorofare, NJ USA
August 10, 2011